CISCO® ASA FIREWALL FU

3RD EDITION

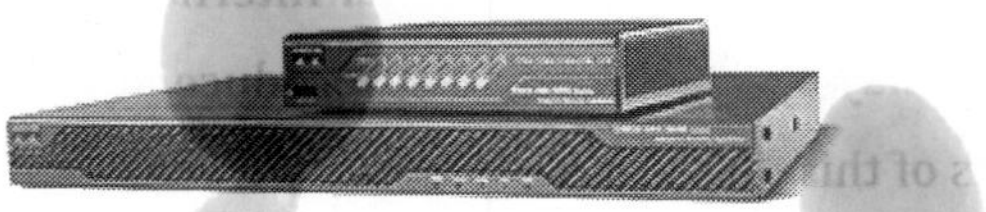

EVERYTHING YOU NEED TO KNOW TO CONFIGURE AND IMPLEMENT

THE BEST FIREWALL IN THE MARKET

WRITTEN BY: HARRIS ANDREA

MSC ELECTRICAL ENGINEERING AND COMPUTER SCIENCE

CISCO CERTIFIED NETWORK ASSOCIATE (CCNA)

CISCO CERTIFIED NETWORK PROFESSIONAL (CCNP)

CISCO CERTIFIED SECURITY PROFESSIONAL (CCSP)

CERTIFIED ETHICAL HACKER (CEH)

EC-COUNCIL CERTIFIED SECURITY ANALYST (ECSA)

http://www.networkstraining.com

Legal Notice:

Email: **admin@networkstraining.com**
Website: **http://www.networkstraining.com/**

The information services and resources provided in this Book are based upon the current Internet environment as well as the author's experience. The techniques presented here have been proven to be successful. Because technologies are constantly changing, the configurations and examples presented in this Book may change, cease or expand with time. We hope that the skills and knowledge acquired from this Book will provide you with the ability to adapt to inevitable evolution of technological services. However, we cannot be held responsible for changes that may affect the applicability of these techniques. The opinions expressed in this Book belong to the author and are not necessarily those of Cisco Systems, Inc. The author is not affiliated with Cisco Systems, Inc.

ISBN-10: 1-4973-9190-3
ISBN-13: 978-1-4973-9190-1

Table of Contents:

About the Author:

Harris Andrea is a Senior Network Security Engineer working for a leading Internet Service Provider in Europe. He graduated from the University of Kansas USA in 1998 with a B.S and M.S degrees in Electrical Engineering and Computer Science. Since then, he has been working in the Networking field, designing, implementing and managing large scale networking projects with Cisco products and technologies. His main focus is on Network Security based on Cisco ASA Firewalls, Firewall Service Modules (FWSM) on 6500/7600 models, VPN products, IDS/IPS products, AAA services etc. To support his knowledge and to build a strong professional standing, Harris pursued and earned several Cisco Certifications such as CCNA, CCNP, CCSP and other security related certifications such as CEH and ECSA. He is also a technology blogger owing a networking blog about Cisco technologies which you can visit for extra technical information and tutorials.

http://www.networkstraining.com

Introduction:

Thank you for purchasing this technical Book about configuring Cisco ASA Firewalls. I firmly believe that you have made an important step towards your career in network security, which is a fast developing and exciting field in the networking area.

Information Security threats are on the rise, and although several products and technologies have been developed to mitigate these threats, the long-proven and trusted hardware firewall is still the heart of security for any network. Firewall administrators and designers are therefore in high demand. Cisco has a large market share in the hardware firewall market, so by learning to configure and implement one of the best firewall appliances you are guaranteed a successful career in this field.

This Book is the result of my working experience with the Cisco Adaptive Security Appliance (ASA), and summarizes the most important features and most frequent configuration scenarios that a security engineer will encounter in real world networks. I have tried to "squeeze" the vast volume of information about Cisco ASA firewalls into a handy, directly applicable book that will get you on track right away. You can use this Book in conjunction with other documentation resources or as a reference guide for the most common configuration concepts of the Cisco ASA Firewall.

This Third Edition of the book is completely updated to cover the latest ASA version 9.x. All configuration commands, features etc will work on the newest ASA 9.x (in addition to older 8.x versions) and also on the newest ASA 5500-X models. This updated book Edition includes also extensive new content, making it one of the most complete ASA books available in the market. I believe that the Third Edition book will be a valuable resource for both beginners and experienced ASA professionals.

For any questions that you may have or clarifications about the information presented in this Book, please contact me at: admin@networkstraining.com

Have fun reading my Book. I hope it will be a valuable resource for you.

Chapter 1 Getting Started With Cisco Firewalls

1.1 User Interface

This lesson describes the access modes and commands associated with the operation of Cisco ASA security appliances. We assume that you know how to connect to the appliance using a console cable (the blue flat cable with RJ-45 on one end, and DB-9 Serial on the other end) and a Terminal Emulation software (e.g HyperTerminal or Putty), and how to use basic Command Line Interface.

1.1.1 Security Appliance Access Modes

A Cisco security appliance (PIX or ASA) has four main administrative access modes:

- **Monitor Mode**: Displays the **monitor>** prompt. A special mode that enables you to update the image over the network or to perform password recovery. While in the monitor mode, you can enter commands to specify the location of a TFTP server and the location of the software image or password recovery binary image file to download. You access this mode by pressing the "Break" or "ESC" keys immediately after powering up the appliance.
- **Unprivileged Mode**: Displays the > prompt. Available when you first access the appliance. If the appliance is a Cisco PIX 500 series, the prompt for unprivileged mode is **pixfirewall>** and if the appliance is the new Cisco ASA 5500 Series, the prompt is **ciscoasa>**
  This mode provides restricted view of the security appliance. You cannot configure anything from this mode. To get started with configuration, the first command you need to know is the **enable** command. Type **enable** and hit Enter. The initial password is empty, so hit Enter again to move on the next access mode (Privileged Mode).

```
ciscoasa> enable          ← Unprivileged Mode
password:                 ← Enter a password here (initially its blank)
ciscoasa#                 ← Privileged Mode
```

- **Privileged Mode**: Displays the # prompt. Enables you to change the current settings. Any unprivileged command also works in this mode. From this mode you can see the current configuration by using **show running-config**. Still, you cannot configure anything yet until you go to **Configuration Mode.** You access the Configuration Mode using the **configure terminal** command from the Privileged Mode.

- **Configuration Mode**: This mode displays the **(config)#** prompt. Enables you to change all system configuration settings. Use **exit** from each mode to return to the previous mode.

```
ciscoasa> enable                      ← Unprivileged Mode
password:                             ← Enter a password here (initially its blank)
ciscoasa# configure terminal          ← Privileged Mode
ciscoasa(config)#                     ← Configuration Mode
ciscoasa(config)# exit
ciscoasa# exit                        ← Back to Privileged Mode
ciscoasa>                             ← Back to Unprivileged Mode
```

The **(config)#** mode is sometimes called **Global Configuration Mode**. Some configuration commands from this mode enter a command-specific mode and the prompt changes accordingly. For example the **interface** command enters interface configuration mode as shown below:

```
ciscoasa(config)# interface GigabitEthernet0/1
ciscoasa(config-if)#                  ← Configure Interface specific parameters
```

1.2 File Management

This lesson describes the file management system in the security appliance. Each ASA device contains flash memory and also RAM which is used to store the currently running configuration.

1.2.1 Viewing and saving your configuration

There are two configuration instances in the Cisco security appliances:

- **running-configuration** (stored in RAM)
- **startup-configuration** (stored in Flash)

The first one (running-configuration) is the one currently running on the appliance, and its stored in the RAM of the firewall. You can view this configuration by typing (in Privileged Mode):

ciscoasa# show running-config

Any command that you enter in the firewall is directly written in the running-config and takes effect immediately. Since the running-config is written in the RAM memory, if the appliance loses power it will lose also any configuration changes that were not previously saved.

To save the currently running configuration, use the command:
ciscoasa# copy run start
or
ciscoasa# write memory

The above two commands copy the running-config into the startup-config.

As mentioned above, the **startup-configuration** is the backup configuration of the running one. It is stored in Flash Memory, so it is not lost when the appliance is rebooted. Also, the **startup-configuration** is the one which is loaded when the appliance boots-up. To view the stored startup-configuration type **show startup-config.**

1.3 ASA Image Software Management

The ASA image is basically the operating system of the appliance. It is like the IOS used in Cisco Routers. When we refer to ASA software version 8.x, 9.x etc we mean the version of the image software.

The ASA image is a compressed binary file and it's pre-installed on the flash of the device. The image gets decompressed into RAM when the appliance boots-up. For example an ASA image filename looks like "**asa911-k8.bin**".

In order to copy a new image file to the ASA (e.g for upgrading the existing software version), follow the steps below:

Step1: Setup a TFTP Server

First copy the ASA image file on a TFTP server computer. Assume that we have already a TFTP server located on the inside network with IP address 192.168.1.10

Step2: Copy image file from TFTP to Flash of ASA

ciscoasa# copy tftp flash

Address or name of remote host []? **192.168.1.10**
Source filename []?**asa911-k8.bin**
Destination filename [asa911-k8.bin]? **←Hit Enter**

Accessing tftp://192.168.1.10/asa911-k8.bin ....

Step3: Set the new image file as boot system file

ciscoasa#config term
ciscoasa(config)# boot system flash:/asa911-k8.bin
ciscoasa(config)# write memory

After rebooting the appliance, the new software image will be **asa911-k8.bin**

1.4 Password Recovery Procedure

If for any reason you are locked out of an ASA appliance and you don't remember the password to log-in, then you need to follow the password recovery procedure below:

Step1:
Connect with a console cable to the ASA and power-cycle the device (switch it OFF and ON again)

Step2:
Press continuously the "**ESC**" key on your keyboard until the device gets into ROMMON mode. This mode shows the following prompt:

rommon #1>

Step3:
Now we need to change the "**configuration register**" which is a special register controlling how the device boots up etc.

rommon #1>confreg

The security appliance displays the current configuration register value, and asks if you want to change the value. Answer **no** when prompt.

Current Configuration Register: 0x00000011
Configuration Summary:
boot TFTP image, boot default image from Flash on netboot failure
Do you wish to change this configuration? y/n [n]: ***n***

Step4:

Now we must manually change the confreg value to **0x41** which means that the appliance will ignore the startup-configuration when booting. Then, reboot the appliance.

rommon #2>confreg 0x41
rommon #3>boot

Step5:

Now the ASA will ignore its startup configuration and boot up without asking for a password.

ciscoasa>enable
Password: <Hit Enter>
ciscoasa#

Step6:

Copy the startup configuration file into the running configuration.

ciscoasa# copy startup-config running-config
Destination filename [running-config]? <Hit Enter>

Step7:

Now configure a new privileged level password (enable password) and also reset the configuration register to its original value (0x01)

ciscoasa#conf term
ciscoasa(config)#enable password *strongpass*
ciscoasa(config)# config-register 0x01
ciscoasa(config)# wr mem

Step8:

Reload the appliance. Now you should be able to log in with the new password.

ciscoasa(config)# reload

1.5 Security Levels

This lesson describes the security levels concept as used in the ASA firewall appliance.

A Security Level is assigned to interfaces (either physical or logical sub-interfaces) and it is basically a number from **0 to 100** designating how trusted an interface is relative to another interface on the appliance. The higher the security level, the more trusted the interface (and hence the network connected behind it) is considered to be, relative to another interface. Since each firewall interface represents a specific network (or security zone), by using security levels we can assign 'trust levels' to our security zones. The primary rule for security levels is that an interface (or zone) with a higher security level can access an interface with a lower security level. On the other hand, an interface with a lower security level cannot access an interface with a higher security level, without the explicit permission of a security rule (Access Control List - ACL).

1.5.1 Security Level Examples

Let us see some examples of security levels below:

- **Security Level 0**: This is the lowest security level and it is assigned by default to the '**Outside**' Interface of the firewall. It is the least trusted security level and must be assigned accordingly to the network (interface) that we don't want it to have any access to our internal networks. This security level is usually assigned to the interface connected to the Internet. This means that every device connected to the Internet can not have access to any network behind the firewall, unless explicitly permitted by an ACL rule.
- **Security Levels 1 to 99**: These security levels can be assigned to perimeter security zones (e.g. DMZ Zone, Management Zone, Database Servers Zone etc).
- **Security Level 100**: This is the highest security level and it is assigned by default to the '**Inside**' Interface of the firewall. It is the most trusted security level and must be assigned accordingly to the network (interface) that we want to apply the most protection from the security appliance. This security level is usually assigned to the interface connecting the Internal Corporate network behind it.

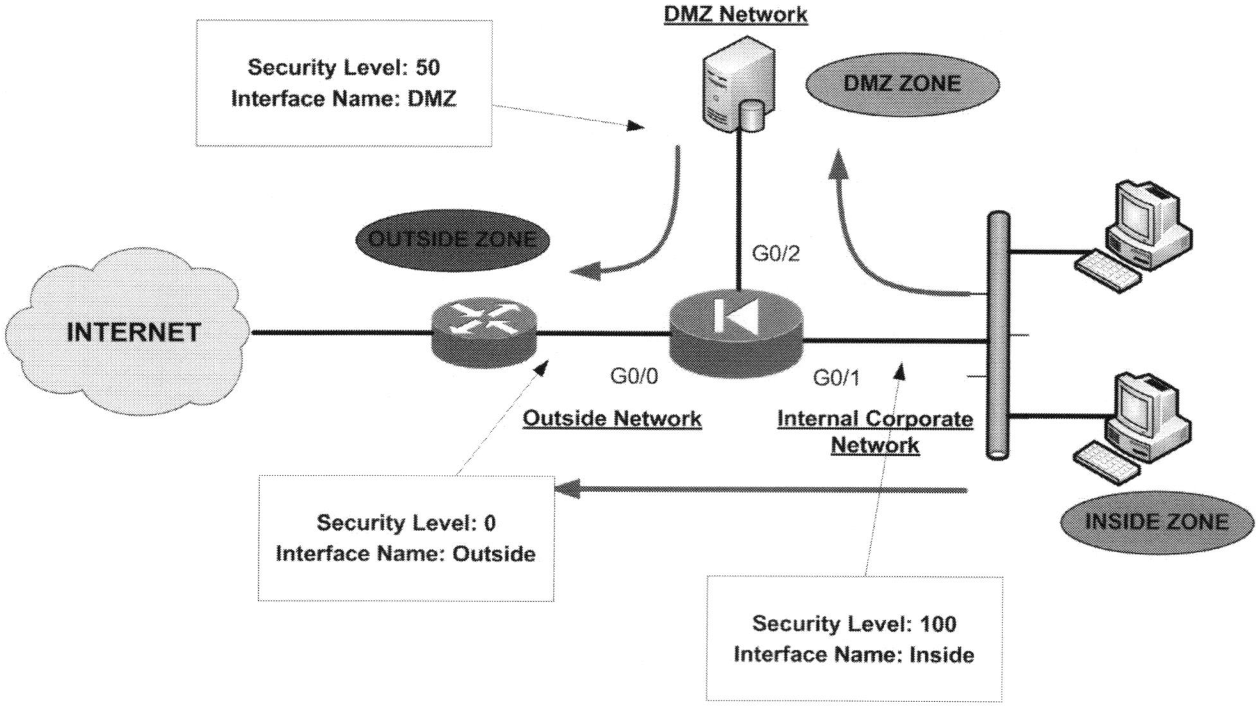

The diagram above illustrates a typical example of security levels assignment in a network with an Inside, Outside, and DMZ zones. Throughout this book we will represent the Cisco Firewall with the "Electrical Diode" symbol. As you can see, the Internal Corporate Network is connected to the Interface with the highest security level (Interface G0/1 with Security Level 100) which is also named as 'Inside'. The Interface name '**Inside**' is given by default to the interface with the highest security level. Also, the INTERNET facing interface (G0/0) is named '**Outside**' and is assigned a security level of 0. A Perimeter Zone (**DMZ**) is also created with a Security Level of 50. The Red Arrows in the diagram represent the flow of traffic. As you can see, the Inside Zone can access both DMZ and Outside Zones (Security Level 100 can access freely the Security Levels 50 and 0). The DMZ Zone can access only the Outside Zone (Security Level 50 can access Level 0), but not the Inside Zone. Lastly, the Outside Zone cannot access either the Inside or the DMZ zones.

What is described in the example above is the default behavior of the Cisco ASA Firewalls. We can override the default behavior and allow access from Lower Security Levels to Higher Security Levels by using Static NAT (only if required) and Access Control Lists, as we will see in the next chapters of this book.

1.5.2 Rules for Traffic Flow between Security Levels

- **Traffic from Higher Security Level to Lower Security Level**: Allow ALL traffic originating from the higher Security Level unless specifically restricted by an Access Control List (ACL). If NAT-Control is enabled on the device, then there must be a **nat/global** translation pair between High-to-Low Security Level interfaces. **NOTE**: "**global**" command is not supported in ASA versions 8.3 and later (more on this later).
- **Traffic from Lower Security Level to Higher Security Level:** Drop ALL traffic unless specifically allowed by an ACL. If NAT-Control is enabled on the device (more on this later), then there must be a **Static NAT** between High-to-Low Security Level interfaces.
- **Traffic between interfaces with same Security Level:** By default this is not allowed, unless you configure the **same-security-traffic permit inter-interface** command (ASA version 7.2 and later).

1.6 Basic Firewall Configuration

The following configuration commands constitute the basic steps for setting up the security appliance from the ground up:

- STEP1: Configure a privileged level password (enable password)

By default there is no password for accessing the ASA firewall, so the first step before doing anything else is to configure a privileged level password, which will be needed to allow subsequent access to the appliance. Configure this under Configuration Mode:

ciscoasa(config)# enable password ***mysecretpassword***

- STEP2: Enable Remote Command Line Management

You can access the security appliance remotely for Command Line Interface management (CLI) using either Telnet or SSH, and for Web-based graphical management using HTTPS (ASDM management). It is recommended to use SSH for CLI management since all communication with the firewall will be encrypted, compared with using Telnet which is not encrypted. To enable SSH on the firewall, we need first to create a username/password for authentication, then generate encryption keys (RSA keys), and also specify the IP address of the management host/network.

! Create a username "ciscoadmin" with password "adminpassword" and use this LOCAL username to !authenticate for SSH connections. Privilege 15 is the highest privilege level for a user.
ciscoasa(config)#username *ciscoadmin* password *adminpassword* privilege 15
ciscoasa(config)#aaa authentication ssh console LOCAL

! Generate a 1024 bit RSA key pair for the firewall which is required for SSH
ciscoasa(config)# crypto key generate rsa modulus 1024
Keypair generation process begin. Please wait...
ciscoasa(config)#

! Specify the hosts allowed to connect to the security appliance.
ciscoasa(config)#ssh 10.1.1.1 255.255.255.255 inside
ciscoasa(config)#ssh 200.200.200.1 255.255.255.255 outside

- **STEP3: Configure a Firewall Hostname**

The default hostname for Cisco ASA appliances is **ciscoasa**, and for the Cisco PIX appliance is **pixfirewall**. It is advisable to configure a unique hostname for a new firewall so that you can differentiate it from other firewalls that you may have in the network.

ciscoasa(config)# hostname NewYork-FW
NewYork-FW(config)#

Notice how the CLI prompt has changed to the new Hostname that you just configured.

- **STEP4: Configure Interface Commands**

The Cisco ASA interfaces are numbered as **GigabitEthernet0/0, GigabitEthernet0/1, GigabitEthernet0/2** etc (for Cisco ASA 5510 model, the interfaces are numbered as Etherne0/0, Ethernet0/1 etc). The **"Interface"** command will put you into a special configuration mode for the interface you specify (**interface configuration mode**), and then allow you to configure other interface sub-commands inside the interface mode. For Cisco ASA 5505, the interface commands are configured under the **"Interface Vlan x"** mode.

ciscoasa(config)# interface GigabitEthernet0/1
ciscoasa(config-if)# ← Configure Interface specific sub-commands

For Cisco ASA 5505:

ciscoasa(config)# interface Vlan *[vlan number]*
ciscoasa(config-if)# ← Configure Interface specific sub-commands

The absolutely necessary Interface Sub-commands that you need to configure in order for the interface to pass traffic are the following:

- **nameif *"interface name"*:** Assigns a name to an interface
- **ip address *"ip_address"* *"subnet_mask"* :** Assigns an IP address to the interface
- **security-level *"number 0 to 100"* :** Assigns a security level to the interface
- **no shutdown :** By default all interfaces are shut down, so enable them.

The configuration snapshot below shows all necessary interface sub-commands:

ciscoasa(config)# interface GigabitEthernet0/1
ciscoasa(config-if)# nameif inside
ciscoasa(config-if)# ip address 10.0.0.1 255.255.255.0
ciscoasa(config-if)# security-level 100 ← By default "inside" interface is sec-level 100
ciscoasa(config-if)# no shutdown

ciscoasa(config)# interface GigabitEthernet0/0
ciscoasa(config-if)# nameif outside
ciscoasa(config-if)# ip address 10.1.1.1 255.255.255.0
ciscoasa(config-if)# security-level 0 ← By default "outside" interface is sec-level 0
ciscoasa(config-if)# no shutdown

- STEP5: Configure NAT Control as needed (This is for versions lower than 8.3)

Another important configuration step is **nat-control**. NAT (Network Address Translation) was a mandatory configuration in older Cisco PIX firewalls (PIX version 6.x) but with ASA Firewalls it is not. **Nat-Control** (which is disabled by default) specifies whether or not the security appliance will enforce address hiding (i.e address translation) to ALL traffic passing from a high security level to a lower one. If you stay with the default configuration (i.e **nat-control** disabled), this will allow you to apply NAT (address hiding) to only selected traffic as you require. If you enable nat-control (using the command: **asa(config)#nat-control**) then you MUST have a NAT rule for ALL traffic passing from a high security interface to a lower security interface. The NAT rule must match a corresponding "**global**" command (more on NAT later). With the default configuration (nat-control disabled) the ASA passes traffic between interfaces with no need to configure any NAT statements. You just need to have the proper Access Control Lists applied on each interface to enforce traffic flow policies.

NOTE: From ASA version 8.3 and later, "**nat-control**" and "**global**" commands are no longer supported.

- **STEP6: Configure routing**

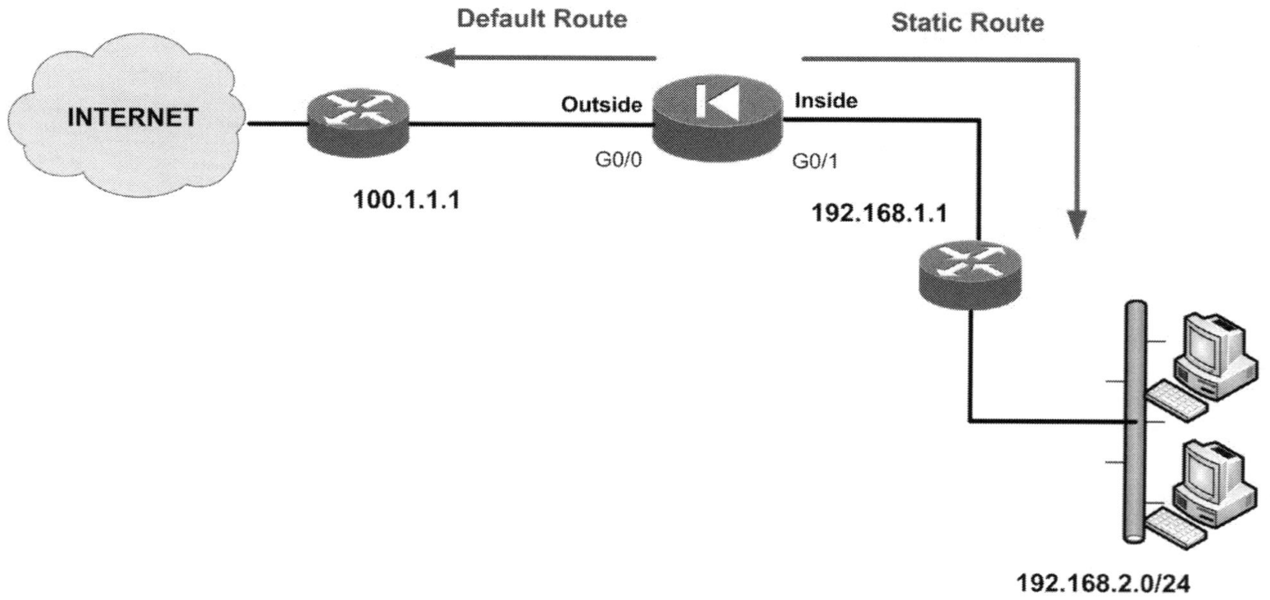

Routing is an essential step to configure, otherwise the Firewall appliance will not know how to send traffic to its destination. In the example above we show only default and static routing although dynamic routing protocols (RIP, OSPF, EIGRP) can be configured also. My recommendation is to use only default or static routing and avoid dynamic protocols in small networks. However, dynamic routing protocols on the ASA are also useful in larger and complex networks. More on dynamic routing protocols in a later Chapter.

Use the **route** command to enter either a static or default route for an interface. The command format is:
ciscoasa(config)# route *"interface-name" "destination-ip-address" "netmask" "gateway"*

Let's see an example configuration below:

ciscoasa(config)# route outside 0.0.0.0 0.0.0.0 100.1.1.1 ← Default Route
ciscoasa(config)# route inside 192.168.2.0 255.255.255.0 192.168.1.1 ← Static Route required on ASA to reach network 192.168.2.0 via gateway 192.168.1.1

For the default route (usually towards the Internet), you set both the *destination-ip-address* and *netmask* to 0.0.0.0. Create also static routes to access specific known networks beyond the locally connected networks, as shown on the diagram above.

The routing configuration concludes the "Minimum Mandatory" steps needed for the security appliance to become operational. Next we will get into more details for further configuration features that will enhance the security of the networks protected by the firewall.

Chapter 2 Configuring Network Address Translation

In this Chapter we will talk about a very important security mechanism that has to do with IP address translation (address hiding), its different types, and how the firewall appliance handles the translation mechanisms. From Cisco ASA version 8.3 and later, the Network Address Translation (NAT) configuration has been completely redesigned to allow for greater flexibility. In this Chapter we will describe Network Translation for versions prior to 8.3 and for versions 8.3 and later as well.

NOTE: For all the NAT scenarios that will follow below, when we say "**ASA Versions 8.3 and Later**" it includes also ASA versions 9.x.

2.1 Network Address Translation (NAT) Overview

The depletion of the public IPv4 address space has forced the Internet Community to think about alternative ways of addressing networked hosts. NAT therefore was created to overcome these addressing problems that occurred with the expansion of the Internet.

Some of the advantages of using NAT in IP networks are the following:

- NAT helps to mitigate global public IP address depletion.
- Networks can use the RFC 1918 private address space internally.
- NAT increases security by hiding the internal network topology and addressing.

The figure below shows a basic topology with an "inside" network for which the ASA Firewall performs a NAT operation to translate the "inside" address into an "outside" address, thus hiding the internal IP range. Note that the translation is usually applied to the "source" IP address of the packets.

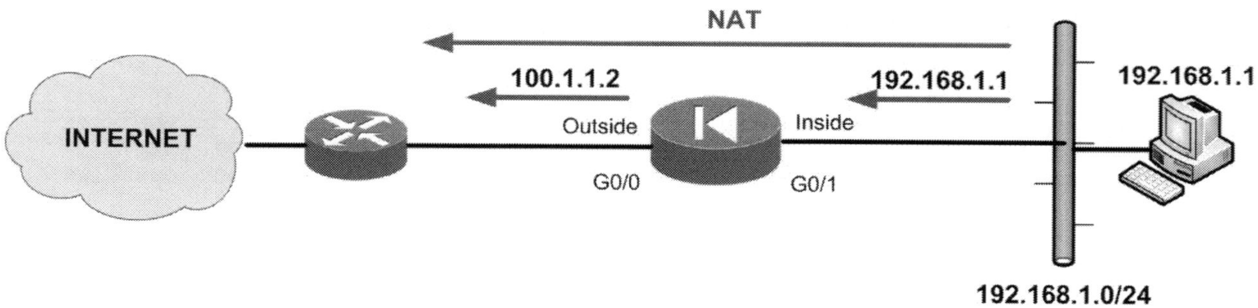

The above is an example of dynamic NAT which is always used for OUTBOUND traffic, that is, traffic from an internal network (higher security level) towards an outside network (lower security level). In the figure above, traffic from the host with private IP address 192.168.1.1 is translated into a public, routable address, 100.1.1.2 in order to be routed towards the Internet. Now, the reply packets from the Internet back to our internal host will have as destination address the IP 100.1.1.2, for which the firewall already has a translation rule established. The firewall will then translate the public address 100.1.1.2 back into 192.168.1.1 and deliver it to the internal host. The "**nat**" and "**global**" commands work together (versions prior to 8.3) to create the translation rules which enable your internal network to use any IP addressing scheme and at the same time remain hidden from the outside world.

Let's see some terminology that will be used in this Chapter:

- **Real IP address/Interface**: The Real IP address is the address which is actually configured on the host (the untranslated address). From our example diagram above, the Real IP address is 192.168.1.1 and the Real Interface is the Inside ASA interface.
- **Mapped IP address/Interface**: The mapped IP address is the address that the Real address is translated to. From our example diagram above, the Mapped IP address is 100.1.1.2 and the Mapped Interface is the Outside ASA interface.

Cisco ASA firewalls support four types of address translations:

- **Dynamic NAT translation**: Translates source addresses on higher security interfaces into a range (or pool) of IP addresses on a less secure interface, for outbound connections. The "**nat**" command defines which internal hosts will be translated, and the "**global**" command (ASA versions prior to 8.3) defines the address pool (mapped addresses) on the outgoing interface. Dynamic NAT is used for outbound communication only.

- **Dynamic Port Address Translation (PAT)**: This is also called "Many-to-One" Translation. A group of Real IP addresses are mapped to a Single IP address using a unique source port of that address.
- **Static NAT translation**: Provides a permanent, one-to-one address mapping between a Real IP address and a Mapped IP address. The Real IP should be on a higher security interface and the Mapped IP on a lower security interface. With the appropriate Access Control List (ACL), static NAT allows hosts on a less secure interface (e.g Internet) to access hosts on a higher security interface (e.g Web Server on DMZ) without exposing the actual IP address of the host on the higher security interface. Static NAT is used for Bidirectional communication.
- **Identity NAT**: Identity NAT lets you translate a Real IP address to itself, essentially bypassing NAT. Identity NAT is useful in VPN configuration where we need to exempt VPN traffic from the NAT operation.

2.1.1 Configuring Dynamic NAT Translation

Cisco ASA Versions prior to 8.3

In this section we will describe **Dynamic NAT translation** with several scenarios. Dynamic NAT is implemented using a combination of two commands: "**nat**" and "**global**". The Real IP network to be translated is defined by the "**nat**" command and the Mapped IP pool that will be used for translation is defined by the "**global**" command. The format of the "**nat**" and "**global**" commands as used in Dynamic NAT is shown below:

ciscoasa(config)# nat (*Real_interface_name*) *"nat-id" "internal network IP subnet"*
ciscoasa(config)# global (*Mapped_interface_name*) *"nat-id" "external IP pool range"*

Cisco ASA Versions 8.3 and later

In Cisco ASA version 8.3 (announced on March 8, 2010), the NAT configuration has been completely changed. The "**nat-control**", "**static**" and "**global**" commands are not available anymore. Also, the new version's syntax uses the "**nat**" command differently as we will describe below. If you are running a version prior to 8.3 (e.g 7.x, 8.0, 8.1, 8.2) and you want to upgrade to 8.3, then keep in mind that a memory upgrade is also required for models 5505, 5510, 5520, 5540. Also, after upgrading, there will be a migration of the old NAT statements to the new ones.

In versions 8.3 and later (including 9.x versions), the ASA firewall implements NAT in two ways:

- ***"Network object NAT"***
- ***"Twice NAT"***

Cisco recommends using "**Network object NAT**" instead of "**Twice NAT**" because is easier to configure and more reliable. Twice NAT on the other hand is more scalable and has some extra features but is more complex than network object NAT. In this Chapter we will focus only on Network Object NAT.

2.1.1.1 Network Object NAT Configuration

Basically you configure NAT under a network object. The network object itself defines the Real IP address/subnet which is going to be translated. Also, inside the network object you configure the "**nat**" command which specifies a pair of interfaces between which the NAT will take place and the Mapped IP address pool.

Step1:

Create network objects to define the Real IP addresses and the Mapped IP addresses. The network objects can contain a single IP address (host), a network subnet, or a range of IP addresses. The network object which defines the Real IP addresses must contain also the "**nat**" statement.

ciscoasa(config)# object network *[obj-name]*

ciscoasa(config-network-object)# {host *ip-addr* **| subnet** *net-addr net-mask* **| range** *ip1-ip2***}**

Step2:

Then we configure the "**nat**" statement inside the network object which defines the Real IP addresses.

ciscoasa(config-network-object)# nat (real if , mapped if) dynamic [*mapped-ip* **|** *mapped-obj***]**

The "**real if**" and "**mapped if**" define the internal and external interfaces respectively between which the Dynamic NAT will take place. After the "**dynamic**" keyword, we use a mapped IP or a mapped network object which define the IP addresses that the real addresses will be translated to. In place of "**real if**" or "**mapped if**" we can use the keyword "**any**" to specify any interface.

Scenario 1: Simple Dynamic Inside NAT Translation

Cisco ASA Versions prior to 8.3

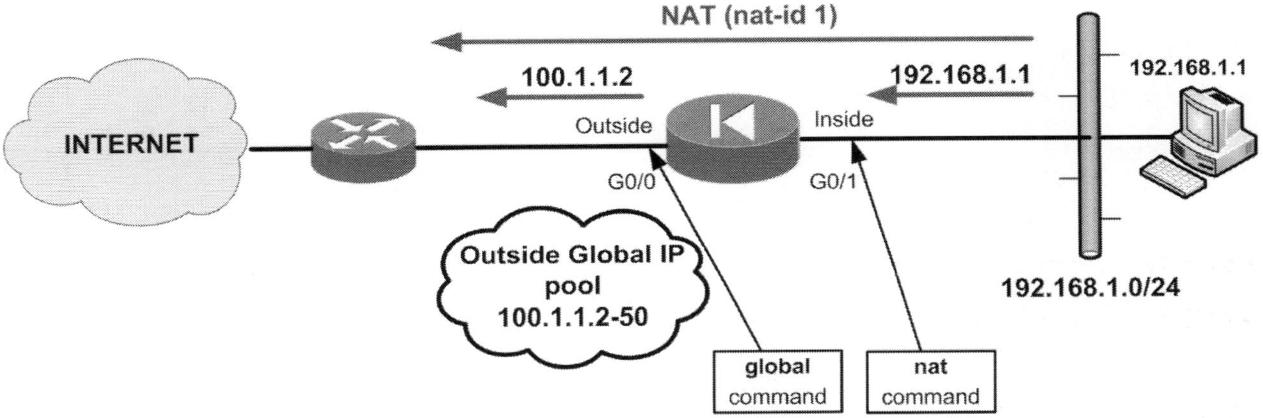

ciscoasa(config)# nat (inside) 1 **192.168.1.0 255.255.255.0** ←**Inside net to be translated**
ciscoasa(config)# global (outside) 1 **100.1.1.2-100.1.1.50 netmask 255.255.255.0** ←**Outside pool**

In the scenario above the firewall will perform dynamic NAT to all inside hosts (192.168.1.0/24). The source IP addresses of outbound traffic from inside to outside will be translated into addresses from the Outside Global pool 100.1.1.2 up to 100.1.1.50. Notice the **nat-id** value (1). This number binds the **nat** command with the **global** command. Its importance will be clearer in our next scenarios.

Also note the names "**inside**" and "**outside**" used in the **nat** and **global** commands. These names are the ones assigned under the interface configuration with the "**nameif**" command.

Cisco ASA Versions 8.3 and later

ciscoasa(config)# object network mapped_public_pool←Create the Mapped addresses object
ciscoasa(config-network-object)# range 100.1.1.2 100.1.1.50 ← Outside public pool

ciscoasa(config)# object network my_internal_lan←Create the Real IP addresses object
ciscoasa(config-network-object)# subnet 192.168.1.0 255.255.255.0 ← LAN to be translated
ciscoasa(config-network-object)# nat (inside,outside) dynamic mapped_public_pool
The example above will hide the internal subnet 192.168.1.0/24 behind a range of public outside addresses in the range 100.1.1.2 up to 100.1.1.50. The dynamic NAT translation will take place between inside and outside interfaces.

NOTE: Because the internal network has more IP addresses than the Mapped Public Pool, we can use the outside interface IP as NAT fallback. After the mapped IP addresses are used up, then the IP address of the mapped interface (outside ASA interface) will be used. See below how to configure dynamic NAT fallback:

ciscoasa(config)# object network my_internal_lan←Create the Real IP addresses object
ciscoasa(config-network-object)# subnet 192.168.1.0 255.255.255.0 ← LAN to be translated
ciscoasa(config-network-object)# nat (inside,outside) dynamic mapped_public_pool interface

Note the usage of the "**interface**" keyword just after the "**mapped_public_pool**" network object.

Scenario 2: Dynamic NAT Translation of two internal networks

Cisco ASA Versions prior to 8.3

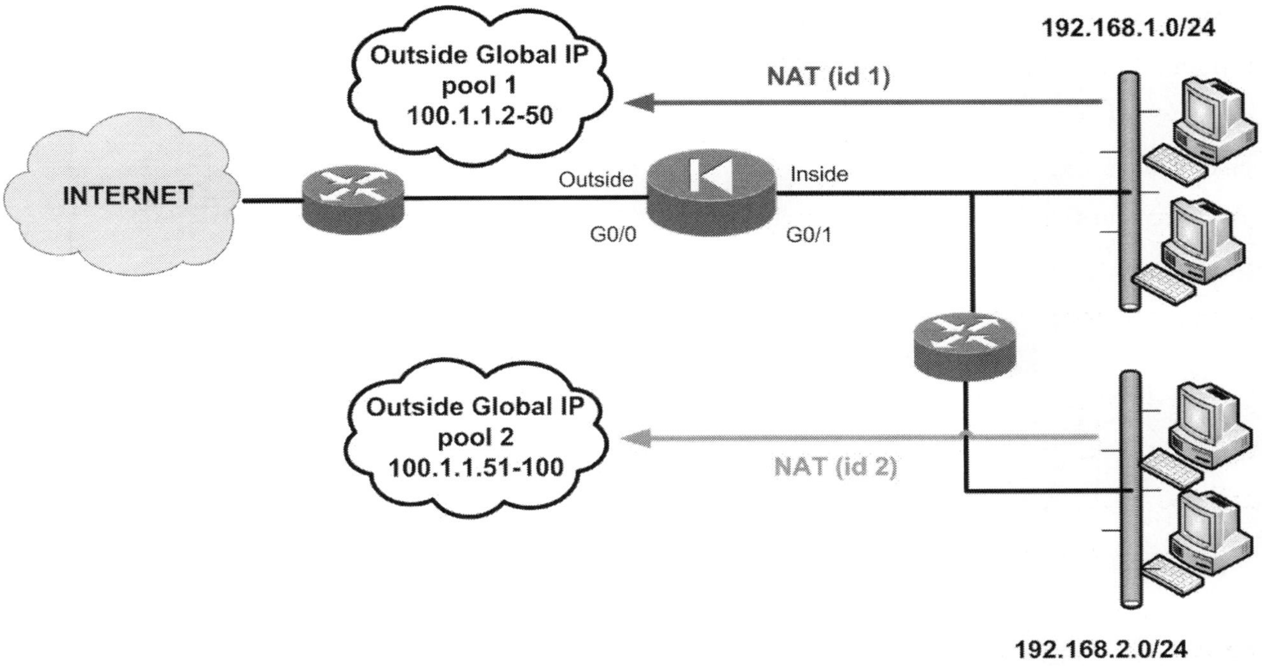

ciscoasa(config)# nat (inside) 1 192.168.1.0 255.255.255.0 ←First Internal Network
ciscoasa(config)# nat (inside) 2 192.168.2.0 255.255.255.0 ←Second Internal Network
ciscoasa(config)# global (outside) 1 100.1.1.2-100.1.1.50 netmask 255.255.255.0
ciscoasa(config)# global (outside) 2 100.1.1.51-100.1.1.100 netmask 255.255.255.0

The scenario here shows the importance of the **nat-id** parameter and how this is used to bind together a **nat/global** command pair. The **nat-id** (1) in the first **nat** command statement tells the firewall to translate the internal network 192.168.1.0/24 addresses into those in the mapped global IP pool containing the same nat-id (i.e 100.1.1.2 up to 100.1.1.50). Similarly, the nat-id (2) in the second **nat** statement tells the firewall to translate addresses for hosts in 192.168.2.0/24 to the addresses in the mapped global pool 2 with nat-id (2) (i.e 100.1.1.51 up to 100.1.1.100).

Cisco ASA Version 8.3 and later

Let's see how to configure the scenario above with ASA version 8.3 or later. Hosts from internal network 192.168.1.0/24 will be translated to addresses from Outside IP pool 1 (100.1.1.2 up to 100.1.1.50) and hosts from internal network 192.168.2.0/24 will be translated to addresses from Outside IP pool 2 (100.1.1.51 up to 100.1.1.100).

ciscoasa(config)# object network mapped_IP_pool_1← Create the Mapped 1 addresses object
ciscoasa(config-network-object)# range 100.1.1.2 100.1.1.50 ← Outside IP pool 1

ciscoasa(config)# object network lan_1
ciscoasa(config-network-object)# subnet 192.168.1.0 255.255.255.0 ←LAN1 to be translated
ciscoasa(config-network-object)# nat (inside,outside) dynamic mapped_IP_pool_1

ciscoasa(config)# object network mapped_IP_pool_2← Create the Mapped 2 addresses object
ciscoasa(config-network-object)# range 100.1.1.51 100.1.1.100 ← Outside IP pool 2

ciscoasa(config)# object network lan_2
ciscoasa(config-network-object)# subnet 192.168.2.0 255.255.255.0 ←LAN2 to be translated
ciscoasa(config-network-object)# nat (inside,outside) dynamic mapped_IP_pool_2

Scenario 3: Dynamic NAT Translation with three interfaces

Cisco ASA Versions prior to 8.3

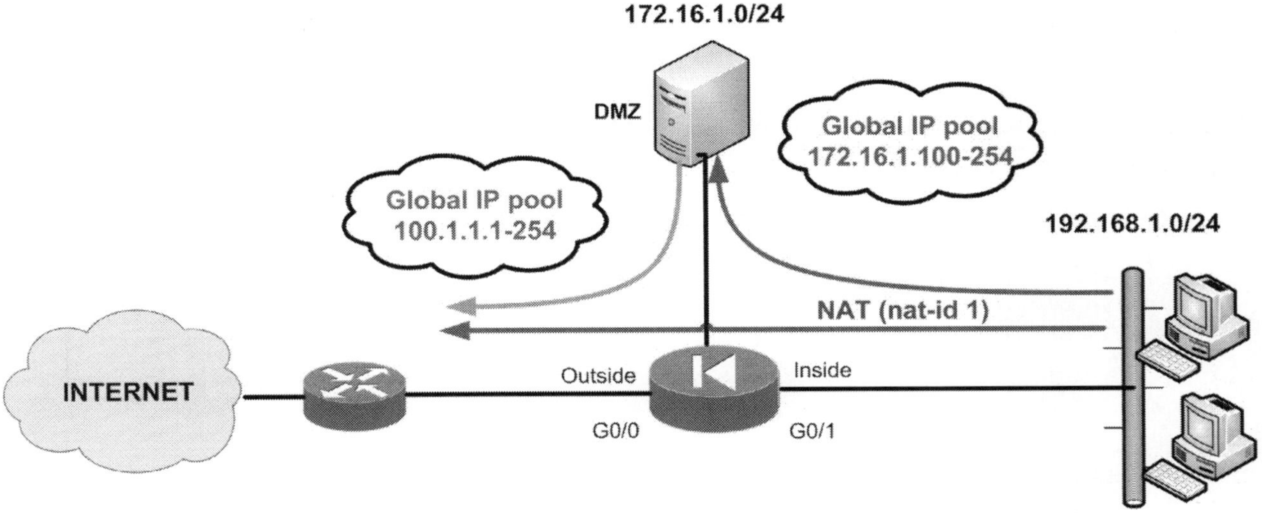

ciscoasa(config)# nat (inside) 1 **192.168.1.0 255.255.255.0** ←Inside Subnet
ciscoasa(config)# nat (DMZ) 1 **172.16.1.0 255.255.255.0** ←DMZ Subnet
ciscoasa(config)# global (outside) 1 100.1.1.1-100.1.1.254 netmask 255.255.255.0
ciscoasa(config)# global (DMZ) 1 172.16.1.100-172.16.1.254 netmask 255.255.255.0

In the scenario above, assume that "inside" interface has security level 100, "DMZ" interface has security level 50, and "outside" interface has security level 0. This means that "inside" hosts can initiate connections to lower security level interfaces (i.e to both "DMZ" and "outside"). Also, these security levels allow hosts on the DMZ interface to initiate connections towards the outside interface.

Because both of the mapped pools (global commands) and the **nat(inside)** command use the same nat-id of 1, addresses for hosts on the inside network (192.168.1.0/24) can be translated to those in either mapped pool, depending on the direction of the traffic. Therefore, when hosts on the inside interface access hosts on the DMZ, the **global(DMZ)** command causes their source addresses to be translated to addresses in the range 172.16.1.100 – 172.16.1.254. Similarly, when inside hosts access hosts on the outside, the **global (outside)** command will cause their source addresses to be translated into the range 100.1.1.1 – 100.1.1.254.

Moreover, the configuration above allows also hosts on the DMZ to use NAT when accessing outside hosts. The **nat (DMZ)** together with **global (outside)** commands will cause the source addresses of DMZ hosts (172.16.1.0/24) to be translated into the outside range 100.1.1.1 – 100.1.1.254.

Monitoring NAT Translations

The "**ciscoasa# show xlate**" command displays the contents of the NAT translation table.

e.g *Global 100.1.1.10 Local 192.168.1.10*

The output above shows that a private local address 192.168.1.10 is assigned a global pool address of 100.1.1.10.

Cisco ASA Version 8.3 and later

For version 8.3 and later this scenario becomes more complicated to configure. We have three firewall network zones. Inside, DMZ, and Outside. Traffic from Inside going to DMZ network must be translated to Mapped IP Pool 172.16.1.100-254 and traffic from Inside going to Outside must be translated to Mapped IP Pool 100.1.1.1-254. Moreover, traffic from DMZ going to Outside must also be translated to outside Mapped IP Pool 100.1.1.1-254.

Let's first create the two network objects for the two Mapped IP pools.

ciscoasa(config)# object network mapped_IP_pool_1← Create the Mapped 1 addresses object
ciscoasa(config-network-object)# range 172.16.1.100 172.16.1.254 ← DMZ IP pool 1

ciscoasa(config)# object network mapped_IP_pool_2← Create the Mapped 2 addresses object
ciscoasa(config-network-object)# range 100.1.1.1 100.1.1.254 ← Outside IP pool 2

Then create the network objects for the Real IP addresses. We will have to create a different object for the three traffic flows (**inside_to_dmz**, **inside_to_outside**, **dmz_to_outside**).

ciscoasa(config)# object network inside_to_dmz←translation when going from inside to dmz
ciscoasa(config-network-object)# subnet 192.168.1.0 255.255.255.0
ciscoasa(config-network-object)# nat (inside,dmz) dynamic mapped_IP_pool_1

ciscoasa(config)# object network inside_to_outside←translation when going from in to out
ciscoasa(config-network-object)# subnet 192.168.1.0 255.255.255.0
ciscoasa(config-network-object)# nat (inside,outside) dynamic mapped_IP_pool_2

ciscoasa(config)# object network dmz_to_outside←translation when going from dmz to out
ciscoasa(config-network-object)# subnet 172.16.1.0 255.255.255.0
ciscoasa(config-network-object)# nat (dmz,outside) dynamic mapped_IP_pool_2

2.1.2 Configuring Dynamic Port Address Translation (PAT)

With Dynamic NAT we assume that we have a range (pool) of public addresses that we use to translate our internal network private addresses. In real situations, an enterprise receives only a limited number of public addresses from its ISP, whereas the number of internal private addresses is much bigger. This means that if we use Dynamic NAT in such a situation, the external public address pool (Mapped IP pool) will be depleted really fast when many internal hosts access the internet simultaneously.

To overcome this problem, we can use a "**many-to-one**" address translation, called also Port Address Translation (PAT). Using PAT, multiple connections from different internal hosts can be **multiplexed** over a single global (public) IP address using different source port numbers. Let's see an example below:

Cisco ASA Versions prior to 8.3

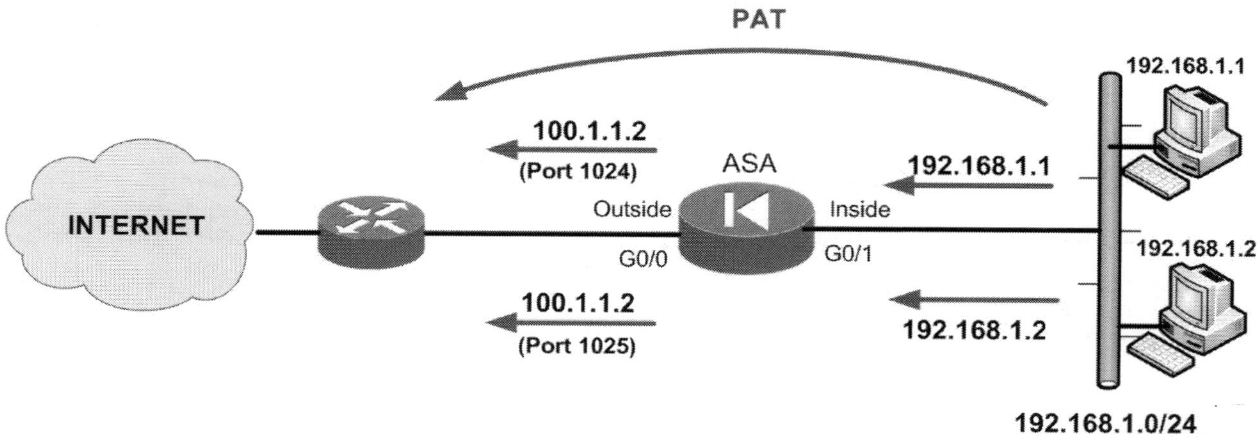

ciscoasa(config)# nat (inside) 1 192.168.1.0 255.255.255.0 ←**Inside Subnet to use PAT**
ciscoasa(config)# global (outside) 1 100.1.1.2 netmask 255.255.255.255 ← **Use a single global IP address for PAT**

In the example above, all internal private addresses (192.168.1.0/24) will use a single public IP address (100.1.1.2) with different source port numbers. For example, when host 192.168.1.1 connects on an Internet outside host, the firewall will translate its source address and port into 100.1.1.2 with source port 1024. Similarly, host 192.168.1.2 will be translated again into 100.1.1.2 but with a different source port (1025). The source ports are dynamically changed to a unique number greater than 1023. A single PAT address can support around 64,000 inside hosts.

Monitoring PAT Translations

The **ciscoasa# show xlate** command displays the contents of the PAT translation table.

e.g *PAT Global 100.1.1.2 (1024) Local 192.168.1.1 (4513)*

The output above shows that a connection from the private local address 192.168.1.1 with source port 4513 is translated into address 100.1.1.2 with source port 1024.

The firewall keeps track of all NAT sessions using its **xlate** table, so that when a reply packet comes back from outside, the firewall will check its translation table to see which port number belongs to the particular reply packet in order to deliver it to the correct internal host.

Cisco ASA Version 8.3 and later

You can configure the single Mapped IP address either as a network object or within the "**nat**" statement. For example, assume that we want to hide our internal network 192.168.1.0/24 behind the public IP address 100.1.1.2.

DYNAMIC PAT

```
ciscoasa(config)# object network internal_lan
ciscoasa(config-network-object)# subnet 192.168.1.0 255.255.255.0
ciscoasa(config-network-object)# nat (inside,outside) dynamic 100.1.1.2
```

There are several different scenarios in which PAT can be used in a network. We will describe them next.

Scenario 1: PAT using outside interface IP address

Instead of configuring a specific IP address in the global command to be used for PAT (as the example above), we can specify the outside Interface as the PAT address. This scenario is important when our firewall obtains a dynamic public IP address from the Internet Service Provider (ISP), in which case we don't know the exact address to configure it on the global command.

Refer to the diagram below for a configuration example using DHCP outside address for PAT:

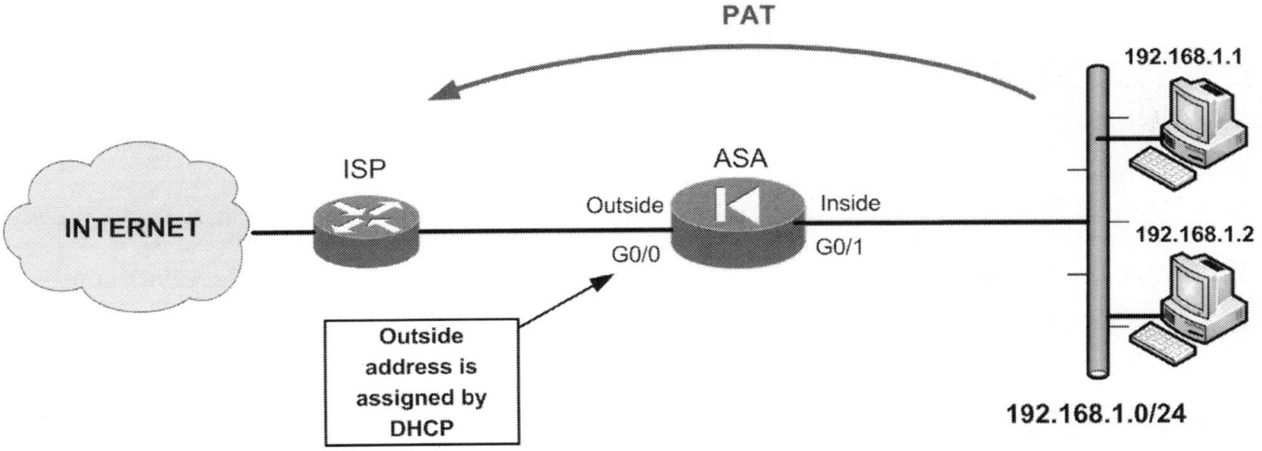

Cisco ASA Versions prior to 8.3

ciscoasa(config)# interface G0/0
ciscoasa(config-if)# ip address dhcp setroute ←Get outside address and gateway from ISP
ciscoasa(config)# nat (inside) 1 192.168.1.0 255.255.255.0 ←Inside Subnet to use PAT
ciscoasa(config)# global (outside) 1 interface ← Use the outside IP address for PAT

The "**ip address dhcp setroute**" interface command configures the firewall to work as a DHCP client for the ISP and obtain a public address automatically. The "**setroute**" parameter tells the Cisco Firewall to set its default route using the default gateway value that the DHCP server provides. **Do not** configure a default route when using the **setroute** option.

Cisco ASA Version 8.3 and later

To use the outside ASA interface address to perform PAT in version 8.3 and later do the following:

ciscoasa(config)# interface G0/0

ciscoasa(config-if)# ip address dhcp setroute ←Get outside address and gateway from ISP

ciscoasa(config)# object network internal_lan

ciscoasa(config-network-object)# subnet 192.168.1.0 255.255.255.0

ciscoasa(config-network-object)# nat (inside,outside) dynamic interface

Scenario 2: Mapping different internal subnets to different PAT addresses

Cisco ASA Versions prior to 8.3

Using the **nat-id** parameter we can bind two or more **nat/global** statement pairs in order to map different internal network subnets to different PAT addresses, as shown in the diagram below:

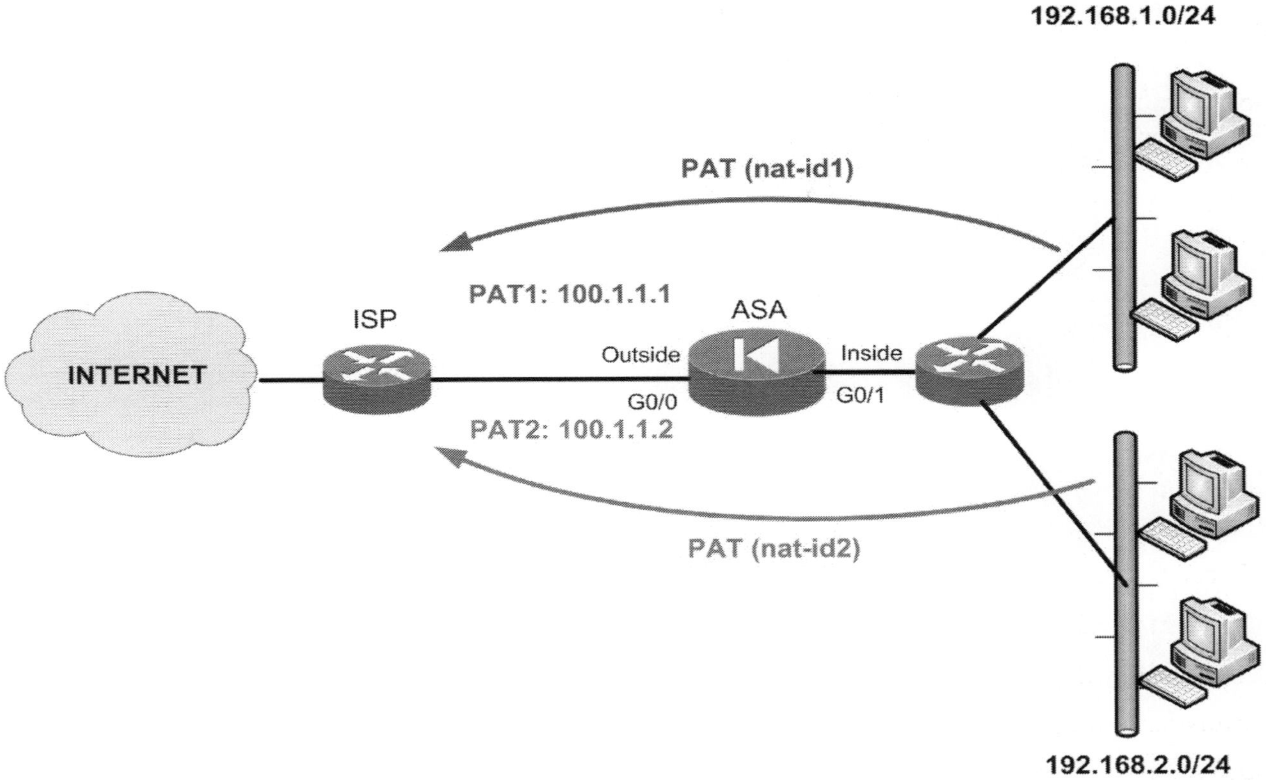

ciscoasa(config)# nat (inside) 1 192.168.1.0 255.255.255.0
ciscoasa(config)# global (outside) 1 100.1.1.1 netmask 255.255.255.255

ciscoasa(config)# nat (inside) 2 192.168.2.0 255.255.255.0
ciscoasa(config)# global (outside) 2 100.1.1.2 netmask 255.255.255.255

Outbound connections from internal subnet 192.168.1.0/24 will seem to originate from address 100.1.1.1 and outbound connections from subnet 192.168.2.0/24 will seem to originate from address 100.1.1.2.

Cisco ASA Version 8.3 and later

In this scenario, internal network 192.168.1.0/24 will be hidden behind PAT address 100.1.1.1 and also internal network 192.168.2.0/24 will be hidden behind PAT address 100.1.1.2.

ciscoasa(config)# object network internal_lan1

ciscoasa(config-network-object)# subnet 192.168.1.0 255.255.255.0

ciscoasa(config-network-object)# nat (inside,outside) dynamic 100.1.1.1

ciscoasa(config)# object network internal_lan2

ciscoasa(config-network-object)# subnet 192.168.2.0 255.255.255.0

ciscoasa(config-network-object)# nat (inside,outside) dynamic 100.1.1.2

Scenario 3: Combining Dynamic NAT with PAT Translation

We can use a pool of external public IP addresses for Dynamic NAT translation, and augment this pool with a single PAT address in case the addresses in the global pool are exhausted.

Cisco ASA Versions prior to 8.3

ciscoasa(config)# nat (inside) 1 192.168.1.0 255.255.255.0
ciscoasa(config)# global (outside) 1 100.1.1.100-100.1.1.253 netmask 255.255.255.0
ciscoasa(config)# global (outside) 1 100.1.1.254 netmask 255.255.255.255

Outbound connections from the internal network 192.168.1.0/24 are assigned addresses from the range 100.1.1.100 up to 100.1.1.253. If the firewall assigns all addresses from its dynamic pool, it will overflow to its PAT address 100.1.1.254.

Cisco ASA Version 8.3 and later

The mapped IP pool 100.1.1.100-100.1.1.253 will be used for Dynamic NAT translation of the internal network 192.168.1.0/24. If the Mapped pool is exhausted, the single PAT address 100.1.1.254 will be used for translation.

ciscoasa(config)# object network mapped_IP_pool
ciscoasa(config-network-object)# range 100.1.1.100 100.1.1.253
ciscoasa(config)# object network PAT_IP
ciscoasa(config-network-object)# host 100.1.1.254

ciscoasa(config)# object-group network nat_pat
ciscoasa(config-network-object)# network-object object mapped_IP_pool
ciscoasa(config-network-object)# network-object object PAT_IP

ciscoasa(config)# object network internal_lan
ciscoasa(config-network-object)# subnet 192.168.1.0 255.255.255.0
ciscoasa(config-network-object)# nat (inside,outside) dynamic nat_pat

2.1.2.1 Per-Session PAT and Multi-Session PAT (For ASA 9.x and later)

In ASA version 9.x, Port Address Translation (PAT) was enhanced with two types of PAT mechanisms: **Per-session PAT** and **Multi-Session PAT**.

- **Per-Session PAT**: This PAT mechanism is enabled by default for all TCP traffic and for UDP DNS Traffic. Per-Session PAT improves greatly the scalability of PAT because at the end of each per-session PAT connection, the ASA sends a reset and immediately removes the translation, thus tearing down the connection and hence freeing up resources on the device. For "hit-and-run" traffic, such as HTTP or HTTPS, the per-session feature is very efficient. However, for real time traffic (such as VoIP, H323, SIP etc) Per-Session PAT is not good.

As we've said above, per-session PAT is enabled by default. The following PAT rules are configured by default:

```
xlate per-session permit tcp any4 any4
xlate per-session permit tcp any4 any6
xlate per-session permit tcp any6 any4
xlate per-session permit tcp any6 any6
xlate per-session permit udp any4 any4 eq domain
xlate per-session permit udp any4 any6 eq domain
xlate per-session permit udp any6 any4 eq domain
xlate per-session permit udp any6 any6 eq domain
```

NOTE: In ASA version 9.x, the configuration keyword "**any4**" means ALL IPv4 traffic, and the keyword "**any6**" means ALL IPv6 traffic. If you use the keyword "**any**" it means ALL IPv4 and IPv6 traffic.

- **Multi-Session PAT:** Multi-session PAT, on the other hand, uses the PAT timeout, by default 30 seconds, before tearing down the translation and hence the connection. Multi-Session PAT is useful for VoIP, H323, SIP and Skinny traffic. Therefore whenever you have this kind of traffic in your network it's recommended to deny Per-Session PAT in order to use Multi-Session PAT.

Example:

Assume we have a VoIP server (or H323, SIP server etc) in our network (with IP 10.10.10.10) and we want to disable Per-Session PAT for this server. Here is how to do it below:

ASA(config)# xlate per-session deny tcp any4 10.10.10.10 eq 1720
ASA(config)# xlate per-session deny udp any4 10.10.10.10 range 1718 1719

The above configuration creates a deny rule for H.323 traffic for server 10.10.10.10, so that it uses multi-session PAT.

2.1.3 Configuring Static Address Translation (Static NAT)

The two translation types that we've discussed in the previous sections (Dynamic NAT and PAT) are used for Outbound communication only (i.e from higher security level to lower security level). However, if an outside host (let's say a host on the Internet) wants to initiate communication to an Internal host behind the firewall, this is not possible if we have only Dynamic NAT or PAT configured. This is very good in terms of security, but there are several cases that we must allow Inbound access as well (i.e access from lower security to higher security levels – Outside to Inside). To achieve this, we MUST use a **Static NAT** translation and also configure an appropriate **Access Control List**. Static NAT maps permanently a host address to a fixed global (outside) address.

The most important reasons to use Static NAT are the following:

- We have an internal server with private IP address (e.g our company's email or web server) that must always appear with a fixed public IP address on the Outside interface of the firewall.
- We want to allow hosts from the Outside (e.g Internet) to initiate connections to a local internal server (e.g our Web or email server).
- We want to use Port Redirection (more on this later).

Static NAT in Cisco ASA Versions prior to 8.3

The command format of Static NAT is:

ciscoasa(config)# static (*real_interface_name , mapped_interface_name*) "mapped_IP" "real_IP" netmask "subnet_mask"

To configure static NAT we need to know the following parameters:

1. Between which two interfaces the translation will take place. The two interfaces are defined as the **real_interface** and the **mapped_interface**. The real interface (e.g DMZ interface or Inside interface) must have higher security level than the mapped interface (e.g Outside interface).
2. The **real_IP** address of the host (the IP actually configured on the Network Card of the host).
3. The **mapped_IP** (or translated) IP address of the host (i.e the address that the host will be known to the Outside networks).

A little "catch" that you need to be careful with the **static** command is the following: when entering the interface names in the parenthesis, you enter the **real_interface** name first followed by the **mapped_interface** name (see command format above). However, when you configure the IP addresses after the interface names, you enter the **mapped_IP** address first followed by the **real_IP** address. Let's see some example scenarios for making things clear:

Scenario 1: Static NAT with a Web Server and Email Server on DMZ

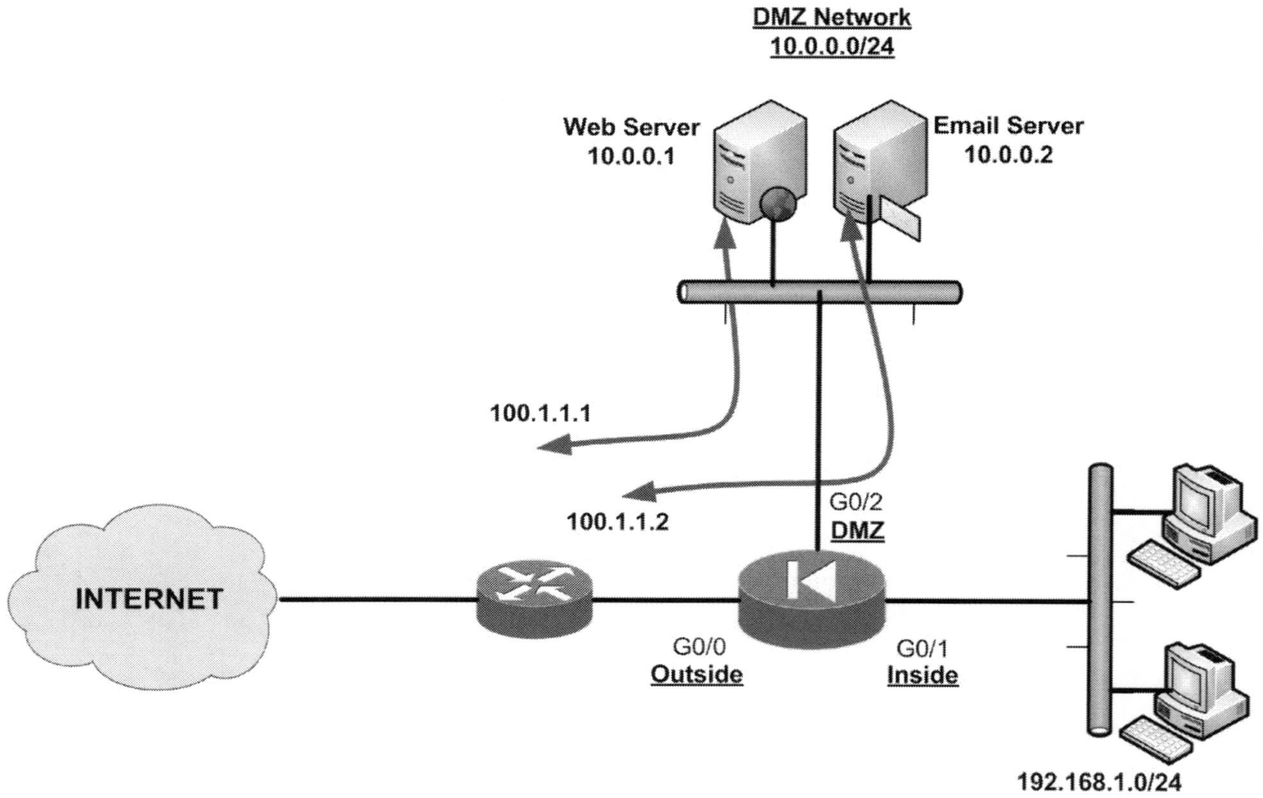

The network topology above is classic in many enterprises. Usually there is an Inside network on the firewall which hosts all internal employees' computers, an Outside network that connects to the Internet, and there is also a Demilitarized Zone (DMZ) that hosts servers which should be accessible from the Internet (in our example, a Web Server and an email Server). In this scenario static NAT must be used for the DMZ servers so that their real private IP address is always translated to a fixed public IP address (10.0.0.1 translated to 100.1.1.1 and 10.0.0.2 translated to 100.1.1.2).

In our scenario above we have the following:

- Real Interface name : **DMZ**
- Mapped Interface name: **Outside**
- Real IP addresses: **10.0.0.1** and **10.0.0.2**
- Mapped IP adresses: **100.1.1.1** and **100.1.1.2**

Static NAT in Cisco ASA Versions prior to 8.3

Let's see the configuration snapshot below:

ciscoasa(config)# static (DMZ , outside**)** 100.1.1.1 10.0.0.1 **netmask 255.255.255.255**
ciscoasa(config)# static (DMZ , outside**)** 100.1.1.2 10.0.0.2 **netmask 255.255.255.255**

The above statements enable bi-directional communication for the web and email servers. Now Internet hosts can access our web and email servers via their public address 100.1.1.1 and 100.1.1.2 Of course an ACL is still needed on the outside interface to allow communication.

Static NAT in Cisco ASA Version 8.3 and later

Now let's see how to configure the scenario above in ASA version 8.3 and later. Static NAT configuration uses the same concept as Dynamic NAT (i.e using network objects) but instead of using the keyword "**dynamic**" in the "**nat**" statement we use the keyword "**static**". The command format of the "**nat**" statement for static NAT is:

ciscoasa(config-network-object)# nat (real if , mapped if) static [*mapped-ip* **|** *mapped-obj***]**

To configure scenario 1 above in versions 8.3 and later execute the following commands:

ciscoasa(config)# object network web_server_static
ciscoasa(config-network-object)# host 10.0.0.1 ← Real IP of Web Server
ciscoasa(config-network-object)# nat (DMZ , outside) static 100.1.1.1 ← Mapped IP

ciscoasa(config)# object network email_server_static
ciscoasa(config-network-object)# host 10.0.0.2 ← Real IP of Email Server
ciscoasa(config-network-object)# nat (DMZ , outside) static 100.1.1.2 ← Mapped IP

Scenario 2: Static NAT for a whole network range (Net Static)

Cisco ASA Versions prior to 8.3

Instead of permanently translating single host addresses, we can create permanent address mappings to a whole subnet with just one command. Referring to the previous diagram in scenario 1 above, assume that we have a whole class C public address range 100.1.1.0/24. We can translate the whole DMZ range 10.0.0.0/24 to 100.1.1.0/24.

ciscoasa(config)# static (DMZ , outside) 100.1.1.0 10.0.0.0 netmask 255.255.255.0

Any packet sourced from a server address on subnet 10.0.0.0/24 on the DMZ will be translated to a host address on the 100.1.1.0/24 subnet on the outside interface (e.g. host 10.0.0.20 will be translated to 100.1.1.20).

Cisco ASA Version 8.3 and later

To configure scenario 2 above (i.e static NAT of whole network) in versions 8.3 and later:

ciscoasa(config)# object network mapped_static_range
ciscoasa(config-network-object)# subnet 100.1.1.0 255.255.255.0

ciscoasa(config)# object network dmz_network
ciscoasa(config-network-object)# subnet 10.0.0.0 255.255.255.0 ← DMZ subnet
ciscoasa(config-network-object)# nat (DMZ , outside) static mapped_static_range

Scenario 3: Static Port Address Translation (Port Redirection)

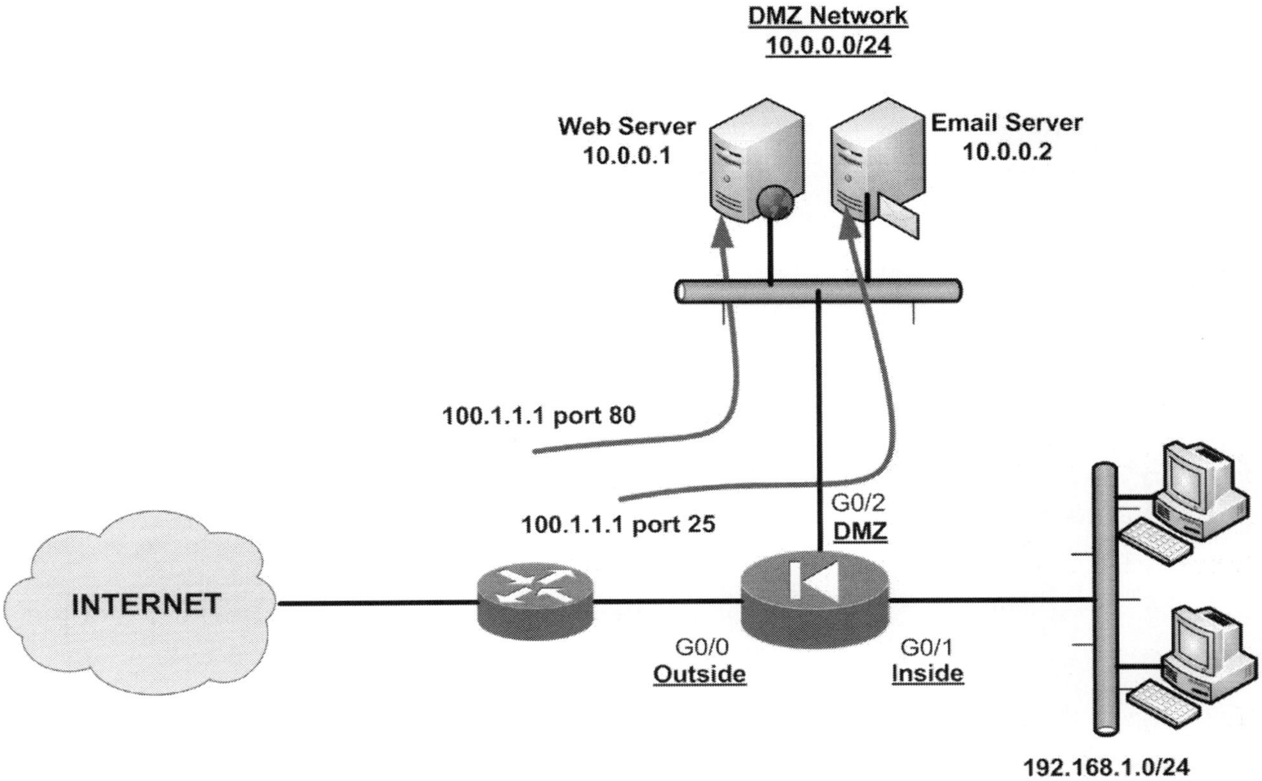

A pretty common scenario is the one shown on the diagram above. Assume we have only one public IP address available (100.1.1.1) but we have two (or more) servers that we need to provide public access for. We know that our Web Server listens to port 80 and our email Server listens to port 25. All inbound traffic hitting address 100.1.1.1 port 80 will be redirected by the firewall to 10.0.0.1 port 80, and all traffic hitting address 100.1.1.1 port 25 will be redirected to 10.0.0.2 port 25.

Cisco ASA Versions prior to 8.3

The command format for Port Redirection is the following:

ciscoasa(config)# static (*real_interface_name , mapped_interface_name*) [tcp|udp] "mapped_IP" "mapped_port" "real_IP" "real_port" netmask "subnet_mask"

For the network topology in our example scenario above, the port redirection commands are the following:

ciscoasa(config)# static (DMZ , outside) tcp 100.1.1.1 80 10.0.0.1 80 netmask 255.255.255.255
ciscoasa(config)# static (DMZ , outside) tcp 100.1.1.1 25 10.0.0.2 25 netmask 255.255.255.255

Another popular case is to do port redirection using the outside interface. If for example the ASA receives IP address dynamically from the ISP (using DHCP on the outside), then the outside address is not known. So we can configure the ASA so that traffic hitting its outside interface on port 80 to be redirected to DMZ Web Server 10.0.0.1 and also traffic hitting its outside interface on port 25 to be redirected to DMZ Email Server 10.0.0.2.

ciscoasa(config)# static (DMZ , outside) tcp interface 80 10.0.0.1 80 netmask 255.255.255.255
ciscoasa(config)# static (DMZ , outside) tcp interface 25 10.0.0.2 25 netmask 255.255.255.255

Now, what if we have two web servers that both listen to port 80? We can configure the firewall to redirect a different public mapped port (e.g. 8080 for example) to our second web server.

We can use also the Port Redirection feature to translate a well-known port to a lesser-known port or vice-versa. This will help to increase security. For example you can tell your web users to connect to a lesser-known port 5265 and then translate them to the correct port 80 on the local network.

Cisco ASA Version 8.3 and later

To configure Port Redirection in version 8.3 and later (using the same diagram above):

ciscoasa(config)# object network web_server_static

ciscoasa(config-network-object)# host 10.0.0.1

ciscoasa(config-network-object)# nat (DMZ , outside) static 100.1.1.1 service tcp 80 80

ciscoasa(config)# object network email_server_static

ciscoasa(config-network-object)# host 10.0.0.2

ciscoasa(config-network-object)# nat (DMZ , outside) static 100.1.1.1 service tcp 25 25

NOTES:

- The first port number (**25 or 80**) : This is the Real Port (actual port listening on th
- The second port number (**25 or 80**) : This is the Mapped Port (port visible from ou
- Instead of using a mapped IP (e.g 100.1.1.1) you can use the keyword "**interface**".

2.1.4 Configuring Identity NAT

<u>Cisco ASA Versions prior to 8.3</u>

It is worth mentioning another type of NAT mechanism called Identity NAT (or **nat 0**). If you enabled **nat-control** on your firewall, it is mandatory that all packets traversing the security appliance must match a translation rule (either **nat/global** or **static nat** rules). If we want to have some hosts (or whole networks) to pass through the firewall <u>without</u> translation, then the **nat 0** command must be used. This creates a transparent mapping. If Identity NAT is used on an interface, IP addresses on this interface translate to themselves on all lower security interfaces.

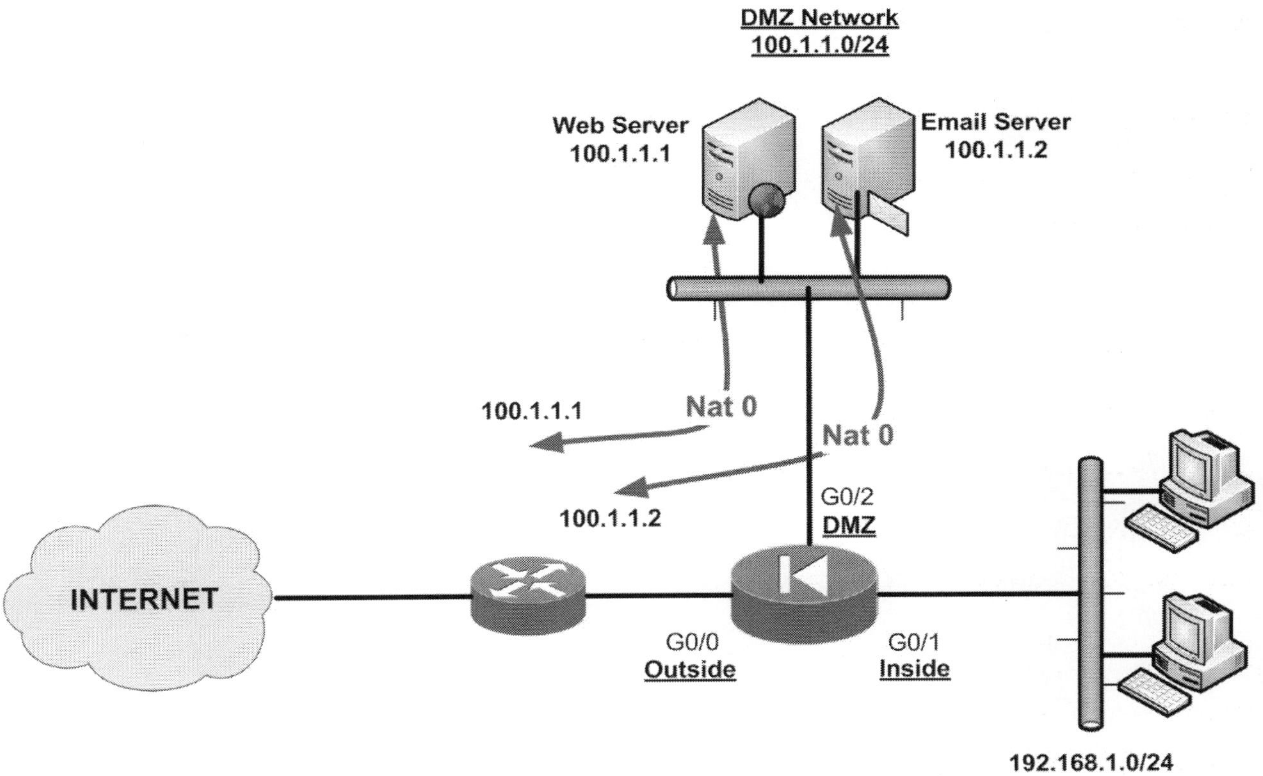

sume that our DMZ network is assigned a public IP address range (100.1.1.0/24). This means that the servers located on the DMZ have public IP addresses configured on their Network Interface cards. Therefore, we don't need to translate the DMZ real IP addresses into mapped global addresses.

ciscoasa(config)# nat (DMZ) 0 100.1.1.0 255.255.255.0

You still need to have an ACL on the Outside interface in order to allow users from the internet to connect with the DMZ servers.

Another way to configure Identity NAT is by using static NAT as shown below:

ciscoasa(config)# static (DMZ , outside) 100.1.1.0 100.1.1.0 netmask 255.255.255.0

Cisco ASA Version 8.3 and later

To configure Identity NAT in version 8.3 and later:

ciscoasa(config)# object network identity_nat_range
ciscoasa(config-network-object)# subnet 100.1.1.0 255.255.255.0

ciscoasa(config)# object network dmz_network
ciscoasa(config-network-object)# subnet 100.1.1.0 255.255.255.0
ciscoasa(config-network-object)# nat (DMZ , outside) static identity_nat_range

Another example with a single host:

ciscoasa(config)# object network no_nat
ciscoasa(config-network-object)# host 100.1.1.1
ciscoasa(config-network-object)# nat (DMZ , outside) static 100.1.1.1

2.1.4.1 Identity NAT Used for VPN Configurations

Cisco ASA Versions prior to 8.3

One important issue to consider is the case of using NAT on the firewall when there is also IPSEC VPN configured. Because IPSEC does not work with NAT, we need to exclude the traffic to be encrypted by IPSEC from the NAT operation. We can use the "**nat 0**" command for this. Although we will see this technique in more detail later (in the IPSEC VPN Chapter), let's talk briefly about it here.

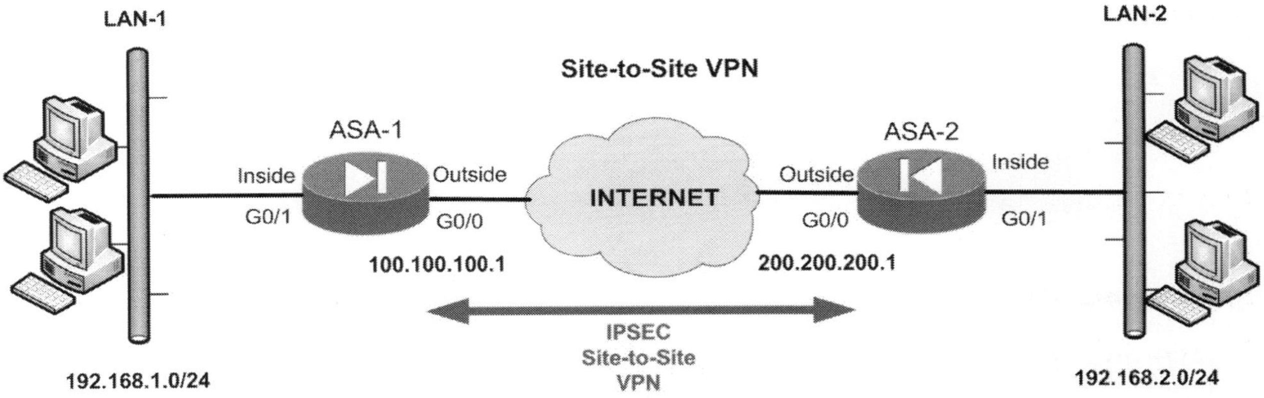

From example diagram above (which we will describe in more detail in a later Chapter), we need to establish a secure IPSEC VPN (Site-to-Site VPN) over the Internet between two internal LAN networks (LAN-1: 192.168.1.0/24 and LAN-2: 192.168.2.0/24). Both LAN1 and LAN2 will also have local Internet access. Therefore we need to configure Dynamic NAT on the ASA firewalls to allow the private LAN networks to access the Internet. However, traffic from LAN-1 to LAN-2 (and vice-versa) which will pass through the VPN tunnel, MUST be excluded from any NAT operation.

To achieve the above, we must configure a "**nat 0**" command using an Access Control List:

ASA 1:
ASA-1(config)# access-list NONAT extended permit ip 192.168.1.0 255.255.255.0 192.168.2.0 255.255.255.0

ASA-1(config)# nat (inside) 0 access-list NONAT ← Exclude traffic from LAN1 to LAN2 from NAT operation

ASA 2:
ASA-2(config)# access-list NONAT extended permit ip 192.168.2.0 255.255.255.0 192.168.1.0 255.255.255.0

ASA-2(config)# nat (inside) 0 access-list NONAT ← Exclude traffic from LAN2 to LAN1 from NAT operation

Cisco ASA Version 8.3 and later

To implement the functionality above in ASA version 8.3 and later, we must use the "Twice NAT" method, as shown below:

ASA 1:
ASA-1(config)# object network obj-local
ASA-1(config-network-object)# subnet 192.168.1.0 255.255.255.0
ASA-1(config-network-object)# exit

ASA-1(config)# object network obj-remote
ASA-1(config-network-object)# subnet 192.168.2.0 255.255.255.0
ASA-1(config-network-object)# exit

ASA-1(config)# nat (inside,outside) 1 source static obj-local obj-local destination static obj-remote obj-remote

ASA 2:
ASA-2(config)# object network obj-local
ASA-2(config-network-object)# subnet 192.168.2.0 255.255.255.0
ASA-2(config-network-object)# exit

ASA-2(config)# object network obj-remote
ASA-2(config-network-object)# subnet 192.168.1.0 255.255.255.0
ASA-2(config-network-object)# exit

ASA-2(config)# nat (inside,outside) 1 source static obj-local obj-local destination static obj-remote obj-remote

Chapter 3 Using Access Control Lists (ACL)

In Chapter 2 we have described the Network Address Translation (NAT) security mechanism, which is one of the two major elements that an administrator needs to configure in order to enable communication through the firewall. The second major element needed to enable traffic flow communication is the Access Control mechanism, also called **Access Control List (ACL)**.

3.1 ACL Overview

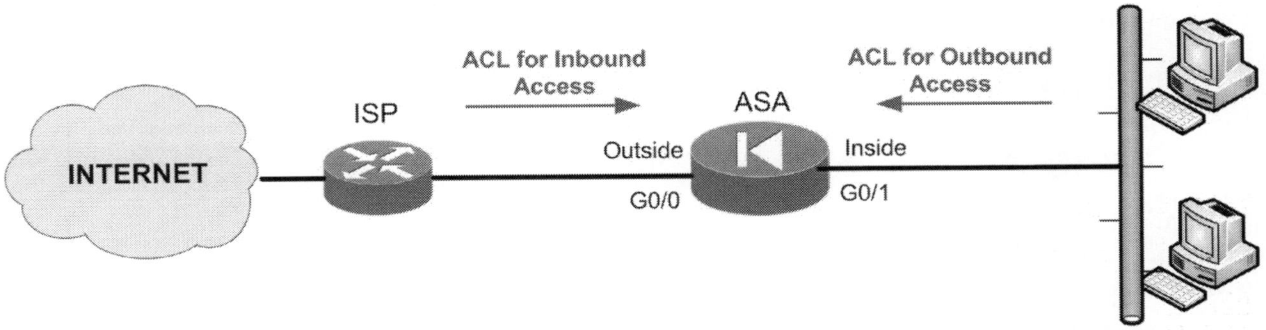

The Access Control List, as the name implies, is a List of statements (called Access Control Entries) that permit or deny traffic from a source to a destination. After an ACL is configured, it is applied to an interface using the "**access-group**" command. If no ACL is applied to an interface, outbound access traffic (from inside to outside) is permitted by default, and inbound access traffic (from outside to inside) is denied by default. The ACL can be applied (using the **access-group** command) both to the "**in**" and "**out**" direction of the traffic with respect to the interface. The "**in**" direction of ACL controls traffic entering an interface, and the "**out**" direction of ACL controls traffic exiting an interface. In the diagram above, both ACLs shown (for Inbound and for Outbound Access) are applied to the "**in**" direction of Outside and Inside interfaces respectively.

The following are guidelines for designing and implementing ACLs:

- For **Outbound Traffic** (Higher to Lower Security Levels), the source address argument of an ACL entry is the actual real address of the host or network.
- For **Inbound Traffic** (Lower to Higher Security Levels), the destination address argument of an ACL entry is the translated Mapped IP address. (**For ASA versions prior to 8.3**)

- In ASA Version 8.3 and later: Always use the Real IP address in the Access List when NAT is configured (i.e the IP actually configured on the host).
- ACLs are always checked before translation is performed on the security appliance.
- ACLs, in addition to restricting traffic flow through the firewall, they can be used also as a traffic selection mechanism for applying several other actions to the selected traffic, such as encryption, translation, policing, Quality of Service etc.

3.2 ACL Configuration

The command format of an Access Control List is the following:

ciscoasa(config)# access-list *"access_list_name"* [line *line_number*] [extended] *{deny | permit} protocol "source_address" "mask" [operator source_port] "dest_address" "mask" [operator dest_port]*

The command format of an Access-Group command used to apply an ACL is the following:

ciscoasa(config)# access-group *"access_list_name"* [in|out] interface *"interface_name"*

Let's see all the elements of the ACL command below:

- ***access_list_name*** : Give a descriptive name of the specific ACL. The same name is used in the access-group command.
- **line *line_number*** : Each ACL entry has its own line number.
- **extended**: Use this when you specify both source and destination addresses in the ACL.
- ***deny/permit*** : Specify whether the specific traffic is permitted or denied.
- ***protocol:*** Specify here the traffic protocol (IP, TCP, UDP etc).
- ***source_address mask:*** Specify the source IP address/network that the traffic originates. If it's a single IP address, you can use the keyword "**host**" without a mask. You can also use the keyword "**any**" to specify any address.
- ***[operator source_port]:*** Specify the source port number of the originating traffic. The "operator" keyword can be "**lt**" (less than), "**gt**" (greater than), "**eq**" (equal), "**Neq**" (Not equal to), "**range**" (range of ports). If no ***source_port*** is specified, the firewall matches all ports.

- ***dest_address mask:*** This is the destination IP address/network that the source address requires access to. You can use also the "**host**" or "**any**" keywords.
- ***[operator dest_port]:*** Specify the destination port number that the source traffic requires access to. The "operator" keyword can be "**lt**" (less than), "**gt**" (greater than), "**eq**" (equal), "**Neq**" (Not equal to), "**range**" (range of ports). If no ***dest-port*** is specified, the firewall matches all ports.

The ACL examples below will give us a better picture of the command format:

Example1

ciscoasa(config)# access-list DMZ_IN extended permit ip any any
ciscoasa(config)# access-group DMZ_IN in interface DMZ

The above will allow ALL traffic from DMZ network to go through the firewall.

Example2

ciscoasa(config)# access-list INSIDE_IN extended deny tcp 192.168.1.0 255.255.255.0 200.1.1.0 255.255.255.0
ciscoasa(config)# access-list INSIDE_IN extended deny tcp 192.168.1.0 255.255.255.0 host 210.1.1.1 eq 80
ciscoasa(config)# access-list INSIDE_IN extended permit ip any any
ciscoasa(config)# access-group INSIDE_IN in interface inside

The above example will deny ALL TCP traffic from our internal network 192.168.1.0/24 towards the external network 200.1.1.0/24. Also, it will deny HTTP traffic (port 80) from our internal network to the external host 210.1.1.1. All other traffic will be permitted from inside.

Example3

Cisco ASA Version prior to 8.3

ciscoasa(config)# access-list OUTSIDE_IN extended permit tcp any host 100.1.1.1 eq 80
ciscoasa(config)# access-group OUTSIDE_IN in interface outside

The ACL above will allow ANY host on the Internet to access our Web Server host (100.1.1.1). For ASA versions prior to 8.3, the address 100.1.1.1 is the public global translated address of our Web server.

Cisco ASA Version 8.3 and Later

If the Web Server has a private IP configured on its interface (Real IP address), then for ASA versions 8.3 and later the command will be (assume private IP of Web Server is **192.168.1.1**):

ciscoasa(config)# access-list OUTSIDE_IN extended permit tcp any host 192.168.1.1 eq 80
ciscoasa(config)# access-group OUTSIDE_IN in interface outside

3.2.1 Editing Access Control Lists

As we have said above, an ACL consists of one or more Access Control Entries (ACEs) which are command lines with permit or deny statements. By default, when you add new ACE lines, these are appended to the end of the ACL. Also, you can delete or insert new ACE lines anywhere in the ACL by using the "**line**" parameter in the access-list command.

You can see the line numbers of each ACE entry by using the "**show access-list [name]**" command.

Example:

Assume we have an ACL with name "INSIDE-IN". We can see the line numbers in the ACL as shown below:

ASA1# **show access-list INSIDE-IN**

access-list INSIDE-IN; 3 elements; name hash: 0xf1656621
access-list INSIDE-IN line 1 extended deny tcp host 10.1.1.12 any eq www (hitcnt=12) 0x410c3b92
access-list INSIDE-IN line 2 extended deny tcp host 10.1.1.12 any eq https (hitcnt=5) 0xefe6d38a
access-list INSIDE-IN line 3 extended permit ip any any (hitcnt=3791) 0xece2599d

As shown from the command output above, we have 3 lines in the ACL.

Now, let's say we want to insert a new ACE entry between lines 2 and 3 of the ACL above:

ASA1#conf t
ASA1(config)# **access-list INSIDE-IN line 3 extended deny tcp host 10.1.1.2 any eq smtp**
ASA1(config)# **show access-list INSIDE-IN**
access-list INSIDE-IN; 4 elements; name hash: 0xf1656621
access-list INSIDE-IN line 1 extended deny tcp host 10.1.1.12 any eq www (hitcnt=12) 0x410c3b92
access-list INSIDE-IN line 2 extended deny tcp host 10.1.1.12 any eq https (hitcnt=5) 0xefe6d38a
access-list INSIDE-IN line 3 extended deny tcp host 10.1.1.2 any eq smtp (hitcnt=0) 0xa0087167
access-list INSIDE-IN line 4 extended permit ip any any (hitcnt=3791) 0xece2599d

As you can see from the output above, a new ACE entry has been inserted at line 3 and the previous "line 3" entry has become "line 4".

In order to delete a specific ACE entry, just use the "**no**" keyword in front of the ACE entry:

ASA1(config)# **no access-list INSIDE-IN extended deny tcp host 10.1.1.12 any eq www**

3.3 New ACL Features in ASA 8.3 and Later

In ASA versions 8.3 and later there have been a few important new features regarding Access Control Lists. We will see them below.

3.3.1 Global Access Control List

As we've seen above, ACLs are applied on interfaces using the "access-group" command.
In newer ASA versions (8.3 and later) you can also apply an ACL globally as following:

ciscoasa(config)# access-group *"access_list_name"* global

An ACL applied globally with the "**access-group global"** command applies a single set of global rules on all traffic, no matter which interface the traffic arrives at the security appliance. However, it affects only traffic in the ingress (input) direction (i.e into the interface).

<u>Example</u>

! The configuration below will allow all internal hosts to access only the internal SMTP server (192.168.1.10) for sending emails and deny all other SMTP traffic from our internal network.

ciscoasa(config)# access-list SMTP extended permit tcp any host 192.168.1.10 eq 25
ciscoasa(config)# access-list SMTP extended permit tcp host 192.168.1.10 any eq 25
ciscoasa(config)# access-list SMTP extended deny tcp any any eq 25
ciscoasa(config)# access-list SMTP extended permit ip any any

! Apply the rules above globally no matter from which interface the traffic comes from. Useful when we have many interfaces on the ASA.

ciscoasa(config)# access-group SMTP global

3.3.2 ACL Changes in ASA Versions 9.x (9.0, 9.1 and later)

In Cisco ASA Version 9.x there were some changes in Access Control Lists regarding IPv4 and IPv6 traffic. Now, on the same ACL you can have both IPv4 and IPv6 addresses (as source and destination addresses on the ACL).

Also, the "**any**" keyword in an ACL has a different meaning in version 9.x. Now, if you have the "**any**" keyword in an ACL entry in version 9.x and later, it represents "ALL IPv4 AND IPv6 addresses". If you want to reference "all IPv4 addresses only" in an ACL, then you must use the keyword "**any4**". Similarly, if you want to reference "all IPv6 addresses only", then you must use the keyword "**any6**". If you are migrating from version 8.x and you had a keyword "any" in your ACL configuration, this will be changed to "any4" in the new configuration running under version 9.x.

Example:

! The rule below will allow only IPv4 traffic to access host 10.1.1.1 from the Internet

ASA(config)# access-list OUTSIDE extended permit ip any4 host 10.1.1.1
ASA(config)# access-group OUTSIDE in interface outside

3.4 Controlling Inbound and Outbound Traffic with ACLs

A picture is a thousand words. Refer to the picture diagram below for the example scenarios that will follow. These examples will show you how to control Inbound and Outbound Traffic flow:

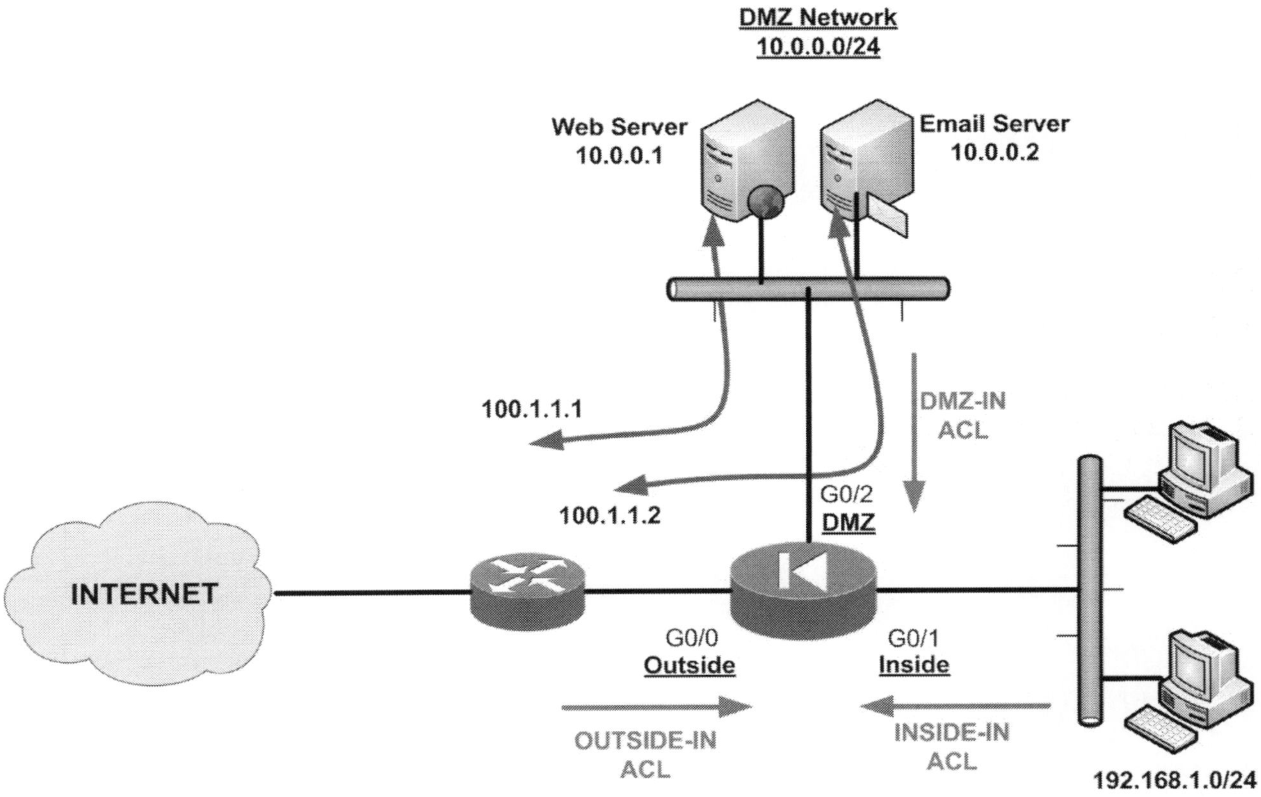

Scenario 1: Allow Inbound Access to DMZ Servers

For the Web and email Servers above, we have created static NAT mappings in order to translate their real private addresses into public addresses that are accessible from the Internet. In addition to the static NAT statements, we have to use also ACLs to allow the appropriate Inbound traffic towards our servers.

Cisco ASA Version Prior to 8.3

ciscoasa(config)# static (DMZ , outside) 100.1.1.1 10.0.0.1 netmask 255.255.255.255
ciscoasa(config)# static (DMZ , outside) 100.1.1.2 10.0.0.2 netmask 255.255.255.255

ciscoasa(config)# access-list OUTSIDE-IN extended permit tcp any host 100.1.1.1 eq 80
ciscoasa(config)# access-list OUTSIDE-IN extended permit tcp any host 100.1.1.2 eq 25
ciscoasa(config)# access-group OUTSIDE-IN in interface outside

ciscoasa(config)# access-list DMZ-IN extended deny ip any any log
ciscoasa(config)# access-group DMZ-IN in interface DMZ

As you can see from the ACL statements, we allow "any" traffic (i.e all internet traffic) to access the public IP addresses of our Web and email servers on the appropriate ports only (80 and 25). Also, all traffic originating from the DMZ servers is denied and logged using the DMZ-IN ACL. This is a good security practice to follow because if a DMZ server is compromised from outside, the attacker will not be able to access anything else from the DMZ zone.

Cisco ASA Version 8.3 and later

From Cisco ASA version 8.3 and later, you must specify the Real IP address in the ACL instead of the Mapped public IP address. From example above we have the following configuration:

! First create the static NAT translations

ciscoasa(config)# object network web_server_static
ciscoasa(config-network-object)# host 10.0.0.1 ← Real IP of Web Server
ciscoasa(config-network-object)# nat (DMZ , outside) static 100.1.1.1 ← Mapped IP

ciscoasa(config)# object network email_server_static
ciscoasa(config-network-object)# host 10.0.0.2 ← Real IP of Email Server
ciscoasa(config-network-object)# nat (DMZ , outside) static 100.1.1.2 ← Mapped IP

! Now allow only the absolutely necessary ports (80 and 25) from Internet

ciscoasa(config)# access-list OUTSIDE-IN extended permit tcp any host 10.0.0.1 **eq 80**
ciscoasa(config)# access-list OUTSIDE-IN extended permit tcp any host 10.0.0.2 **eq 25**
ciscoasa(config)# access-group OUTSIDE-IN in interface outside

Notice that we have used the Real IP addresses (**10.0.0.1** and **10.0.0.2**) in the access list entry and NOT the mapped public IP addresses.

Scenario 2: Apply Identity NAT to Inside Network when accessing DMZ

As we have mentioned earlier, ACLs, in addition to restricting traffic flow, they can be used also to identify traffic for applying other actions to it. For our diagram above, assume that we want to apply Identity NAT to our Inside network when this communicates with the DMZ. In other words, when hosts in network 192.168.1.0/24 initiate communication to network 10.0.0.0/24, then we don't want to translate them. To disable NAT translation from a specific high security interface to a lower security interface, we can use the **nat 0** command (**Only in versions prior to 8.3**). An ACL can be used together with the **nat 0** command to identify which traffic flow will not be translated.

Cisco ASA Version Prior to 8.3

ciscoasa(config)# access-list NO-NAT extended permit ip 192.168.1.0 255.255.255.0 10.0.0.0 255.255.255.0 ←**Match Traffic from Inside to DMZ**
ciscoasa(config)# nat (inside) 0 access-list NO-NAT ←**Do not translate traffic matched by this ACL**

ciscoasa(config)# nat (inside) 1 192.168.1.0 255.255.255.0
ciscoasa(config)# global (outside) 1 interface ←**Use PAT when going from Inside to Outside**

The configuration above applies for versions prior to 8.3. The next scenario is much more popular, so let's proceed with this.

Scenario 3: Bidirectional Communication between Inside and DMZ Networks

The previous scenario 2 above works only for traffic going from Inside to DMZ (and not vice-versa). If we want to have bidirectional communication between Inside Network and DMZ, then we must configure Static NAT translation between the two networks. Specifically, we can create a static Identity NAT of the Inside LAN (192.168.1.0/24) when communicating with DMZ. This means that source IP addresses of Inside LAN hosts will not be translated when communicating with DMZ (Identity NAT). Since we will use static mapping, this will allow also access from DMZ to Inside (controlled by an ACL ofcourse).

Referring again to the previous diagram in scenario 1 above, we will create a Static Identity NAT of Inside LAN. Let's see the commands needed for this scenario:

Cisco ASA Version Prior to 8.3

ciscoasa(config)# static (inside , DMZ) 192.168.1.0 192.168.1.0 netmask 255.255.255.0

The above creates a Static Identity NAT of inside LAN (between inside and DMZ zones). The hosts in Inside Zone will not be translated when going to DMZ Zone. Moreover, this configuration will allow access from DMZ to Inside if needed.

! Now allow access from DMZ to Inside as needed. This access is controlled by "dmzin" ACL.

ciscoasa(config)# access-list dmzin extended permit tcp host 10.0.0.2 host 192.168.1.3 eq 25
ciscoasa(config)# access-group dmzin in interface DMZ
The ACL "dmzin" will allow access from DMZ host 10.0.0.2 to Inside host 192.168.1.3 port 25.

Cisco ASA Versions 8.3 and later

To configure scenario 3 above in versions 8.3 and later:

! Configure the static Identity NAT

ciscoasa(config)# object network inside_identity_nat
ciscoasa(config-network-object)# subnet 192.168.1.0 255.255.255.0

ciscoasa(config)# object network inside_network
ciscoasa(config-network-object)# subnet 192.168.1.0 255.255.255.0 ← Internal subnet
ciscoasa(config-network-object)# nat (inside, DMZ) static inside_identity_nat

! Now allow access from DMZ to Inside as needed. This access is controlled by "dmzin" ACL.

ciscoasa(config)# access-list dmzin extended permit tcp host 10.0.0.2 host 192.168.1.3 eq 25
ciscoasa(config)# access-group dmzin in interface DMZ

Scenario 4: Apply Outbound Restrictions from Inside to DMZ

Now, assume that users on the Inside network (192.168.1.0/24) are only allowed to access the email Server at port 25 on the DMZ (to retrieve email) but should not have any access to the rest of the DMZ network. All access however towards the Internet should be allowed.

```
ciscoasa(config)# access-list INSIDE-IN extended  permit tcp 192.168.1.0 255.255.255.0 host 10.0.0.2 eq 25
ciscoasa(config)# access-list INSIDE-IN extended  deny ip 192.168.1.0 255.255.255.0 10.0.0.0 255.255.255.0
ciscoasa(config)# access-list INSIDE-IN extended  permit ip 192.168.1.0 255.255.255.0 any

ciscoasa(config)# access-group INSIDE-IN in interface inside
```

3.5 Configuring Object Groups for ACLs

Imagine that you are responsible for a huge network with hundreds of hosts protected by a Cisco Firewall. Imagine also that your organization's security policy dictates that there should be strict access control for all hosts in your network. Creating and maintaining Access Control Lists in such an environment could be a daunting task.

Fortunately, Cisco introduced the **object-group** command which allows the firewall administrator to group together objects such as hosts, networks, ports etc. These object groups can then be used in an access-list command to reference all objects within the group. This helps to reduce multiple lines in the access list and makes ACL administration much easier. Also, any changes in hosts, ports etc are done inside the **object-group** and are automatically reflected in the access-list.

There are six types of object groups:

- **Network**: Used to group together hosts or subnets.
- **Service**: Used to group TCP or UDP port numbers.
- **Protocol**: Used to group protocols.
- **ICMP-type**: Used to group ICMP message types.
- **User**: Creates Local User Groups (used in Identity Firewall feature)
- **Security** object group (Version 9.x): Used with Cisco TrustSec.

We will describe the first two types (Network and Service object groups) since they are the most important and popular types used in ACLs.

3.5.1 Network Object Groups

The command format of the Network Object Group is the following:

ciscoasa(config)# object-group network *"group_name"* ←**First Define a name of the object group. This will put you in a subcommand mode (config-network)**
ciscoasa(config-network)# network-object host *"ip_addr"* ←**Define a single Host**
ciscoasa(config-network)# network-object *"net_addr netmask"* ←**Define a whole subnet**
ciscoasa(config-network)# exit
ciscoasa(config)#

Example:

- Create the Network Object Group:

ciscoasa(config)# object-group network WEB_SRV
ciscoasa(config-network)# network-object host 10.0.0.1
ciscoasa(config-network)# network-object host 10.0.0.2

ciscoasa(config)# object-group network DMZ_SUBNET
ciscoasa(config-network)# network-object 10.0.0.0 255.255.255.0

- Using the object group with an ACL:

ciscoasa(config)# access-list OUT-IN extended permit tcp any object-group WEB_SRV eq 80

In the example above, we created a network object group (WEB_SRV) for our Web Servers (10.0.0.1 and 10.0.0.2). With a single ACL statement, we allowed TCP access from Outside towards this specific object-group for port 80. Notice that the network object-group in the access-list command is used in place of the destination address. It could be used also in place of the source address accordingly.

3.5.2 Service Object Groups

The command format of the Service Object Group is the following:

ciscoasa(config)# object-group service *"group_name"* {tcp | udp | tcp-udp} ←**First Define a name of the obj. group and specify what kind of service ports will follow (tcp, udp or both)**
ciscoasa(config-service)# port-object {eq | range} *"port_number"* ←**Define service ports**
ciscoasa(config-service)# exit
ciscoasa(config)#

Example:

- Create the Service Object Group:

ciscoasa(config)# object-group service DMZ_SERVICES tcp
ciscoasa(config-service)# port-object eq http
ciscoasa(config-service)# port-object eq https
ciscoasa(config-service)# port-object range 21 23

ciscoasa(config)# object-group network DMZ_SUBNET
ciscoasa(config-network)# network-object 10.0.0.0 255.255.255.0

- Using the object group with an ACL:

ciscoasa(config)# access-list OUTSIDE-IN extended permit tcp any object-group DMZ_SUBNET object-group DMZ_SERVICES

In our example above, assume that we have a DMZ network 10.0.0.0/24 hosting servers with tcp services of http, https, ftp (port 21), ssh (port 22) and telnet (port 23). For this scenario we created a DMZ network object group (DMZ_SUBNET) together with a service object group (DMZ_SERVICES). The DMZ_SUBNET group is used in place of the destination address, and the DMZ_SERVICES group is used in place of the destination port.

3.6 Time Based Access Lists

Another important feature of ACLs that is very useful is "**Time-Based ACLs**". You can append to an ACL command a time-range period which means that this specific ACL entry will be valid only during the specified time-range. First you need to define the "time-range" and then use this time range on an ACL entry.

Example1:

Assume we want to restrict web access for the Internal network during working hours from 09:00 to 17:00.

Step1: Define the time-range period

You can use absolute time ranges (such as January 1 to January 20) or periodic ranges (such as weekdays or every Sunday for example).

ASA1(config)# time-range workhours
ASA1(config-time-range)# periodic weekdays 09:00 to 17:00
ASA1(config-time-range)# exit

Step2: Create an ACL which will use the time range above

ASA1(config)# access-list INSIDE-IN extended deny tcp any any eq www time-range workhours
ASA1(config)# access-list INSIDE-IN extended permit ip any any

ASA1(config)# access-group INSIDE-IN in interface inside

From the configuration above, if a user tries to access the web and the time-range is within the "workhours" period, then the first ACL entry will be enabled and therefore the user will be blocked. If the time-range is outside the "workhours" period then the first ACL entry will be disabled and therefore the second ACL entry will permit the traffic.

Example2:

Assume we want to allow web access for a specific DMZ server in order to download security updates every Sunday between 08:00 – 11:00. For all other time the access to Internet will be blocked.

ASA1(config)# time-range updatehours
ASA1(config-time-range)# periodic Sunday 08:00 to 11:00
ASA1(config-time-range)# exit

ASA1(config)# access-list DMZ-IN extended permit ip host 10.1.1.1 any time-range updatehours
ASA1(config)# access-list DMZ-IN extended deny ip any any

ASA1(config)# access-group DMZ-IN in interface DMZ

Chapter 4 Configuring VLANs and Subinterfaces

In this Chapter we will focus on Interface Layer 2 connectivity of the Cisco ASA firewall. Let me remind you that each interface (physical or logical) of the ASA appliance is used to create a security zone, which is basically a network segment (Layer 3 subnet) hosting PCs, Servers etc. Each security zone is protected by the firewall from the other security zones on the appliance or the Internet.

In order to build a secure network that follows the principles of "**Layered Security**", it is a good practice to segment your network into different security zones (Layer 3 subnets) which are controlled and protected by the firewall. To create security zones, you can use either Physical or Logical Interfaces on the appliance. However, in order to create Layer 3 subnets, you must have also a different Layer 2 VLAN for each subnet.

Cisco ASA firewalls support multiple 802.1q VLANs on a Physical interface. This means that an administrator can configure multiple Logical interfaces (subinterfaces) on a single physical interface and assign each logical interface to a specific VLAN. For example, a Cisco firewall appliance with 4 physical interfaces is not limited to having only 4 security zones. We can create for example 3 logical subinterfaces on each physical interface, which will give us 12 (4x3) different security zones (12 VLANs and 12 Layer 3 subnets). Depending on the ASA model, up to 1024 maximum VLANs can be configured on a single appliance (the ASA 5585-X supports 1024 VLANS).

If you configure subinterfaces (VLANs) on a physical interface, then this physical interface must be connected to a Trunk Port on a Layer 2 switch. In addition, if you enable subinterfaces, you typically do not want the main physical interface to also be passing traffic. You can achieve this by omitting the **nameif** command (**no nameif**) on the physical interface.

To configure logical subinterfaces, use the *subinterface* argument of the **interface** command in global configuration mode. This will put you in subinterface configuration mode, where you have to assign a VLAN ID using **vlan** *id* command. As we mentioned in "**Basic Configuration Steps**" Section of Chapter 1, we also have to configure a name for the subinterface (**nameif**), a security level, and an IP address.

The command format for configuring VLAN logical subinterfaces is shown below:

ciscoasa(config)# interface "*physical_interface.subinterface*" ←Use the *subinterface* argument
ciscoasa(config-subif)# ←This is the subinterface configuration mode
ciscoasa(config-subif)# vlan "*id*" ←Assign a VLAN to the subinterface
ciscoasa(config-subif)# nameif "*subif_name*" ←Assign a name to the subinterface
ciscoasa(config-subif)# security-level "*0-100*" ←Assign a security level to the subinterface
ciscoasa(config-subif)# ip address "*IP*" "*netmask*" ←Assign IP address

Let's see an example scenario below with a network diagram.

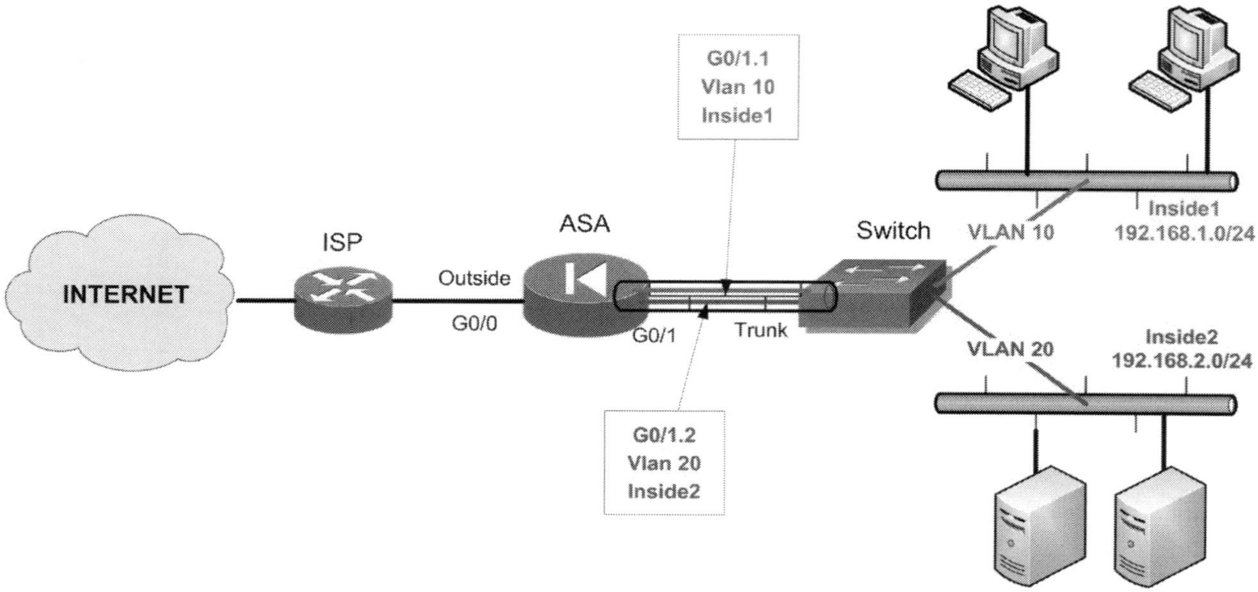

In the example above, assume that we wanted to segment our internal network into two security zones (**Inside1** and **Inside2**). Maybe Inside1 zone will host all user PCs, and Inside2 zone will host all internal corporate servers (email server, domain server etc). To build this topology, we need to create two VLANs on the switch (10 and 20), one for each network subnet. Instead of using two Physical Interfaces of the ASA firewall (one for each zone), we used one physical interface with two logical interfaces, as shown below:

- G0/1 = Physical Interface
- G0/1.1 = Logical Interface (subinterface) assigned to VLAN 10
- G0/1.2 = Logical Interface (subinterface) assigned to VLAN 20

The two logical interfaces (G0/1.1 and G0/1.2) behave just like the physical interface, and they are two separate "legs" of the firewall.

See the sample configuration below for details:

ciscoasa(config)# interface gigabitethernet 0/1
ciscoasa(config-if)# no nameif ←**Disable the physical interface from passing traffic**
ciscoasa(config-if)# no security-level
ciscoasa(config-if)# no ip address
ciscoasa(config-if)# exit

ciscoasa(config)# interface gigabitethernet 0/1.1
ciscoasa(config-subif)# vlan 10
ciscoasa(config-subif)# nameif inside1
ciscoasa(config-subif)# security-level 80
ciscoasa(config-subif)# ip address 192.168.1.1 255.255.255.0

ciscoasa(config)# interface gigabitethernet 0/1.2
ciscoasa(config-subif)# vlan 20
ciscoasa(config-subif)# nameif inside2
ciscoasa(config-subif)# security-level 90
ciscoasa(config-subif)# ip address 192.168.2.1 255.255.255.0

Chapter 5 Configuring Threat Detection

5.1 Threat Detection Overview

Threat detection was introduced to allow the security appliance to monitor threatening packet flows. This feature can inform administrators about a possible attack and also has enough intelligence to automatically block threatening IP addresses or ranges (mainly for scanning threats).

Threat Detection is a tool to identify, understand, and stop attacks before they reach the internal network infrastructure. It relies on a number of different triggers and statistics on the firewall which are fired and calculated as the traffic passes through the ASA.

Threat detection feature is supported from software versions 8.0(2) so you can enable it on any ASA which is running 8.0(2) or higher version. Advanced Threat Detection statistics for TCP intercept are only available in ASA 8.0(4) and later. You should note that **threat detection is not a substitute of a dedicated IDS/IPS solution**; it can be used in environments where an IPS is not available to provide an added layer of protection to the core functionality of ASA.

The threat detection feature has three main components:

1. **Basic Threat Detection** (enabled by default)
2. **Advanced Threat Detection** (only ACL statistics are enabled by default)
3. **Scanning Threat Detection** (you can shun hosts which scan the protected network)

Let's walk through each one of them below.

5.2 Basic Threat Detection

Basic threat detection provides very basic security where it monitors the rates at which packets are dropped for various reasons by the ASA as a whole. As the name suggests, it provides basic functionality and is applicable on the entire device because it does not give you the granularity to monitor anything very specific. In general, it uses the ASP-Drop engine on the firewall to generate the statistics.

With Basic threat detection, ASA monitors dropped packets for these events:

- **Packes denied by Access Lists** (ACL Drop).
- **Bad packet format** (such as invalid-ip-header or invalid-tcp-hdr-length).
- **Connection limits exceeded** (both system-wide resource limits, and limits set in the configuration).
- **DoS attack detected** (such as an invalid SPI, Stateful Firewall check failure).
- **Basic firewall checks failed** (This option is a combined rate that includes all firewall-related packet drops in this bulleted list. It does not include non-firewall-related drops such as interface overload, packets failed at application inspection, and scanning attack detected.)
- **Suspicious ICMP packets detected**.
- **Packets failed application inspection**.
- **Interface overload**.
- **Scanning attack detected** (This option monitors scanning attacks; for example, the first TCP packet is not a SYN packet, or the TCP connection failed the 3-way handshake. Full scanning threat detection takes this scanning attack rate information and acts on it by classifying hosts as attackers and automatically shunning them, for example.)
- **SYN Attack Detection**. Incomplete session detection such as TCP SYN attack detected or no data UDP session attack detected.

When the ASA detects a threat, it immediately sends a system log message (733100).

For each event, basic threat detection measures the rates at which drops occur over a defined period of time which is known as the **average rate interval (ARI)** which ranges from 600 seconds to 30 days. If the number of events that occur within the ARI exceeds the configured rate thresholds, the ASA considers these events a threat.

Basic threat detection has two configurable thresholds for when it considers events to be a threat: the **average rate** and the **burst rate**. The average rate is simply the average number of drops per second within the time period of the configured ARI. For example, if the average rate threshold for ACL drops is configured for 300 with an ARI of 600 seconds, the ASA calculates the average number of packets that were dropped by ACLs in the last 600 seconds. If this number turns out to be greater than 300 per second, the ASA logs a threat.

As we have said above, whenever a basic threat is detected, the ASA simply generates syslog message **%ASA-4-733100** to alert the administrator that a potential threat has been identified. The

ASA can be configured to send these alert messages in email. If I am an administrator and if I want to get alerted then I will receive an email from the ASA stating this alert number and then I can act over it. The average, current, and total number of events for each threat category can be seen with the **show threat-detection rate** command. Since Basic threat detection works on the overall drops on the firewall, it does not take any actions to stop the offending traffic or prevent future attacks. Basic threat detection is purely informational and can be used as a monitoring or reporting mechanism.

5.2.1 Configuration and Monitoring of Basic Threat Detection

Simply enable basic threat detection statistics using the following command:

ciscoasa(config)# threat-detection basic-threat

Note: Basic threat detection statistics are enabled by default and have no performance impact. You can enable it from the ASDM by going to **Configuration→Firewall→Threat Detection** to enable or disable this feature.

A sample log that is generated after enabling this command can be seen below:

Aug 25 2013 08:38:19: %ASA-4-733100: [Scanning] drop rate-1 exceeded. Current burst rate is 10 per second, max configured rate is 10; Current average rate is 8 per second, max configured rate is 5; Cumulative total count is 4860

Aug 25 2013 08:38:21: %ASA-4-733100: [Scanning] drop rate-2 exceeded. Current burst rate is 8 per second, max configured rate is 8; Current average rate is 5 per second, max configured rate is 4; Cumulative total count is 20163

Aug 25 2013 08:42:15: %ASA-4-733100: [Scanning] drop rate-1 exceeded. Current burst rate is 10 per second, max configured rate is 10; Current average rate is 7 per second, max configured rate is 5; Cumulative total count is 4531

Aug 25 2013 08:42:28: %ASA-4-733100: [Scanning] drop rate-2 exceeded. Current burst rate is 8 per second, max configured rate is 8; Current average rate is 5 per second, max configured rate is 4; Cumulative total count is 20880

Aug 25 2013 08:42:40: %ASA-4-733100: [Scanning] drop rate-1 exceeded. Current burst rate is 10 per second, max configured rate is 10; Current average rate is 7 per second, max configured rate is 5; Cumulative total count is 4591

When you enable basic threat detection using the **threat-detection basic-threat** command, you can view statistics using the **show threat-detection rate** command in privileged EXEC mode.

ciscoasa# show threat-detection rate

Following is a sample output from the **show threat-detection rate** command:

	Average(eps)	Current(eps)	Trigger	Total events
10-min ACL drop:	*0*	*0*	*0*	*165*
1-hour ACL drop:	*0*	*0*	*0*	*123*
1-hour SYN attck:	*4*	*0*	*5*	*51332*
10-min Scanning:	*0*	*0*	*29*	*193*
1-hour Scanning:	*106*	*0*	*10*	*384776*
10-min Firewall:	*0*	*0*	*3*	*22*
1-hour Firewall:	*76*	*0*	*2*	*274844*
10-min DoS attck:	*0*	*0*	*0*	*6*
1-hour DoS attck:	*0*	*0*	*0*	*42*

The output shows the following:

- The average rate in events/sec over fixed time periods.
- The current burst rate in events/sec over the last completed burst interval, which is 1/30th of the average rate interval or 10 seconds, whichever is larger
- The number of times the rates were exceeded (Trigger).
- The total number of events over the fixed time periods.

Default Values of Basic Threat Detection

In order to see the default values of Basic Threat Detection events, run the following command:

ciscoasa# show running-config all threat-detection

threat-detection rate dos-drop rate-interval 600 average-rate 100 burst-rate 400

threat-detection rate dos-drop rate-interval 3600 average-rate 80 burst-rate 320

threat-detection rate bad-packet-drop rate-interval 600 average-rate 100 burst-rate 400

threat-detection rate bad-packet-drop rate-interval 3600 average-rate 80 burst-rate 320

threat-detection rate acl-drop rate-interval 600 average-rate 400 burst-rate 800

threat-detection rate acl-drop rate-interval 3600 average-rate 320 burst-rate 640

threat-detection rate conn-limit-drop rate-interval 600 average-rate 100 burst-rate 400

threat-detection rate conn-limit-drop rate-interval 3600 average-rate 80 burst-rate 320

threat-detection rate icmp-drop rate-interval 600 average-rate 100 burst-rate 400

threat-detection rate icmp-drop rate-interval 3600 average-rate 80 burst-rate 320

threat-detection rate scanning-threat rate-interval 600 average-rate 5 burst-rate 10

threat-detection rate scanning-threat rate-interval 3600 average-rate 4 burst-rate 8

---Output Omitted---

You can fine tune the default values as following:

Let's say we want to change the DoS event trigger rates from the default values:

ciscoasa(config)#threat-detection rate dos-drop rate-interval 600 average-rate 60 burst-rate 100

In the example above, the ASA will issue a syslog message (%ASA-4-73310) when the number of DoS events exceeds 60 per second over 600 seconds. Also, if the DoS events are more than 100 per second over 20 seconds (1/30 of 600) it will issue again a syslog message.

5.3 Advanced Threat Detection

Advanced threat detection statistics show both allowed and dropped traffic rates for individual objects such as hosts, ports, protocols, or ACLs. Therefore it offers a more granular control in monitoring threats. By default, Advanced Threat Detection is enabled only for ACL statistics. Depending on the type of statistics enabled, it can have performance impact on the device. The **threat-detection statistics host** command affects performance in a significant way; if you have a high traffic load, you might consider enabling this type of statistics temporarily. The **threat-detection statistics port** command, however, has modest impact.

For host, port, and protocol objects, Threat Detection keeps track of the number of packets, bytes, and drops that were both sent and received by that object within a specific time period. Threat Detection keeps track of the top 10 ACEs (both permit and deny) that were hit the most within a specific time period.

Like Basic Threat Detection, the Advanced Threat Detection is purely informational. No actions are taken to block traffic based on the Advanced Threat Detection statistics.

5.3.1 Configuration and Monitoring of Advanced Threat Detection

To configure Advanced Threat Detection use the command "**threat-detection statistics**". If no specific feature keyword is provided, the command enables tracking for all statistics.

ciscoasa(config)# threat-detection statistics { access-list|host|port|protocol|tcp-intercept}

- **access-list**: Enables statistics for ACLs (enabled by default).
- **host number-of rate {1|2|3}** : Enable statistics for host with specified number-of-rate interval. The number-of-rate keyword sets the number of rate intervals maintained for host statistics. The default number of rate intervals is 1, which keeps the memory usage low. To view more rate intervals, set the value to 2 or 3. For example, if you set the value to 3, then you view data for the last 1 hour, 8 hours, and 24 hours. If you set this keyword to 1 (the default), then only the shortest rate interval statistics are maintained. NOTE: The "host" monitoring may affect ASA performance.

- **port number-of rate {1|2|3} :** Enable statistics for TCP and UDP ports. For the "**number-of-rate**" keyword see the explanation above.
- **protocol number-of rate {1|2|3} :** Enable statistics for non-TCP/UDP IP protocols.
- **tcp-intercept:** Enable statistics for attacks intercepted by TCP intercept feature.

To monitor the advanced threat detection statistics use the following:

ciscoasa(config)# show threat-detection statistics {host| min-display-rate|port|protocol|top}

It is very useful to use the "**top**" keyword on the command above to monitor the top 10 statistics for various elements.

Example1:

ciscoasa(config)# show threat-detection statistics top access-list

The command above will show you the top 10 Access Control Entries that match packets, including both permit and deny.

Example2:

ciscoasa(config)# show threat-detection rate acl-drop

With the command above you can track ACL denies on the firewall.

Example3:

ciscoasa(config)# show threat-detection statistics host

If you have enabled the "host" threat detection monitoring, you can see some very interesting statistics such as:

- Total number of sessions from hosts.
- Total number of active sessions for each host (useful to identify if there are hosts in the network infected with worms or viruses which generate a lot of sessions and traffic in the network).
- Firewall drops for each host.
- Application inspection drops for each host.
- Etc

5.4 Scanning Threat Detection

Scanning Threat Detection is the only one which can actively block (shun) attackers which are attempting to scan the network protected by the ASA. Unlike IPS scan detection that is based on traffic signatures, the ASA scanning threat detection feature maintains an extensive database that contains host statistics that can be analyzed for scanning activity. If the scanning threat rate is exceeded, then the ASA sends a syslog message (733101), and optionally shuns the attacker. If a shun is configured, the ASA sends a syslog message 733102 to indicate that an attacker was blocked.

NOTES:

1. The Scanning Threat Detection feature can have a significant impact on ASA performance.
2. Only traffic that is allowed to pass through the ASA is affected by scanning threat detection. Traffic that is denied by ACL is not detected by Scanning Threat mechanism.

5.4.1 Configuration and Monitoring of Scanning Threat Detection

To configure Scanning Threat Detection use the command "**threat-detection scanning-threat**" as we will explain below:

ciscoasa(config)# threat-detection scanning-threat { shun [duration|except] **}**

Example1:

ciscoasa(config)# threat-detection scanning-threat ← **Just enable the scanning threat detection**

Example2:

ciscoasa(config)# threat-detection scanning-threat shun duration 3600← **Enable scanning threat detection and shun attackers for 3600 seconds.**

Example3:

ciscoasa(config)# threat-detection scanning-threat shun except ip-address 10.1.1.1 255.255.255.0 ← Enable scanning threat detection and shun attackers except IP 10.1.1.1

Default Values for Scanning Threat Detection

The following are the default values for scanning threat detection:

Average Rate	Burst Rate
5 drops/sec over the last 600 seconds	10 drops/sec over the last 20 second period
5 drops/sec over the last 3600 seconds	10 drops/sec over the last 120 second period.

To change the default values:

Example:

ciscoasa(config)# threat-detection rate scanning-threat rate-interval 1200 average-rate 10 burst-rate 20

To monitor the scanning threat detection shunned hosts, attackers and targets, use the following:

ciscoasa(config)#show threat-detection shun ← Shows which hosts are shunned

Shunned Host List:

111.222.0.1
200.0.0.2

To unblock one of the shunned hosts above:

ciscoasa(config)#clear threat-detection shun 111.222.0.1

ciscoasa(config)#show threat-detection scanning-threat attacker ← Shows attackers which are identified to be scanning our network.

111.222.0.1
200.0.0.2
195.1.0.2

Chapter 6 IPSec VPNs

This Chapter discusses Virtual Private Networks using the IPSec protocol standard. Cisco ASA appliances, in addition to their core firewall functionality, can be used also to securely connect together distant LAN networks (**Site-to-Site VPN**) or allow remote users/teleworkers to securely communicate with their corporate network (**Remote-Access VPN**). So, with the IPSec technology we can build two types of VPN topologies:

- **Site-to-Site VPNs** (or **Hub-and-Spoke** between a hub site and several branch spoke sites)
- **Remote Access VPNs**.

In this Chapter we will focus on the above two types of VPN topologies.

The majority of IPSec VPNs operating today are built using the legacy **IKEv1 IPSEC** technology. However, a new **IKEv2 IPSEC** implementation has been introduced which will be discussed also in this Chapter. Specifically, we will see how to setup Site-to-Site VPNs using both IKEv1 and IKEv2 IPSEC. Moreover, we will also discuss Remote Access VPN using the legacy IPSEC VPN client software.

Before proceeding with the technical details of configuring IPSEc VPNs, it will be very useful to briefly summarize the VPN technologies supported by Cisco ASA. These VPN technologies will be discussed in this Chapter and in the next one.

6.1 Overview of Cisco ASA VPN Technologies

Cisco supports several types of VPN implementations on the ASA but they are generally categorized as either "**IPSec Based VPNs**" or "**SSL Based VPNs**". The first category uses the IPSec protocol for secure communications while the second category uses SSL. SSL Based VPNs are also called **WebVPN** in Cisco terminology and will be discussed in the next Chapter when we talk about the Anyconnect VPN client solution. The two general VPN categories supported by Cisco ASA are further divided into the following VPN technologies.

- **IPSec Based VPNs:**
    - *Site-to-Site IPSec VPN*: Used to connect two or more remote LAN networks over unsecure media (e.g Internet). It runs between ASA-to-ASA or ASA-to-Cisco Router.
    - *Remote Access with IPSec VPN Client*: A VPN client software is installed on user's PC to provide remote access to the central network. It uses the IPSec protocol and provides full network connectivity to the remote user. The users use their applications at the central site as they normally would without a VPN in place.

      NOTE: Cisco has announced the **End-of-Life** of the Legacy Cisco IPSec VPN client. It is now replaced by the "**Cisco Anyconnect Secure Mobility Client**" which provides both secure SSL and IPSec/IKEv2 connections to the ASA for remote users.

- **SSL Based VPNs (WebVPN)**:
    - *Clientless Mode WebVPN:* This is the first implementation of SSL WebVPN supported from ASA version 7.0 and later. It lets users establish a secure remote access VPN tunnel using just a Web browser. There is no need for a software or hardware VPN client. However, only limited applications can be accessed remotely.
    - *AnyConnect VPN:* A special Java based client is installed on the user's computer providing an SSL secure tunnel to the central site. Anyconnect provides full network connectivity (similar with IPSec remote access client). All applications at the central site can be accessed remotely. Also, in the newest Anyconnect versions (3.x and above), the client supports also IKEv2 IPSEC to offer remote access.

NOTE: The newest AnyConnect VPN product from Cisco is called "**Cisco Anyconnect Secure Mobility Client**". It is supported on ASA version 8.0(3) and later and provides both SSL VPN connectivity as well as IPSec/IKEv2 VPN connectivity for remote users. You need ASA version 8.4 and later to use the IPSec/IKEv2 VPN feature.

6.2 What is IPSec

Let's now talk about some theory behind IPSEc in order to have a knowledge base for understanding the discussion in later sections of this Chapter.

IP Security (**IPSEc**) is an open IETF standard that enables encrypted communication. It is a suit of protocols that provide data confidentiality, integrity, and authentication. A Virtual Private Network (**VPN**) is a secure private tunnel over an insecure path (e.g over the Internet). IPSEc therefore is ideal to build VPNs over the Internet or any other non-secure networks.

IPSEc works at the network layer, encrypting and authenticating IP packets between a firewall security appliance and other participating IPSEc devices (peers), such as Cisco routers, other Cisco firewalls, VPN software clients etc. Because IPSEc is standardized, all other firewall vendors support it as well, so it is ideal to build VPNs between multivendor devices.

The following IPSEc protocols and standards will be used later in our discussion, so it's a good idea to briefly explain their functionality and usage:

- **ESP (Encapsulation Security Payload):** This is the first of the two main protocols that make up the IPSEc standard. It provides data integrity, authentication, and confidentiality services. ESP is used to encrypt the data payload of the IP packets.
- **AH (Authentication Header):** This is the second of the two main protocols of IPSEc. It provides data integrity, authentication, and replay-detection. It does not provide encryption services, but rather it acts as a "digital signature" for the packets to ensure that tampering of data has not occurred.
- **Internet Key Exchange (IKE):** This is the mechanism used by the security appliance for securely exchanging encryption keys, authenticating IPSEc peers and negotiating IPSEc Security parameters. On the ASA firewall, this is synonymous with **ISAKMP** as we will see in the IPSEc configuration.
- **DES, 3DES, AES:** All these are encryption algorithms supported by the Cisco ASA Firewall. DES is the weakest one (uses 56-bit encryption key), and AES is the strongest one (uses 128, 192, or 256 bit encryption keys). 3DES is a middle choice using 168-bit encryption key.

- **Diffie-Hellman Group (DH):** This is a public-key cryptography protocol used by IKE to establish session keys.
- **MD5, SHA-1:** These are both Hash Algorithms used to authenticate packet data. SHA is stronger than MD5.
- **Security Association (SA):** An SA is a connection between two IPSEc peers. Each IPSEc peer maintains an SA database in its memory containing SA parameters. SAs are uniquely identified by the IPSEc peer address, security protocol, and security parameter index (SPI).

6.3 How IPSec Works

There are five main steps followed by the IPSEc devices:

1. **Interesting Traffic**: The IPSEc devices recognize the traffic to protect.
2. **Phase 1 (ISAKMP)**: The IPSEc devices negotiate an IKE security policy and establish a secure channel for communication.
3. **Phase 2 (IPSEc)**: The IPSEc devices negotiate an IPSEc security policy to protect data.
4. **Data Transfer**: Data is transferred securely between the IPSEc peers based on the IPSEc parameters and keys negotiated during the previous phases.
5. **IPSEc Tunnel Terminated**: IPSEc SAs terminate when timing out or a certain data volume is reached.

The steps above will become clear when we see actual configuration examples. Let's start with the first IPSEc VPN type that we will describe in this Chapter. Site-to-Site VPN (using IKEv1 IPSec).

6.4 Site-to-Site VPN using IKEv1 IPSEC

6.4.1 Site-to-Site IKEv1 IPSEC VPN Overview

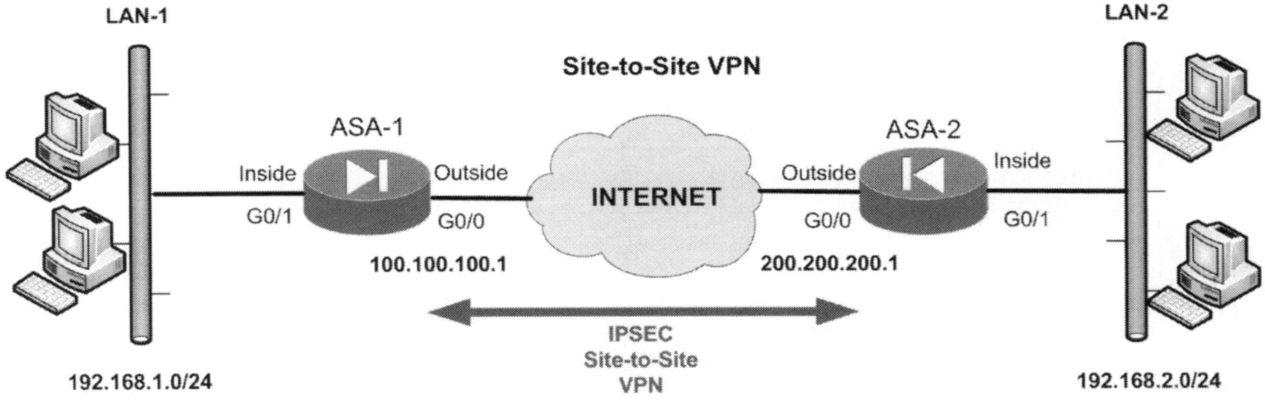

Site-to-Site IPSEc VPN is sometimes called LAN-to-LAN VPN. As the name implies, this VPN type connects together two distant LAN networks over the Internet. Usually, Local Area Networks use private addressing as shown on our diagram above. Without VPN connectivity, the two LAN networks above (LAN-1 and LAN-2) wouldn't be able to communicate. By configuring a Site-to-Site IPSEc VPN between the two ASA firewalls, we can establish a secure tunnel over the Internet, and pass our private LAN traffic inside this tunnel. The result is that hosts in network 192.168.1.0/24 can now directly access hosts in 192.168.2.0/24 network (and vice-versa) as if they were located in the same LAN. The IPSEc tunnel is established between the Public IP addresses of the firewalls (100.100.100.1 and 200.200.200.1).

6.4.2 Configuring Site-to-Site IKEv1 IPSec VPN

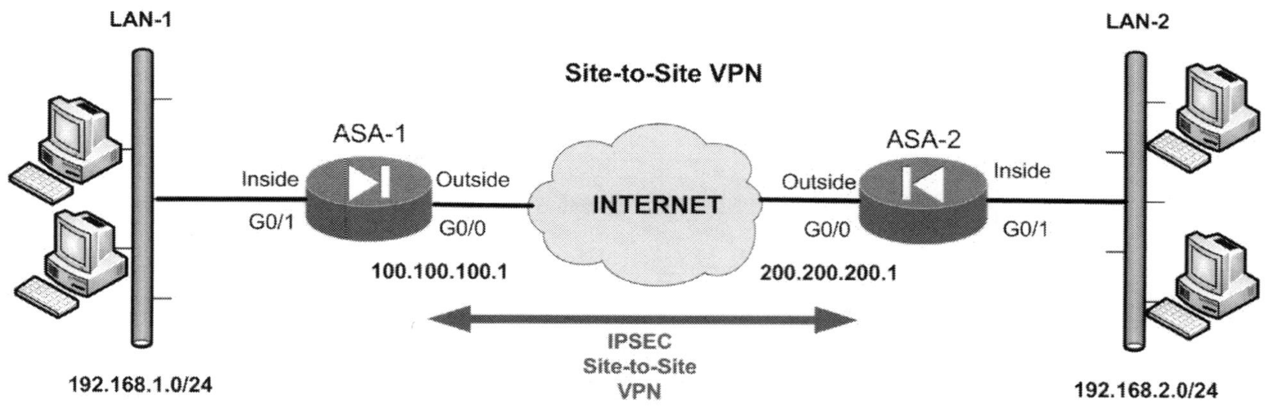

As we've described above in "How IPSEc Works", there are five steps in the operation of IPSEc. Next we will describe the configuration commands needed for each step in order to set up the VPN. All configuration examples below refer to the network diagram for site-to-site VPN. This is for the legacy IKEv1 IPSEC. Later on we will see also how to configure site-to-site IKEv2 IPSEC VPNs.

- STEP 1: Configure Interesting Traffic

We need first to define the Interesting Traffic, that is, traffic that will be encrypted. Using Access-Lists (**Crypto ACL**) we can identify which traffic flow must be encrypted. In our example diagram above, we want all traffic flow between private networks 192.168.1.0/24 and 192.168.2.0/24 to be encrypted.

ASA 1:
ASA-1(config)# access-list LAN1-to-LAN2 extended permit ip 192.168.1.0 255.255.255.0 192.168.2.0 255.255.255.0

ASA 2:
ASA-2(config)# access-list LAN2-to-LAN1 extended permit ip 192.168.2.0 255.255.255.0 192.168.1.0 255.255.255.0

Notice that we have to configure the exact mirror access-list for each ASA firewall participating in the IPSEc VPN. The Crypto ACL needs to identify only outbound traffic. The **permit** statement in the ACL means that the specific traffic must be encrypted.

NAT Exclusion for VPN Traffic

One important issue to consider is the case of using NAT on the firewall for normal Internet access. Because IPSEc does not work with NAT, we need to exclude the traffic to be encrypted from the NAT operation. This means in our example that the Interesting Traffic in the Crypto ACL must not be translated (you can use the **nat 0** command for this if you are running ASA version prior to 8.3). See configuration below:

Cisco ASA Version Prior to 8.3

ASA 1:

ASA-1(config)# access-list NONAT extended permit ip 192.168.1.0 255.255.255.0 192.168.2.0 255.255.255.0
ASA-1(config)# nat (inside) 0 access-list NONAT ← Exclude traffic from LAN1 to LAN2 from NAT operation

ASA 2:

ASA-2(config)# access-list NONAT extended permit ip 192.168.2.0 255.255.255.0 192.168.1.0 255.255.255.0
ASA-2(config)# nat (inside) 0 access-list NONAT ← Exclude traffic from LAN2 to LAN1 from NAT operation

Cisco ASA Version 8.3 and later

ASA 1:

ASA-1(config)# object network obj-local
ASA-1(config-network-object)# subnet 192.168.1.0 255.255.255.0
ASA-1(config-network-object)# exit

ASA-1(config)# object network obj-remote
ASA-1(config-network-object)# subnet 192.168.2.0 255.255.255.0
ASA-1(config-network-object)# exit

ASA-1(config)# nat (inside,outside) 1 source static obj-local obj-local destination static obj-remote obj-remote

ASA 2:

ASA-2(config)# object network obj-local
ASA-2(config-network-object)# subnet 192.168.2.0 255.255.255.0
ASA-2(config-network-object)# exit

ASA-2(config)# object network obj-remote
ASA-2(config-network-object)# subnet 192.168.1.0 255.255.255.0
ASA-2(config-network-object)# exit

ASA-2(config)# nat (inside,outside) 1 source static obj-local obj-local destination static obj-remote obj-remote

- **STEP 2: Configure Phase 1 (IKEv1 or ISAKMP)**

Phase 1 of the IPSEc operation is used to establish a secure communication channel for further data transmission. In Phase 1, VPN peers exchange shared secret keys, authenticate each other, negotiate IKE security policies etc. In this Phase we configure an **ikev1 policy** which MUST match the policy configured on the other peer(s). This **ikev1 policy** tells the other peer(s) what security parameters must be used in the VPN (e.g encryption protocol, hash algorithm, authentication method, Diffie Hellman Group (DH), lifetime threshold for the tunnel etc).

The command format of the ikev1 policy is the following:

ASA(config)# crypto ikev1 policy "*priority number*" ←**Lower number means higher priority**
ASA(config-ikev1-policy)# encryption {*aes |aes-192|aes-256|3des|des*}
ASA(config-ikev1-policy)# hash {*sha | md5*}
ASA(config-ikev1-policy)# authentication {*pre-share | rsa-sig*}
ASA(config-ikev1-policy)# group {*1 | 2 | 5 | 7*} ←**DH Group**
ASA(config-ikev1-policy)# lifetime "*seconds*" ←**Up to 86400 seconds**

ASA(config)# crypto ikev1 enable "*interface-name*" ←**Enable the policy on an interface**
ASA(config)# crypto isakmp identity address ←**Identify the ASA with its address and not FQDN**

NOTE: In ASA versions prior to 8.4, the command keyword "**ikev1**" was named as "**isakmp**".

Several ikev1 policies can be configured to match different requirements from different IPSEc peers. The priority number uniquely identifies each policy. The lower the priority number, the higher the priority will be given to the specific policy.

The following example parameters can be used to create a strong isakmp policy:

- Encryption **aes**
- Hash **sha**
- Authentication **pre-share**
- Group **2 or 5**
- Lifetime **3600** (the Security Association – SA will expire and renegotiate every 1 hour)

The next thing we need to specify is the pre-shared key and the type of the VPN (Lan-to-Lan, or Remote Access). These are configured by the **tunnel-group** command.

ASA(config)# tunnel-group "*peer IP address*" type { *ipsec-l2l | remote-access* }
ASA(config)# tunnel-group "*peer IP address*" ipsec-attributes
ASA(config-tunnel-ipsec)# ikev1 pre-shared-key "*key*"
Note: *The tunnel-group types "**ipsec-ra**" and "**webvpn**" were deprecated from ASA version 8.0(2). These two are replaced by the new "**remote-access**" type.*

Let's see the complete example configuration for both firewalls for Phase 1 setup:

ASA 1:

ASA-1(config)# crypto ikev1 policy 10
ASA-1(config-ikev1-policy)# authentication pre-share← Use pre-shared key for auth
ASA-1(config-ikev1-policy)# encryption aes ← Use AES 128 bit encryption
ASA-1(config-ikev1-policy)# hash sha ← Use SHA for hashing
ASA-1(config-ikev1-policy)# group 2 ← Diffie-Hellman Group 2
ASA-1(config-ikev1-policy)# lifetime 3600 ← Lifetime of SA is 3600 seconds
ASA-1(config-ikev1-policy)# exit

ASA-1(config)# crypto ikev1 enable outside ← Enable the policy on "outside" interface
ASA-1(config)# crypto isakmp identity address

ASA-1(config)# tunnel-group 200.200.200.1 type ipsec-l2l ← Configure a tunnel with peer IP 200.200.200.1 which will be of type Lan-to-Lan
ASA-1(config)# tunnel-group 200.200.200.1 ipsec-attributes
ASA-1(config-tunnel-ipsec)# ikev1 pre-shared-key *somestrongkey* ← pre-shared key

ASA 2:

ASA-2(config)# crypto ikev1 policy 10
ASA-2(config-ikev1-policy)# authentication pre-share← Use pre-shared key for auth
ASA-2(config-ikev1-policy)# encryption aes ← Use AES 128 bit encryption
ASA-2(config-ikev1-policy)# hash sha ← Use SHA for hashing
ASA-2(config-ikev1-policy)# group 2 ← Diffie-Hellman Group 2
ASA-2(config-ikev1-policy)# lifetime 3600 ← Lifetime of SA is 3600 seconds
ASA-2(config-ikev1-policy)# exit

ASA-2(config)# crypto ikev1 enable outside ← Enable the policy on "outside" interface
ASA-2(config)# crypto isakmp identity address

ASA-2(config)# tunnel-group 100.100.100.1 type ipsec-l2l ← Configure a tunnel with peer IP 100.100.100.1 which will be of type Lan-to-Lan
ASA-2(config)# tunnel-group 100.100.100.1 ipsec-attributes
ASA-2(config-tunnel-ipsec)# ikev1 pre-shared-key *somestrongkey* ← pre-shared key

- <u>STEP 3: Configure Phase 2 (IPSEc)</u>

After a secured tunnel is established in Phase 1, the next step in setting up the VPN is to negotiate the IPSEc security parameters that will be used to protect the data and messages within the tunnel. This is achieved in Phase 2 of the IPSEc. In this Phase the following functions are performed:

- Negotiation of IPSEc security parameters and IPSEc **transform sets**.
- Establishment of IPSEc SAs.
- Renegotiation of IPSEc SAs periodically to ensure security.

The ultimate goal of IKE Phase 2 is to establish a secure IPSEc session between peers. Before that can happen, each pair of endpoints negotiates the level of security required (encryption and authentication algorithms for the session). Rather than negotiate each encryption and authentication protocol individually, the protocols are grouped into sets, called **transform sets.** IPSEc transform sets are exchanged between peers and they must match between peers in order for the session to be established.

The command format of configuring a transform set is the following:

ASA(config)# crypto ipsec ikev1 transform-set *"name"* *"transform1"* *"transform2"*

The following transforms (protocols/algorithms) can be used in place of *transform1* and *transform2*:

Transform	Description
esp-des	ESP transform using DES cipher (56 bits)
esp-3des	ESP transform using 3DES cipher (168 bits)
esp-aes	ESP transform using AES-128 cipher
esp-aes-192	ESP transform using AES-192 cipher
esp-aes-256	ESP transform using AES-256 cipher
esp-md5-hmac	ESP transform using HMAC-MD5 authentication
esp-sha-hmac	ESP transform using HMAC-SHA authentication
esp-none	ESP with no authentication
esp-null	ESP with null encryption

The following guidelines might be useful when choosing transform protocols:

- For providing data confidentiality (encryption), use an ESP encryption transform such as the first 5 in the list above.
- Also consider using an ESP authentication transform by choosing MD5-HMAC or SHA-HMAC algorithms.
- SHA is stronger than MD5 but it is slower.

Consider the following example combinations of transform sets:

- ESP-DES for high performance encryption but with no authentication.
- ESP-3DES and ESP-MD5-HMAC for strong encryption and authentication.
- ESP-AES-192 and ESP-SHA-HMAC for stronger encryption and authentication.

After configuring a transform set on both IPSEc peers, we need to configure a **crypto map** which contains all Phase 2 IPSEc parameters. This crypto map is then attached to the firewall interface (usually "outside") on which the IPSEc will be established.

The command format of a crypto map is:

ASA(config)# crypto map "*name*" "*seq-num*" match address "*Crypto-ACL*" ←Assign the Crypto ACL which specifies the Interesting Traffic to be encrypted.
ASA(config)# crypto map "*name*" "*seq-num*" set peer "*Peer_IP_address*" ←Specify the remote peer IP address
ASA(config)# crypto map "*name*" "*seq-num*" set ikev1 transform-set "*Transform_set_name*" ←This is the transform set name configured above
ASA(config)# crypto map "*name*" "*seq-num*" set security-association lifetime seconds {*Seconds*} ←Specify how often the SA will expire and get renegotiated.

ASA(config)# crypto map "*name*" interface "*interface-name*" ←Attach the map to an interface

The *seq-num* parameter in the crypto map is used to specify multiple map entries (with the same name) for cases where we have more than one IPSEc peer for the firewall (e.g three ASA firewalls in a hub-and-spoke configuration). If the above firewall is a Hub firewall in a Hub-and-Spoke VPN configuration with 2 spokes, then there will be two crypto map entries with same "name" but different "sequence numbers".

Let's see the complete example configuration for both firewalls for Phase 2 setup:

ASA 1:

ASA-1(config)# crypto ipsec ikev1 transform-set ASA1TS esp-aes-192 esp-sha-hmac
ASA-1(config)# crypto map ASA1VPN 10 match address LAN1-to-LAN2
ASA-1(config)# crypto map ASA1VPN 10 set peer 200.200.200.1
ASA-1(config)# crypto map ASA1VPN 10 set ikev1 transform-set ASA1TS
ASA-1(config)# crypto map ASA1VPN 10 set security-association lifetime seconds 3600
ASA-1(config)# crypto map ASA1VPN interface outside

ASA 2:

ASA-2(config)# crypto ipsec ikev1 transform-set ASA2TS esp-aes-192 esp-sha-hmac
ASA-2(config)# crypto map ASA2VPN 10 match address LAN2-to-LAN1
ASA-2(config)# crypto map ASA2VPN 10 set peer 100.100.100.1
ASA-2(config)# crypto map ASA2VPN 10 set ikev1 transform-set ASA2TS
ASA-2(config)# crypto map ASA2VPN 10 set security-association lifetime seconds 3600
ASA-2(config)# crypto map ASA2VPN interface outside

- ### STEP 4: Verify Encrypted Data Transfer

With the three steps above we concluded the configuration of a site-to-site IPSEc VPN. An essential step though is to verify that everything is working fine and that our data is actually getting encrypted by the firewalls. There are two important commands that will help you verify if the tunnel is established and if data is bi-directionally encrypted between the IPSEc peers.

Verify that tunnel is established

The **show crypto isakmp sa** command verifies that the Security Association (SA) is established which means that the tunnel is up and running. Let's see an example output of this command below:

ASA-1# show crypto isakmp sa

```
 IKEv1 SAs:

 Active SA: 1
  Rekey SA: 0 (A tunnel will report 1 Active and 1 Rekey SA during rekey)
Total IKE SA: 1

1   IKE Peer: 200.200.200.1
    Type    : L2L          Role    : initiator
    Rekey   : no           State   : MM_ACTIVE

There are no IKEv2 SAs
```

The important point to observe here is the **State : MM_ACTIVE**. This verifies that the IPSEc tunnel is established successfully.

Verify that data is bi-directionally encrypted

The **show crypto ipsec sa** command verifies that data is being encrypted and decrypted successfully by the firewall appliance, as shown below:

ASA-1# show crypto ipsec sa

```
interface: outside
Crypto map tag: ASA1VPN, seq num: 10, local addr: 100.100.100.1

    access-list LAN1-to-LAN2 permit ip 192.168.1.0 255.255.255.0 192.168.2.0 255.255.255.0
    local ident (addr/mask/prot/port): (192.168.1.0/255.255.255.0/0/0)
    remote ident (addr/mask/prot/port): (192.168.2.0/255.255.255.0/0/0)
    current_peer: 200.200.200.1

    #pkts encaps: 2050, #pkts encrypt: 2050, #pkts digest: 2050
    #pkts decaps: 2108, #pkts decrypt: 2108, #pkts verify: 2108
    #pkts compressed: 0, #pkts decompressed: 0
    #pkts not compressed: 2050, #pkts comp failed: 0, #pkts decomp failed: 0
    #pre-frag successes: 0, #pre-frag failures: 0, #fragments created: 0
    #PMTUs sent: 0, #PMTUs rcvd: 0, #decapsulated frgs needing reassembly: 0
    #send errors: 0, #recv errors: 0

    local crypto endpt.: 100.100.100.1, remote crypto endpt.: 200.200.200.1

      ---Output Omitted---
```

The output field **#pkts encrypt:2050** and **#pkts decrypt:2108** show indeed that we have encryption of data bi-directionally.

6.4.2.1 Restricting VPN Traffic between the Two Sites

By default, a site-to-site IPSEC VPN provides full network connectivity between the two LANs. This means that hosts in LAN1 can access all hosts in LAN2 and vice-versa. However, this might not be desirable is some situations. There are cases where we want hosts from one site to access only specific hosts of the other site and not the whole network.

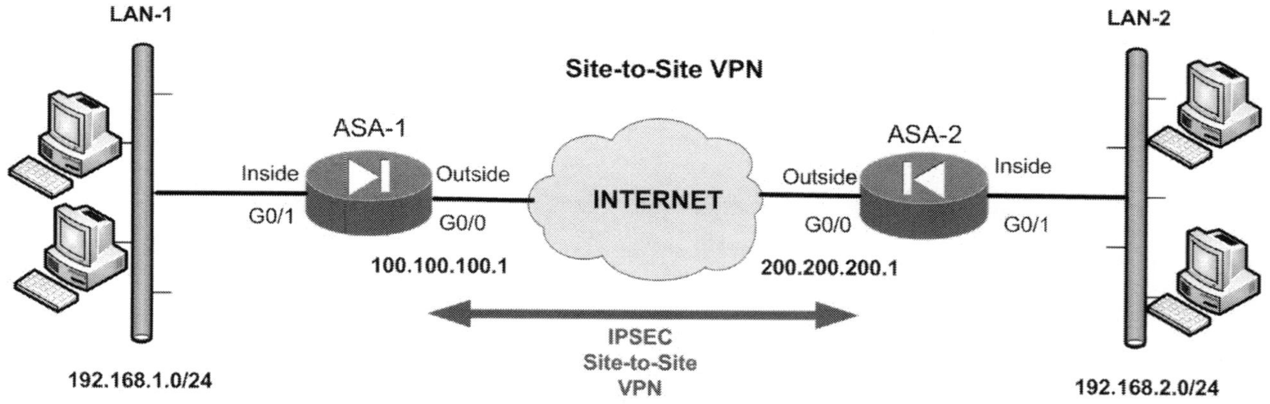

In this section I will show you how to restrict IPSEC VPN traffic so that LAN-2 can access only two hosts on LAN-1 and not the whole network.

The key here is to disable the default command "**sysopt connection permit-vpn**". This command is enabled by default on Cisco ASA and its purpose is to exempt all IPSEC VPN traffic from Access List check on the outside ASA interface. This means that when the above command is enabled, all IPSEC VPN traffic is allowed to pass between the two sites without restricting anything. If we disable the command above, then we must explicitly allow the IPSEC traffic from the peer site on the outside Access Control List of the ASA. Hence, we can apply fine-grained control of the IPSEC traffic between the two sites.

Note that IPSEC uses three protocols: **ESP**, **AH** and **IKE port UDP 500** (isakmp). Therefore we must allow those protocols on the outside Access List to reach the firewall interface. After that, we need also to explicitly allow which private hosts on LAN-1 can be accessed from LAN-2.

Let's see how to restrict IPSEC VPN traffic so that LAN-2 can access only two hosts (192.168.1.10 and 192.168.1.2) on LAN-1. This configuration will be performed on ASA-1

ASA-1

!First disable the IPSEC traffic exemption from Access List checks. This means that we must explicitly specify which VPN traffic is allowed to pass.
ASA-1(config)#no sysopt connection permit-vpn

!Now let's explicitly allow IPSEC traffic from LAN-2 to LAN-1. We need first to allow the three IPSEC Protocols from ASA-2 to ASA-1
ASA-1(config)#access-list outside_in extended permit esp host 200.200.200.1 host 100.100.100.1
ASA-1(config)#access-list outside_in extended permit ah host 200.200.200.1 host 100.100.100.1
ASA-1(config)#access-list outside_in extended permit udp host 200.200.200.1 host 100.100.100.1 eq isakmp

!Now allow access from LAN-2 to two hosts on LAN-1 only
ASA-1(config)#access-list outside_in extended permit ip 192.168.2.0 255.255.255.0 host 192.168.1.10
ASA-1(config)#access-list outside_in extended permit ip 192.168.2.0 255.255.255.0 host 192.168.1.2

!Apply the ACL to outside interface.
ASA-1(config)#access-group outside_in in interface outside

If you need to restrict traffic from LAN-1 to LAN-2, you must configure ASA-2 similar to the above scenario.

6.4.3 Configuring Hub-and-Spoke IKEv1 IPSec VPN

A Hub-and-Spoke VPN topology is considered an extension of Site-to-Site VPN because we basically have two or more Site-to-Site VPN links between a Central Hub site and two or more remote branch sites (Spokes). Here we will see the configuration required on the Hub ASA device only because the configuration on the Spoke ASA firewalls is the same as Site-to-Site VPN we have seen above.

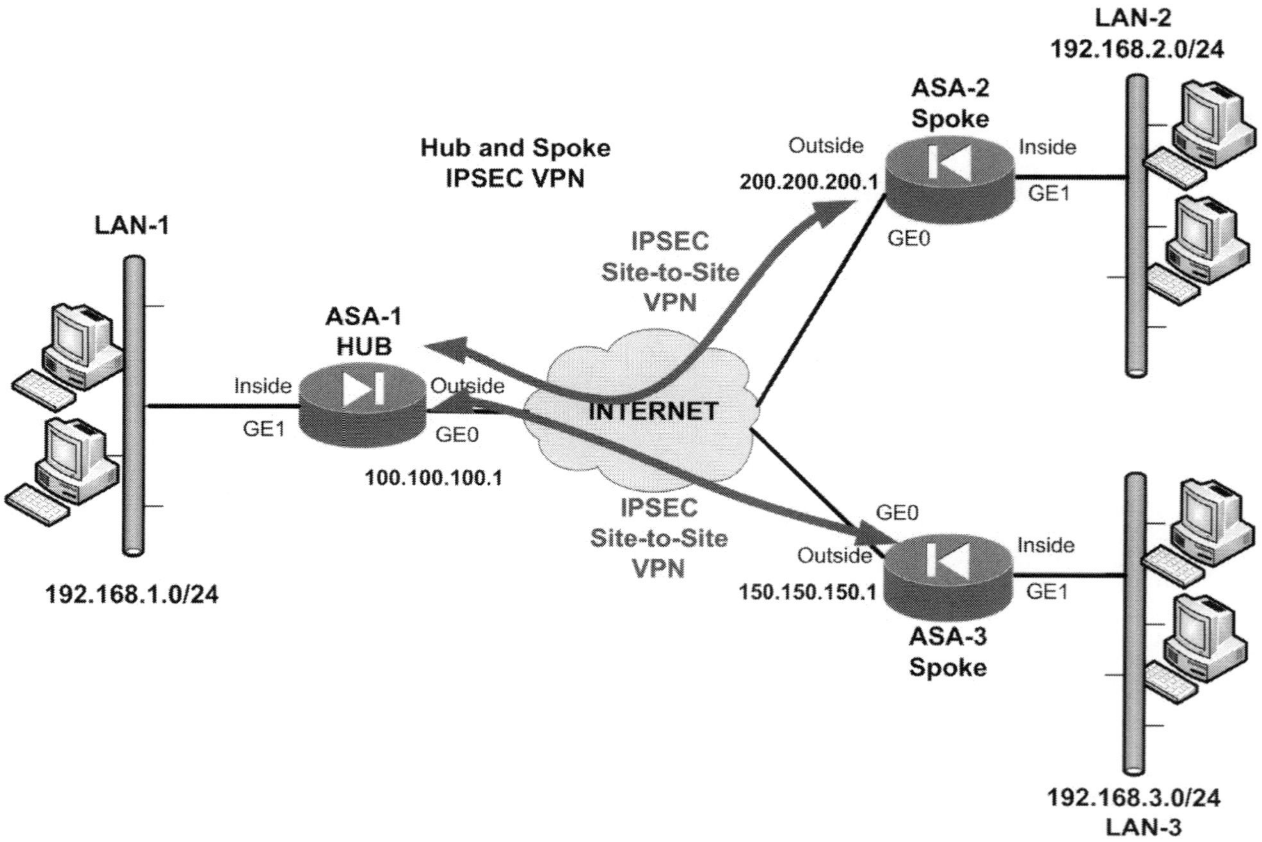

Let's now see how to setup the Hub Site firewall (ASA-1) so that to establish secure VPNs between LAN-1 and LAN-2/LAN-3. Only the configuration that is different from the classical site-to-site VPN is shown below.

ASA-1 (HUB):

- ### STEP 1: Configure Interesting Traffic and NAT Exemption

!First identify the Interesting traffic to be encrypted. We need to have two crypto ACLs, one for each Spoke site.

ASA-1(config)# access-list VPN-ACL1 extended permit ip 192.168.1.0 255.255.255.0 192.168.2.0 255.255.255.0
ASA-1(config)# access-list VPN-ACL2 extended permit ip 192.168.1.0 255.255.255.0 192.168.3.0 255.255.255.0

!Then exclude the VPN Interesting traffic from the NAT operation

ASA-1(config)# object network obj-local
ASA-1(config-network-object)# subnet 192.168.1.0 255.255.255.0 ← Local LAN
ASA-1(config-network-object)# exit

ASA-1(config)# object network obj-remote1
ASA-1(config-network-object)# subnet 192.168.2.0 255.255.255.0 ← Spoke LAN2
ASA-1(config-network-object)# exit
ASA-1(config)# object network obj-remote2
ASA-1(config-network-object)# subnet 192.168.3.0 255.255.255.0 ← Spoke LAN3
ASA-1(config-network-object)# exit

ASA-1(config)# object network internal-lan ← This object will be used for PAT
ASA-1(config-network-object)# subnet 192.168.1.0 255.255.255.0
ASA-1(config-network-object)# exit

ASA-1(config)# nat (inside,outside) 1 source static obj-local obj-local destination static obj-remote1 obj-remote1 ← Exclude traffic from LAN1 to LAN2 from NAT operation

ASA-1(config)# nat (inside,outside) 2 source static obj-local obj-local destination static obj-remote2 obj-remote2 ← Exclude traffic from LAN1 to LAN3 from NAT operation

ASA-1(config)# object network internal-lan
ASA-1(config-network-object)# nat (inside,outside) dynamic interface ← Configure Port Address Translation (PAT) using the outside ASA interface. This will perform dynamic NAT on internal LAN hosts so that they can access the Internet.

- <u>STEP 2: Configure Phase 1 (ISAKMP - ikev1)</u>

!Configure Phase1 isakmp parameters

ASA-1(config)# crypto ikev1 policy 10
ASA-1(config-ikev1-policy)# authentication pre-share
ASA-1(config-ikev1-policy)# encryption 3des
ASA-1(config-ikev1-policy)# hash sha
ASA-1(config-ikev1-policy)# group 2
ASA-1(config-ikev1-policy)# lifetime 86400
ASA-1(config-ikev1-policy)# exit
ASA-1(config)# crypto ikev1 enable outside
ASA-1(config)# crypto isakmp identity address

!Configure static tunnel-groups with the Spoke Sites ASA-2 and ASA-3

ASA-1(config)# tunnel-group 200.200.200.1 type ipsec-l2l ← Tunnel with ASA-2
ASA-1(config)# tunnel-group 200.200.200.1 ipsec-attributes
ASA-1(config-tunnel-ipsec)# ikev1 pre-shared-key *secretkey1* ← pre-shared key with static spoke ASA-2

ASA-1(config)# tunnel-group 150.150.150.1 type ipsec-l2l ← Tunnel with ASA-3
ASA-1(config)# tunnel-group 150.150.150.1 ipsec-attributes
ASA-1(config-tunnel-ipsec)# ikev1 pre-shared-key *secretkey1* ← pre-shared key with static spoke ASA-3

- STEP 3: Configure Phase 2 (IPSEc)

!Now Configure Phase2 Transform Set and Crypto Map. Under the same Crypto Map name you can have two entries representing the two Remote Spoke Sites.

ASA-1(config)# crypto ipsec ikev1 transform-set TRSET esp-3des esp-md5-hmac

!Create the main crypto map "VPNMAP"with two entries (10 and 20)
ASA-1(config)# crypto map VPNMAP 10 match address VPN-ACL1
ASA-1(config)# crypto map VPNMAP 10 set peer 200.200.200.1 ← Static IP Spoke ASA-2
ASA-1(config)# crypto map VPNMAP 10 set ikev1 transform-set TRSET

ASA-1(config)# crypto map VPNMAP 20 match address VPN-ACL2
ASA-1(config)# crypto map VPNMAP 20 set peer 150.150.150.1 ← Static IP Spoke ASA-3
ASA-1(config)# crypto map VPNMAP 20 set ikev1 transform-set TRSET

!Attach the main crypto map to the outside interface
ASA-1(config)# crypto map VPNMAP interface outside

The rest of the configuration is the same as the Site-to-Site VPN we have seen earlier.

6.5 Site-to-Site VPN using IKEv2 IPSEC

The new IPSEC implementation uses the updated version of IKEv2 (RFC 5996 published in Sept 2010) and is now fully supported by ASA firewalls. Cisco has quickly adopted this new standard for several reasons. One of the reasons for implementing IKEv2 is that many customers including existing Cisco VPN Client customers and big customers of Cisco required continuation of support for remote-access and site-to-site VPNs with IPsec. Also, there is a mandate from security compliance bodies to add support for the next generation Internet Key Exchange protocol, IKEv2, to security products to meet higher levels of security requirements.

IKEv2 provides some improvements to the protocol compared to IKEv1:

- Photuris style cookie mechanism: Prevents DoS attacks from forged source addresses.
- Less round trips (down to 2 from 5 for very basic exchange)
- OR'd transforms (reducing complexity and packet size)
- Built-in Dead-Peer-Detection (DPD) mechanism.
- Built-in configuration payload and user authentication mode (EAP)
- Unidirectional authentication methods
- Built-in NAT traversal
- Better re-keying and collision handling

In this section we will discuss some theory and configuration of site-to-site IPSEC VPNs using the IKEv2 standard.

6.5.1 IKEv2 Site-to-Site VPN Overview

The IKEv2 functionality for site-to-site is designed in-line with the existing IKEv1 implementation and it utilizes the existing configuration where appropriate and augments with IKEv2 specific configuration as necessary to allow independent control of each protocol. It provides you the same functionality that we discussed in SITE-TO-SITE IPSEC VPN (using IKEv1) but with few differences.

Specifically, IKEv2 adds the following features for site-to-site VPN:

- Full IKEv2 IPv6 support **for site-to-site ONLY**
- Ability to configure both IKEv1 and IKEv2 configurations in parallel and on the same crypto map.
- For the initiator, it allows fallback from IKEv2 to IKEv1 if a protocol or configuration issue exists with IKEv2 that causes the connection attempt to fail and both protocols are configured for the crypto map. This should make a migration easier.
- General feature parity with IKEv1 for things like the following: (besides the things listed in the "IKEv2 Site-to-Site does not support")
    - Tunnel-group mapping based on: OU, certificate map rules, ike-id, peer-ip via the tunnel-group-map CLIs
    - Dynamic L2L
    - Access-control via vpn-filter setting in the group-policy
    - Peer-id check
    - Delete tunnels on reboot and delete tunnels on crypto map changes etc.

The major differences between IKEv1 and IKEv2 for Site-to-Site VPN

- IKEv2 allows for asymmetric authentication methods to be configured (e.g pre-shared-key authentication for the originator but certificate authentication for the responder) using separate local and remote-authentication CLIs.

- IKEv2 does not negotiate the authentication type (pre-shared-key or certificate/rsa-sig) in the IKE policies as IKEv1 did. Therefore, the authentication type for a responder is determined later when a tunnel-group mapping takes place which makes the IKEv2 policies easier to configure and makes them more global/universal to be used with any tunnel-group.
    - IKEv2 will still allow for both pre-shared-key and certificate-based authentication to be allowed from the remote peer allowing for the peer to choose it's authentication method as was possible with IKEv1.
- IKEv2 maintains the originator authentication model which takes the trustpoint configured in the crypto map as the preferred authentication method, if available, otherwise, it performs a tunnel-group look up based on the peer IP and grabs the pre-shared-key configured for authentication
- IKEv2 does not interoperate with IKEv1.

IKEv2 Site-to-Site does not support

- Multiple peers or backup L2L peers are not supported
- Transport mode which is only used with L2TP isn't supported

Some Advantages of IKEv2:

- Less number of messages are exchanged between peers when compared to IKEv1.
- Aggressive and main mode does not exist anymore
- IKEv2 policies are agnostic to authentication method. Previously you had to define authentication mechanism in a policy.
- Standardized essential features: NAT detection, Dead Peer Detection check, DoS (IP spoofing) protection.
- Informational messages have to be acknowledged. This should address some synchronization issues we saw with IKEv1.
- Asymmetric authentication. You can authenticate yourself with pre-shared-key and authenticate peer with certificates for example.

Some Disadvantages of IKEv2:

- Since it's a new technology, there are still bugs in vendor implementations.
- Interoperability issues between different vendors.
- In case of pure IKEv2, it does not offer services like automatic software updates, profile distribution, posture checks.

Migration from IKEv1 to IKEv2

If you configure both IKEv1 and IKEv2 in parallel on the same device (as we will see in the next configuration scenario), the ASA supports fallback to IKEv1 if the IKEv2 tunnel is not established for any reason with the other site. This will make migration easier.

Also, you can use a single command ("**migrate L2L**") on the ASA to migrate an existing ASA configuration running IKEv1 VPN to IKEv2 VPN (for ASA 8.4 and later versions).

After issuing the above command, ASA uses IKEv1 settings to automatically add the new lines of code required for IKEv2 VPN.

6.5.2 IKEv2 Site-to-Site VPN Configuration

In this scenario, we will describe how IKEv2 will be used to establish a VPN tunnel between ASA-1 and ASA-2 and this will help PC 192.168.10.1 to talk to a remote Host 192.168.11.1. To make the scenario more interesting and useful, we will actually have both IKEv1 and IKEv2 configured on the ASA devices. We will use the diagram below for our scenario:

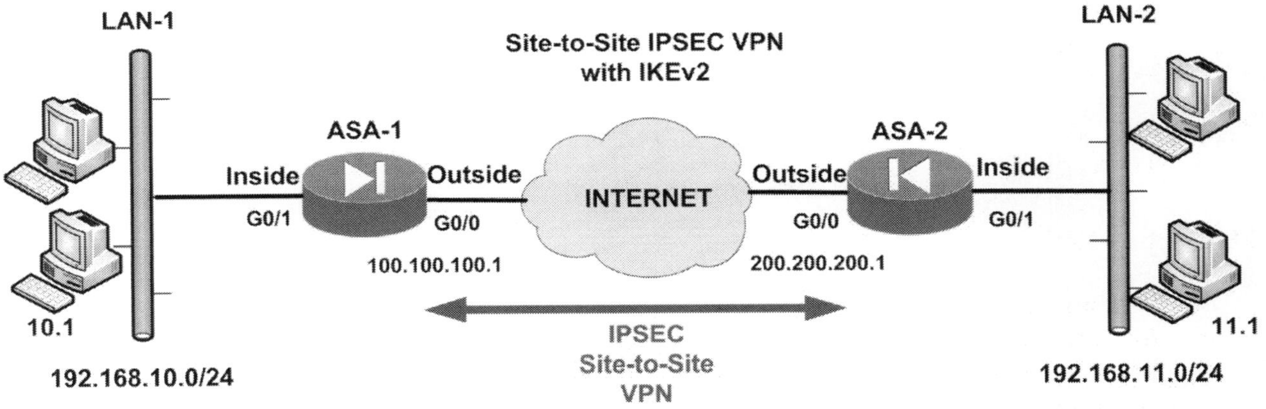

A summary of the steps required is shown on the list below:

1. Configure the ASA's :
    - We assume that Interface addresses and routing is configured already.
    - Configure Interesting Traffic to be encrypted.
    - Configure IKEv2 policies and IPSEC proposals
    - Configure IKEv1 policies and transform-sets
    - Configure Crypto map with both IKEv1 and IKEv2 IPsec policies
    - Allow IKEv2 as a vpn-tunnel-protocol in the group-policy
    - IPsec L2L tunnel-group with pre-shared-keys configured (both IKEv1 and IKEv2) under ipsec-attributes. Configure them to be different in each direction for IKEv2 to illustrate asymmetric authentication behavior.
    - Enable both IKEv1 and IKEv2 on the outside interfaces
2. Configure the workstations.
3. Send traffic across and bring the tunnel up.

Let's now see the actual configuration on the ASA Firewalls.

- **Step1: Configure Interesting Traffic to be encrypted**

Just like the IKEv1 site-to-site VPN example before, we need to define which traffic we want to pass through the VPN tunnel (encrypted) between LAN1 and LAN2. We can allow the whole subnet or only specific hosts. In our example, only traffic between 192.168.10.1 and 192.168.11.1 will pass through the VPN tunnel.

ASA 1:
ASA-1(config)# access-list LAN1-to-LAN2 extended permit ip host 192.168.10.1 host 192.168.11.1

ASA 2:
ASA-2(config)# access-list LAN2-to-LAN1 extended permit ip host 192.168.11.1 host 192.168.10.1

NAT Exclusion for VPN Traffic

If you are using NAT on the firewall (which is very common), you must exclude the VPN interesting traffic above from the NAT operation.

ASA 1:
ASA-1(config)# object network obj-local
ASA-1(config-network-object)# host 192.168.10.1
ASA-1(config-network-object)# exit

ASA-1(config)# object network obj-remote
ASA-1(config-network-object)# host 192.168.11.1
ASA-1(config-network-object)# exit

ASA-1(config)# nat (inside,outside) 1 source static obj-local obj-local destination static obj-remote obj-remote

ASA 2:
ASA-2(config)# object network obj-local
ASA-2(config-network-object)# host 192.168.11.1
ASA-2(config-network-object)# exit

ASA-2(config)# object network obj-remote
ASA-2(config-network-object)# host 192.168.10.1
ASA-2(config-network-object)# exit

ASA-2(config)# nat (inside,outside) 1 source static obj-local obj-local destination static obj-remote obj-remote

- **Step2: Configure IKEv2 Policy (similar to Phase1 in IKEv1)**

Like the older IKEv1 model, we need to configure an IKEv2 policy which is similar to the **Phase1** stage we have described in IKEv1 site-to-site VPN scenario. In this policy, we can have multiple encryption and integrity protocols under the same policy. This is because IKEv2 sends across a single proposal containing multiple ciphers, compared to IKEv1 in which multiple policies must be configured if we have multiple encryption and integrity proposals.

ASA 1:

ASA-1(config)# crypto ikev2 policy 1
ASA-1(config-ikev2-policy)# encryption aes 3des ← **Notice we have 2 ciphers**
ASA-1(config-ikev2-policy)# integrity sha md5 ← **Notice we have 2 integrity algorithms**
ASA-1(config-ikev2-policy)# group 2 ← **Diffie-Hellman group**
ASA-1(config-ikev2-policy)# prf sha ← **Pseudo Random Function Algorithm**
ASA-1(config-ikev2-policy)# lifetime seconds 86400
ASA-1(config-ikev2-policy)# exit

ASA 2:

ASA-2(config)# crypto ikev2 policy 1
ASA-2(config-ikev2-policy)# encryption aes 3des ← **Notice we have 2 ciphers**
ASA-2(config-ikev2-policy)# integrity sha md5 ← **Notice we have 2 integrity algorithms**
ASA-2(config-ikev2-policy)# group 2 ← **Diffie-Hellman group**
ASA-2(config-ikev2-policy)# prf sha ← **Pseudo Random Function Algorithm**
ASA-2(config-ikev2-policy)# lifetime seconds 86400
ASA-2(config-ikev2-policy)# exit

Note:

PRF is the Pseudo Random Function algorithm which is same as the integrity algorithm. It is not mandatory. You must configure at least one encryption algorithm, one integrity algorithm, and one DH group for the proposal to be considered complete.

- **Step3: Configure IKEv2 IPSEC Proposal (similar to transform-set in IKEv1)**

This is similar to the Phase2 stage we had in IKEv1 case where we have configured a "**transform set**". The "**ipsec-proposal**" in IKEv2 is the same as the "**transform-set**" we had in IKEv1.

The IPSEc security parameters in this step will be used to protect the data and messages within the tunnel.

ASA 1:

ASA-1(config)# crypto ipsec ikev2 ipsec-proposal IKEv2-AES-SHA
ASA-1(config-ipsec-proposal)# protocol esp encryption aes
ASA-1(config-ipsec-proposal)# protocol esp integrity sha-1
ASA-1(config-ipsec-proposal)# exit

ASA 2:

ASA-2(config)# crypto ipsec ikev2 ipsec-proposal IKEv2-AES-SHA
ASA-2(config-ipsec-proposal)# protocol esp encryption aes
ASA-2(config-ipsec-proposal)# protocol esp integrity sha-1
ASA-2(config-ipsec-proposal)# exit

- **Step4: Configure IKEv1 Policies and Transform Sets**

On the same ASA device we can have both IKEv1 and IKEv2 configured. If IKEv2 VPN is not successfully established between the two ASA firewalls, they can revert back to IKEv1.
Here we set-up IKEv1 Policies and Transform Sets (as we have seen in previous section for the IKEv1 site-to-site VPN)

ASA 1:

!Configure the Phase1 Policy
ASA-1(config)# crypto ikev1 policy 10
ASA-1(config-ikev1-policy)# authentication pre-share← Use pre-shared key for auth
ASA-1(config-ikev1-policy)# encryption aes ← Use AES encryption
ASA-1(config-ikev1-policy)# hash sha ← Use SHA for hashing
ASA-1(config-ikev1-policy)# group 2 ← Diffie-Hellman Group 2
ASA-1(config-ikev1-policy)# lifetime 86400 ← Lifetime of SA is 3600 seconds
ASA-1(config-ikev1-policy)# exit
ASA-1(config)# crypto isakmp identity address

!Configure the Phase2 Transform Set
ASA-1(config)# crypto ipsec ikev1 transform-set IKEv1-AES-SHA esp-aes esp-sha-hmac

ASA 2:

!Configure the Phase1 Policy
ASA-2(config)# crypto ikev1 policy 10
ASA-2(config-ikev1-policy)# authentication pre-share← Use pre-shared key for auth
ASA-2(config-ikev1-policy)# encryption aes ← Use AES encryption
ASA-2(config-ikev1-policy)# hash sha ← Use SHA for hashing
ASA-2(config-ikev1-policy)# group 2 ← Diffie-Hellman Group 2
ASA-2(config-ikev1-policy)# lifetime 86400 ← Lifetime of SA is 3600 seconds
ASA-2(config-ikev1-policy)# exit
ASA-2(config)# crypto isakmp identity address

!Configure the Phase2 Transform Set
ASA-2(config)# crypto ipsec ikev1 transform-set IKEv1-AES-SHA esp-aes esp-sha-hmac

- ## Step5: Configure a Group Policy to allow both IKEv1 and IKEv2

ASA 1:

ASA-1(config)# group-policy GroupPolicy1 internal
ASA-1(config)# group-policy GroupPolicy1 attributes
ASA-1(config-group-policy)# vpn-tunnel-protocol ikev2 ikev1 ← allow both IKEv2 IKEv1
ASA-1(config-group-policy)# exit

ASA 2:

ASA-2(config)# group-policy GroupPolicy1 internal
ASA-2(config)# group-policy GroupPolicy1 attributes
ASA-2(config-group-policy)# vpn-tunnel-protocol ikev2 ikev1 ← allow both IKEv2 IKEv1
ASA-2(config-group-policy)# exit

- ## Step6: Configure Crypto Maps with both IKEv1 and IKEv2 IPSEC Profiles

The crypto map combines the previously created encryption algorithms, the remote peer, and the phase 2 policy into a single crypto map. Notice that we have both IKEv1 and IKEv2 IPSEC profiles attached on the same crypto map.

ASA 1:

ASA-1(config)# crypto map outside_map 1 match address LAN1-to-LAN2
ASA-1(config)# crypto map outside_map 1 set peer 200.200.200.1
ASA-1(config)# crypto map outside_map 1 set ikev1 transform-set IKEv1-AES-SHA
ASA-1(config)# crypto map outside_map 1 set ikev2 ipsec-proposal IKEv2-AES-SHA
ASA-1(config)# crypto map outside_map interface outside

ASA 2:

ASA-2(config)# crypto map outside_map 1 match address LAN2-to-LAN1
ASA-2(config)# crypto map outside_map 1 set peer 100.100.100.1
ASA-2(config)# crypto map outside_map 1 set ikev1 transform-set IKEv1-AES-SHA
ASA-2(config)# crypto map outside_map 1 set ikev2 ipsec-proposal IKEv2-AES-SHA
ASA-2(config)# crypto map outside_map interface outside

- **Step7: Configure Crypto Maps with both IKEv1 and IKEv2 IPSEC Profiles**

At this point, we will create the tunnel group. Just like IKEv1, the preshared key (or other authentication method) is defined here. However, IKEv2 allows you to use different authentication methods for both local and remote authentication.

ASA 1:

ASA-1(config)# tunnel-group 200.200.200.1 type ipsec-l2l
ASA-1(config)# tunnel-group 200.200.200.1 general-attributes
ASA-1(config-tunnel-general)# default-group-policy GroupPolicy1←Group Policy from Step5
ASA-1(config-tunnel-general)#exit
ASA-1(config)# tunnel-group 200.200.200.1 ipsec-attributes
ASA-1(config-tunnel-ipsec)# ikev1 pre-shared-key cisco123
ASA-1(config-tunnel-ipsec)# ikev2 remote-authentication pre-shared-key cisco1
ASA-1(config-tunnel-ipsec)# ikev2 local-authentication pre-shared-key cisco1234
ASA-1(config-tunnel-ipsec)# exit

ASA 2:

ASA-2(config)# tunnel-group 100.100.100.1 type ipsec-l2l
ASA-2(config)# tunnel-group 100.100.100.1 general-attributes
ASA-2(config-tunnel-general)# default-group-policy GroupPolicy1←Group Policy from Step5
ASA-2(config-tunnel-general)#exit
ASA-2(config)# tunnel-group 100.100.100.1 ipsec-attributes
ASA-2(config-tunnel-ipsec)# ikev1 pre-shared-key cisco123
ASA-2(config-tunnel-ipsec)# ikev2 remote-authentication pre-shared-key cisco1234
ASA-2(config-tunnel-ipsec)# ikev2 local-authentication pre-shared-key cisco1
ASA-2(config-tunnel-ipsec)# exit

NOTE:

Please note that the pre-shared-keys are used to authenticate the remote peer in order to build a trust relationship. If you compare the configuration on ASA1 and ASA2, you will see that the pre-shared-key defined for **remote-authentication** on ASA1 is matching the pre-shared-key defined for **local authentication** on ASA2 and vice versa. This illustrates the asymmetrical authentication allowed on IKEv2.

- **Step8: Enable both IKEv1 and IKEv2 on outside interface**

ASA 1:
ASA-1(config)# crypto ikev2 enable outside
ASA-1(config)# crypto ikev1 enable outside

ASA 2:
ASA-2(config)# crypto ikev2 enable outside
ASA-2(config)# crypto ikev1 enable outside

- **Step9: Verification**

ASA-1# show crypto isakmp sa

```
There are no IKEv1 SAs

IKEv2 SAs:

Session-id:1, Status:UP-ACTIVE, IKE count:1, CHILD count:1

Tunnel-id          Local              Remote     Status       Role
 9807541       100.100.100.1/500        200.200.200.1/500      READY    INITIATOR
    Encr: AES-CBC, keysize: 128, Hash: SHA96, DH Grp:2, Auth sign: PSK, Auth verify: PSK
    Life/Active Time: 86400/58 sec
Child sa: local selector  192.168.10.1/0 - 192.168.10.1/65535
        remote selector 192.168.11.1/0 - 192.168.11.1/65535
        ESP spi in/out: 0x19e57b7b/0x5520a043
```

As you have seen above, the ASA firewall has established an IKEv2 Security Association (SA) with the remote peer. If you have both IKEv1 and IKEv2 on the same device, then IKEv2 is preferred.

ASA-1# show crypto ipsec sa

```
interface: outside
   Crypto map tag: outside_map, seq num: 1, local addr: 100.100.100.1

     access-list LAN1-to-LAN2 extended permit ip host 192.168.10.1 host 192.168.11.1
     [output omitted]......

     #pkts encaps: 7, #pkts encrypt: 7, #pkts digest: 7
     #pkts decaps: 7, #pkts decrypt: 7, #pkts verify: 7
```

6.6 Remote Access IPSec VPNs

6.6.1 Remote Access IPSec VPN Overview

The second topology type of IPSEc VPN that we will describe in this Chapter is **Remote Access IPSEC VPN** (IKEv1) using a Cisco VPN client installed on the remote user. This type of VPN allows remote users/teleworkers with Internet access to establish a secure IPSEc VPN tunnel with their central corporate network. The user must have a Cisco VPN client software installed on his/her computer which will enable a secure communication with the ASA firewall in the central office. After the VPN is established between the remote user and the ASA firewall, the user is assigned a private IP address from a predefined pool, and then gets attached on the Corporate LAN network.

NOTE: Cisco has announced the End-of-Life of its legacy Cisco IPSec VPN client software. It is now replaced by the "**Cisco Anyconnect Secure Mobility Client**" which provides secure SSL and IPSec/IKEv2 connections to the ASA for remote users. We will discuss configuration of Anyconnect in the next Chapter later in this book. Although the legacy Cisco IPSec VPN client is not supported anymore, it's valuable to include it in this book because it is still widely used in networks today.

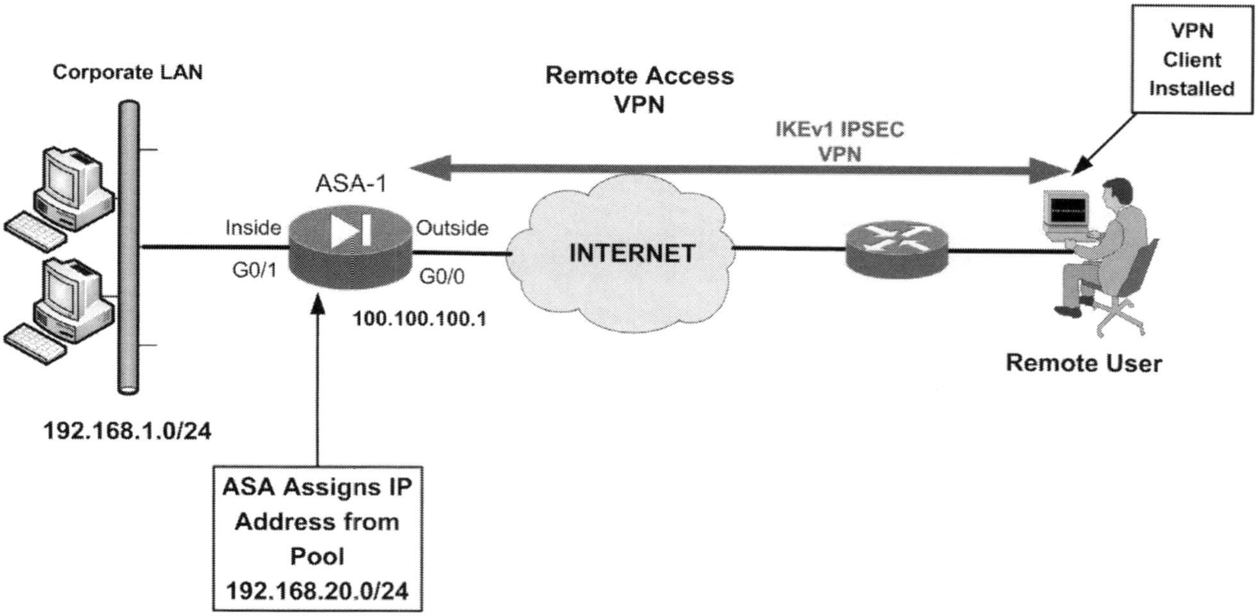

Our example network topology above shows a central ASA firewall protecting the Corporate LAN, and a remote user with a software VPN client establishing a secure connection with the ASA. An IP address in the range 192.168.20.0/24 will be assigned to the VPN client, which will be allowed to communicate with the Internal Corporate network 192.168.1.0/24. Once the Remote Access VPN is established, the remote user by default will not be able to access anything else on the Internet, except the Corporate LAN network. This behavior can be altered by configuring the "**split tunneling**" feature on the Firewall, which however is not recommended for security purposes.

Next we will discuss the configuration required both on the ASA Firewall and the Cisco Software client to build a remote access connection.

6.6.2 Configuring Remote Access IPSec VPN

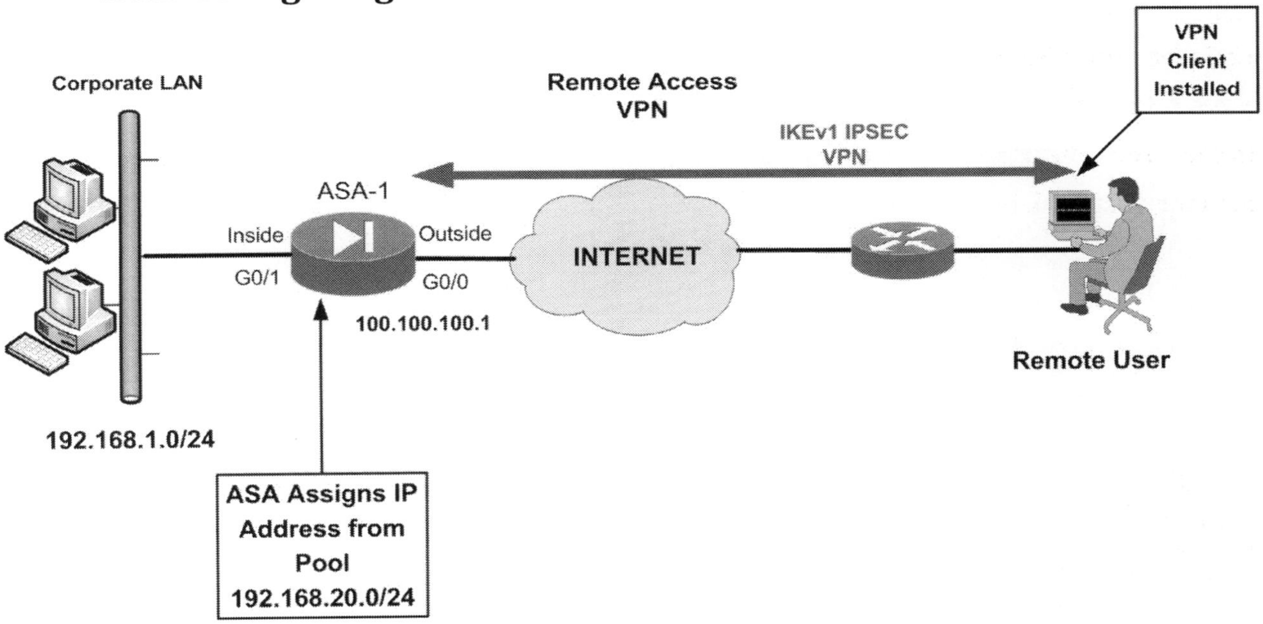

A lot of configuration statements are the same as the site-to-site IKEv1 VPN, especially for IKE Phase 1 and Phase 2 stages. Also, an IP address pool must be configured on the firewall for dynamically assigning addresses to the remote users. Let's get started with the configuration:

- **STEP 1: Configure an IP address Pool**

The command format is the following:

ASA(config)# ip local pool *"name of pool" {first IP address}-{last IP address}*
In our example we want to assign addresses to the remote users from the range 192.168.20.0/24:

Example:

ASA-1(config)# ip local pool VPNPOOL 192.168.20.1-192.168.20.254

Also, we need to specify to the firewall that the IP address assignment for the remote users will be facilitated from a local address pool

ASA-1(config)# vpn-addr-assign local

Configure Split Tunneling (OPTIONAL)

Once the Remote Access VPN is established, the remote user by default will not be able to access anything else on the Internet, except the Corporate LAN network. This behavior can be altered by configuring the "**split tunneling**" feature on the Firewall, which however is not recommended for security purposes. However, if you want to allow users to access the Internet and also access the Corporate LAN network, you must configure a Split-Tunnel Access Control List.

ASA-1(config)# access-list splittunnel standard permit 192.168.1.0 255.255.255.0

Traffic from the remote users towards the network specified in the split-tunnel ACL (192.168.1.0/24) will pass through the VPN tunnel. All other traffic from the remote user will go to the Internet.

- **STEP 2: NAT Exemption (Encrypted Traffic should be excluded from NAT)**

Similarly with site-to-site VPN, we need to identify with an ACL the traffic flow from our Internal LAN network (192.168.1.0/24) towards the Remote Users (192.168.20.0/24) in order to be excluded from NAT.

Example:

Cisco ASA Version Prior to 8.3

ASA-1(config)# access-list NONAT extended permit ip 192.168.1.0 255.255.255.0 192.168.20.0 255.255.255.0

ASA-1(config)# nat (inside) 0 access-list NONAT

Cisco ASA Version 8.3 and later

For ASA 8.3 and later, we need to configure the above NAT exemption as following:

ASA-1(config)# object network obj-local

ASA-1(config-network-object)# subnet 192.168.1.0 255.255.255.0

ASA-1(config-network-object)# exit

ASA-1(config)# object network obj-vpnpool

ASA-1(config-network-object)# subnet 192.168.20.0 255.255.255.0

ASA-1(config-network-object)# exit

ASA-1(config)# nat (inside,outside) source static obj-local obj-local destination static obj-vpnpool obj-vpnpool

- **STEP 3: Configure Group Policy**

The Group Policy allows you to separate different remote access users into groups with different attributes. For example System Administrators can be assigned in a group having 24-hours VPN access, while normal remote user can be in a different group with 9am-5pm VPN access. The Group Policy also provides DNS or WINS server addresses, connection filtering, idle timeout settings etc.

The command format is the following:

ASA(config)# group-policy "*policy name*" internal
ASA(config)# group-policy "*policy name*" attributes

Example:

ASA-1(config)# group-policy company-vpn-policy internal
ASA-1(config)# group-policy company-vpn-policy attributes
ASA-1(config-group-policy)# vpn-idle-timeout 30
ASA-1(config-group-policy)# dns-server value 192.168.1.5
ASA-1(config-group-policy)# wins-server value 192.168.1.6
ASA-1(config-group-policy)# split-tunnel-policy tunnelspecified
ASA-1(config-group-policy)# split-tunnel-network-list value splittunnel ← **This is the Split Tunnel ACL Configured in Step 1 (Optional)**

Assume that all remote users will use the same group policy, with the name "**company-vpn-policy**" as configured above. This policy assigns DNS and WINS server addresses so that users can resolve internal domain and host names. It sets also the idle timeout to 30 minutes. Also, under the Group Policy we assign the Split-Tunnel ACL (**splittunnel**) which will dictate which traffic will pass through the tunnel from the remote clients.

NOTE:

Under Group Policy you can configure also a **VPN Filter** with a purpose of restricting access from remote users to certain IPs or Ports in the Corporate LAN. For example, assume that you want remote VPN users to access only a specific Internal Server at port 80 and disallow anything else. You must configure a filter ACL and apply it under the Group Policy:

ASA-1(config)# access-list VPN-FILTER-ACL **extended permit tcp 192.168.20.0 255.255.255.0 host 192.168.1.10 eq 80** ← **Allow access from remote users to server 192.168.1.10 port 80**

ASA-1(config)# group-policy company-vpn-policy attributes
ASA-1(config-group-policy)# vpn-filter value VPN-FILTER-ACL

- **STEP 4: Configure Usernames for Remote Access authentication**

When remote users connect with the VPN client, they will be presented with a login screen in order to authenticate with the firewall. We need therefore to create username/password combinations for authentication. The command format is:

ASA(config)# username "*name*" password "*password*"

Example:
ASA-1(config)# username user password 1234

- **STEP 5: Configure IPSEC Phase 1 (IKEv1 Policy)**

This is similar with site-to-site VPN.

Example:

ASA-1(config)# crypto ikev1 policy 10
ASA-1(config-ikev1-policy)# encryption 3des
ASA-1(config-ikev1-policy)# hash sha
ASA-1(config-ikev1-policy)# authentication pre-share
ASA-1(config-ikev1-policy)# group 2
ASA-1(config-ikev1-policy)# lifetime 86400
ASA-1(config-ikev1-policy)# exit
ASA-1(config)# crypto ikev1 enable outside
ASA-1(config)# crypto isakmp identity address

- **STEP 6: Configure IPSEC Phase 2 (IPSEC parameters)**

This Step also has similarities with site-to-site IKEv1 VPNs. We need an IPSEC transform set which will specify the encryption and authentication protocols for the Remote Access VPN. Also, we need to configure a dynamic crypto map which will be assigned to a static crypto map.

NOTE: A dynamic crypto map is required whenever we have a remote VPN peer with dynamic public IP address. This applies in remote access VPN users (their IP address is not known) and also in site-to-site VPNs with a site having a dynamic public IP. Also, keep in mind that you must always have a static crypto map in order to attach the dynamic crypto map to it.

Example:

! Configure a Transform Set
ASA-1(config)# crypto ipsec ikev1 transform-set RA-TS esp-3des esp-sha-hmac

! Configure a dynamic crypto map (DYN_MAP)
ASA-1(config)# crypto dynamic-map DYN_MAP **10 set ikev1 transform-set RA-TS**

! Attach the dynamic crypto map (DYN_MAP) to a static crypto map (VPN_MAP)
ASA-1(config)# crypto map VPN_MAP 30 ipsec-isakmp dynamic DYN_MAP
ASA-1(config)# crypto map VPN_MAP interface outside

- **STEP 7: Configure a Tunnel Group for Remote Access**

The tunnel group configuration is the heart of remote access VPN. It binds together the Group Policy configured before, the IP pool assignment, the pre-shared key etc.

The command format of the Tunnel Group is the following:

ASA(config)# tunnel-group "*Group Name*" type remote-access
ASA(config)# tunnel-group "*Group Name*" {*general-attributes* / *ipsec-attributes*}

The ***Group Name*** is important here because we will have to specify the same exact name when configuring the VPN client software, as we will see later.

Example:

ASA-1(config)# tunnel-group vpnclient **type remote-access**
ASA-1(config)# tunnel-group vpnclient **general-attributes**
ASA-1(config-tunnel-general)# address-pool VPNPOOL ←Attach the local IP pool
ASA-1(config-tunnel-general)# default-group-policy company-vpn-policy ←Assign Group Policy from Step 3

ASA-1(config-tunnel-general)#exit

ASA-1(config)# tunnel-group vpnclient **ipsec-attributes**
ASA-1(config-tunnel-ipsec)# ikev1 pre-shared-key *groupkey123*

- **STEP 8: Configure The VPN Client Software**

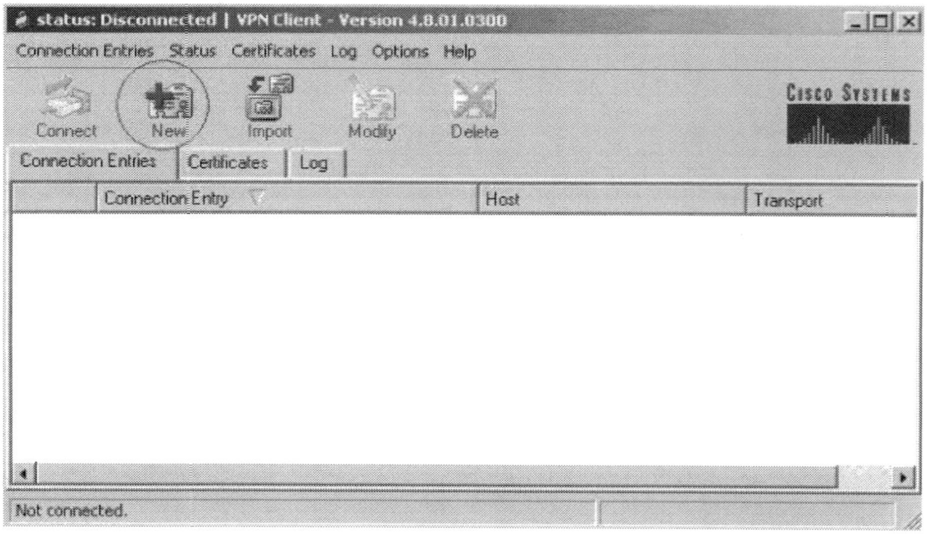

After installing the VPN client, start the application and select "New" (see above) to create a new connection entry.

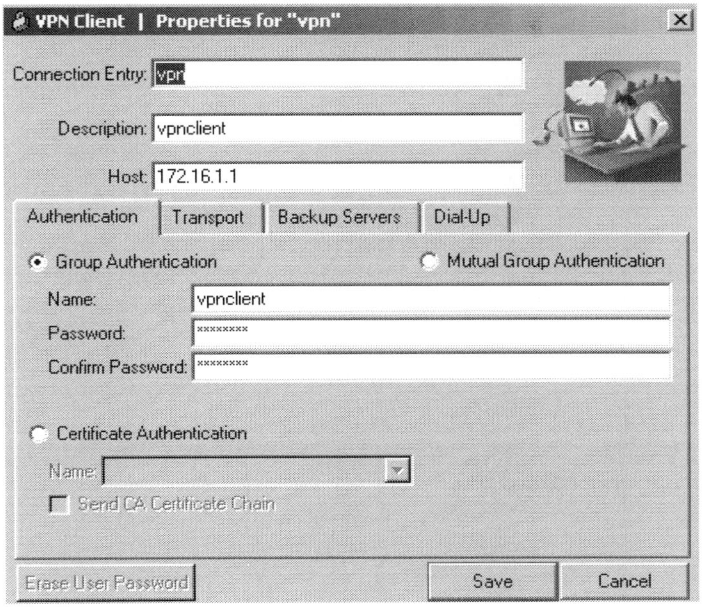

Name the connection entry (e.g "vpn") and provide a description. In the "Host" field, specify the **public IP address** of the outside interface of the central ASA Firewall. The example image above shows 172.16.1.1 but this should be changed accordingly to represent the Outside public IP of the ASA. Also, on the "Group Authentication" Tab, the **Name** and **Password** of the Group must be the same as the **tunnel-group name** and **pre-shared-key** from Step 7 above. In our example configuration, the Group Authentication Name is "**vpnclient**" and the Password (pre-shared-key) is "**groupkey123**". Press "Save" to save the settings.

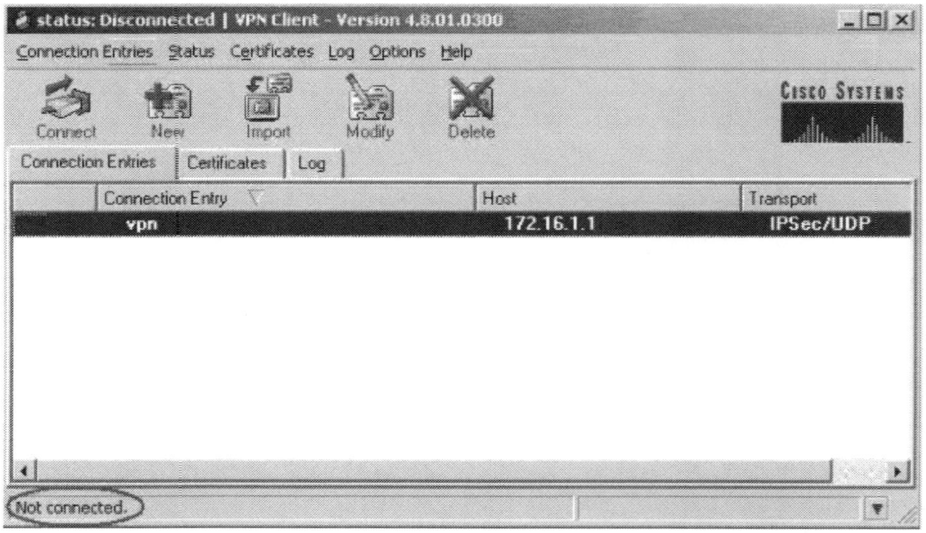

After saving the configuration settings, return to the Connection Entries Tab as shown above. Press the "Connect" button to initiate the Remote Access VPN connection.

After initiating the VPN communication, the remote user will be presented with a login screen in order to authenticate with the firewall. The credentials used in our example configuration (see Step 4 above) are Username: **user** and Password: **1234**

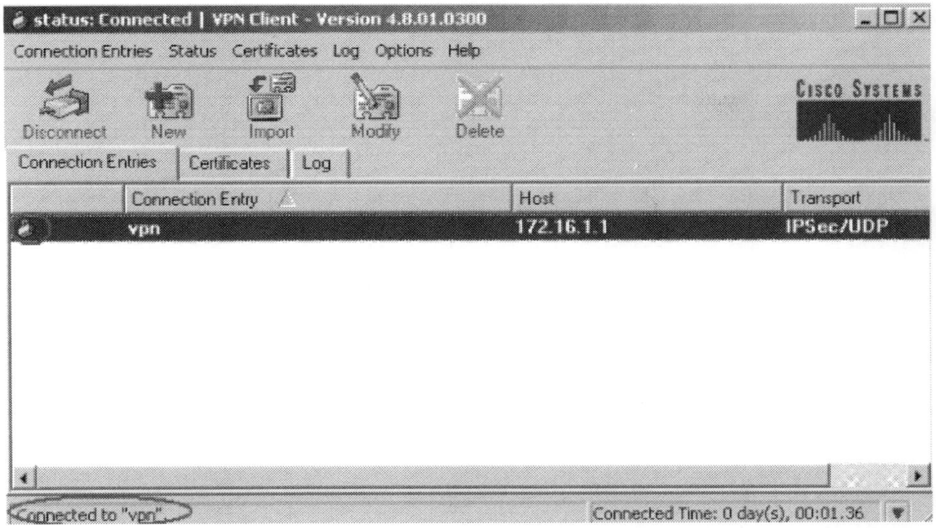

After successfully authenticating with the firewall, the secure VPN Remote Access tunnel is established. If you use the **ipconfig/all** command on the remote user's computer, you will see an IP address in the range 192.168.20.0/24 assigned to the virtual VPN connection interface. This will enable the remote user to have full network access to the central corporate LAN.

- **STEP 9: Verification**

Now let's verify that everything is working fine. Assuming the remote user authenticates successfully, we will see the following on ASA:

ASA-1# show crypto ipsec sa

```
interface: outside
  Crypto map tag: DYN_MAP, seq num: 10, local addr: 172.16.1.1
    local ident (addr/mask/prot/port): (0.0.0.0/0.0.0.0/0/0)
    remote ident (addr/mask/prot/port): (192.168.20.1/255.255.255.255/0/0)
    current_peer: 195.12.101.240, username: user
    dynamic allocated peer ip: 192.168.20.1
    #pkts encaps: 4, #pkts encrypt: 4, #pkts digest: 4
    #pkts decaps: 4, #pkts decrypt: 4, #pkts verify: 4
...Output Omitted...
```

As shown above, the remote user "**user**" has received a dynamic allocated IP of **192.168.20.1**. Also, we have packets encrypted and decrypted.

Chapter 7 AnyConnect Remote Access VPNs

In this Chapter we will describe the newest Remote Access VPN functionality supported by Cisco ASA using the **AnyConnect** client solution. Anyconnect uses either SSL or IKEv2 IPSEC (on Anyconnect version 3.x and above) to offer tunnel mode remote access VPN for users. We will discuss both of these VPN methods in this Chapter (SSL and IKEv2). Before moving on to the details of AnyConnect VPNs, let's first see a comparison between the Remote Access Web VPN technologies supported by Cisco ASA firewalls.

7.1 Comparison between SSL VPN Technologies

In this Chapter we will focus only on the AnyConnect VPN solution (to create either SSL or IKEv2/IPSEC VPNs). I decided not to bother with the Clientless WebVPN solution because I believe that the benefits of using AnyConnect instead of Clientless are much more. To justify what I'm saying, let's see the differences between the two SSL VPN modes and I'm sure you will understand why I focus only on AnyConnect!

Clientless WebVPN does not require any VPN client to be installed on user's computer. It uses a normal web browser. By pointing the browser to **https://[outside address of ASA]** the user authenticates with the firewall and gets access to a Web Portal. Through this Web Portal, the user can then access a limited number of internal applications. Specifically, only internal Web applications (HTTP, HTTPs), email servers (POP3, SMTP, IMAP), Windows file shares and a small number of TCP legacy applications (e.g Telnet) can be accessed. That is, there is no full network connectivity with Clientless WebVPN for the remote users.

AnyConnect VPN, on the other hand, provides FULL network connectivity to the remote user. The ASA firewall, working as AnyConnect VPN server, assigns an IP address to the remote user and attaches the user to the network. Thus, all IP protocols and applications function across the SSL or IKEv2/IPSEC VPN tunnel without any problems. By pointing the browser to **https://[outside address of ASA]** the user authenticates first with the firewall. After successful authentication, the user communicates through the AnyConnect VPN tunnel and has full access to the central site. For example, the user can open a Remote Desktop connection and access a Windows Terminal Server inside the central network. Although a special Java-based client is required to be installed on the user's desktop, this client can be supplied and installed dynamically to the user from the ASA during the first connection of the user. The Java client can remain installed or even get removed from the user's desktop when disconnected from the ASA appliance. This Java client is small in size (around 3MB) and is stored on the ASA flash memory.

7.2 AnyConnect VPN Overview

The AnyConnect VPN client protects traffic at the network layer and above (tunnel-mode). It provides the same remote access connectivity as the legacy Cisco IPSec VPN client (i.e full network access). The history of the WebVPN client versions is shown below:

WebVPN Client	**Operating System Supported**	**ASA version**
SSL VPN Client (SVC)	Windows 2000 and XP	7.0-7.2
Original AnyConnect Client	Windows 2000, XP, VISTA, MAC OS X, Linux	8.0+
New "**Cisco Anyconnect Secure Mobility Client**" (supports both SSL VPN and IPSEC/IKEv2 VPN)	• Windows 7 32-bit (x86) and 64-bit (x64) • Windows Vista 32-bit (x86) and 64-bit (x64), including Service Packs 1 and 2 • XP SP2+ 32-bit (x86) and 64-bit (x64) • Mac OS X 10.6 and later • Linux Intel	8.0(3) and later for SSL VPN 8.4 and later for both SSL and IPSEC/IKEv2 VPN

On the older ASA versions 7.0 up to 7.2, the WebVPN client was called SVC (SSL VPN Client). From ASA version 8.0 and later, the client was called AnyConnect WebVPN client. The newest Anyconnect product as we've said above is called now "**Cisco Anyconnect Secure Mobility Client**".

Overview of AnyConnect VPN operation:

The diagram below shows a network topology with ASA and a remote user with AnyConnect VPN.

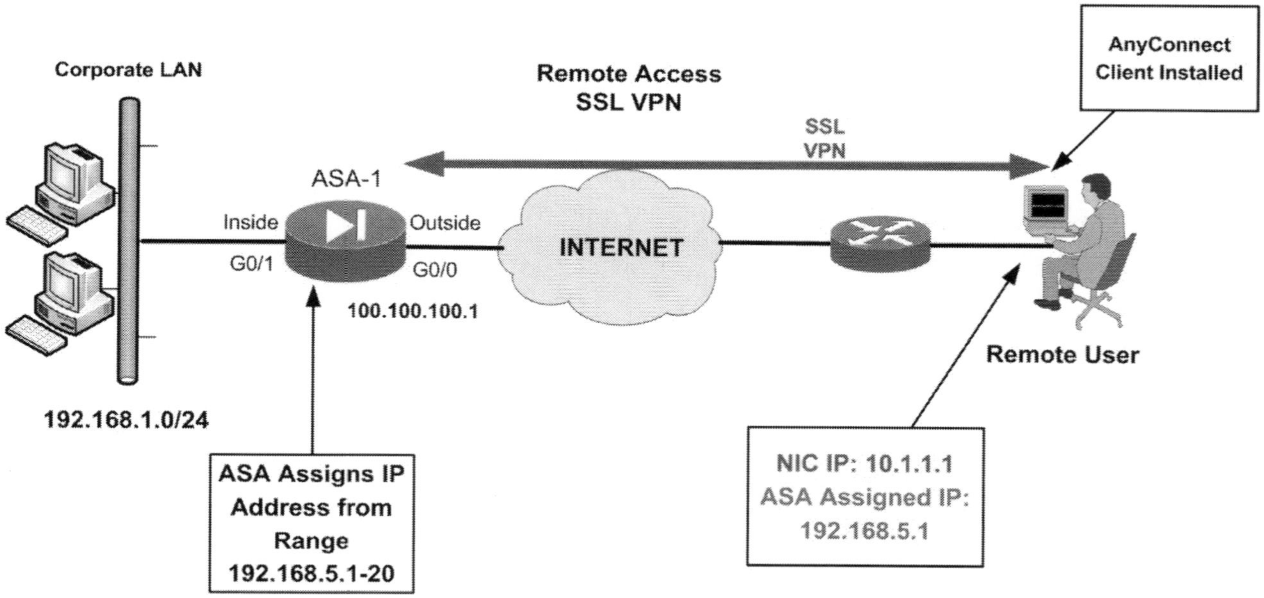

From the diagram above, the ASA firewall is configured as AnyConnect WebVPN server. A remote user has access to the Internet and has an IP address on his/her laptop interface card of 10.1.1.1 (NIC IP). The user can also be behind a router doing NAT/PAT and have his private IP address translated to a public IP by the Internet router. When the remote user connects and successfully authenticates to the ASA with the AnyConnect client, the ASA will assign an internal IP address to the user from a preconfigured IP address range (in our example above, this address range is 192.168.5.1 up to 192.168.5.20). From the diagram above, the ASA assigns IP 192.168.5.1 to the remote user. This means that the remote user is virtually attached to the corporate LAN behind the ASA firewall.

The operation overview described above assumes that the AnyConnect client is already installed on the user's computer. Let's see below the available options how to initially install the AnyConnect client.

There are two Initial Installation options for AnyConnect client:

- Using clientless WebVPN portal.
- Manual installation by the user or administrator.

Using the clientless Web portal, the user first connects and authenticates to the ASA with a secure web browser and the Java Anyconnect client is automatically downloaded and installed on the user's computer. This means that the Java client (**.pkg extension**) is already stored on the ASA flash memory by the administrator (you need to download it from Cisco site). This is the preferred method in my opinion because it automates the distribution of the client to the remote users.

With the manual installation method, the network administrator must download the Anyconnect package from Cisco site and provide the file to the users for manual installation on their laptop. With this method, the user does not need to log in via clientless mode to start the SSL VPN tunnel. Instead, the users can start up the AnyConnect client manually from their desktop and provide their authentication credentials.

7.3 Basic AnyConnect SSL VPN Configuration

We will focus on the automatic Anyconnect installation option, i.e the AnyConnect client is located on the ASA flash memory and is downloaded by the remote users. The diagram below will be used to describe a basic Anyconnect configuration. Note that in our scenario here we will setup an SSL VPN with authentication using the ASA local user database. In the next sections later on we will describe also SSL VPNs using Self-Signed Certificate (ASA working as Local CA Server), using 3rd Party CA Certificate, and also a Remote Access VPN using IKEv2/IPSEC with the Anyconnect client.

Let's now move on to the steps required to setup a basic Anyconnect SSL VPN.

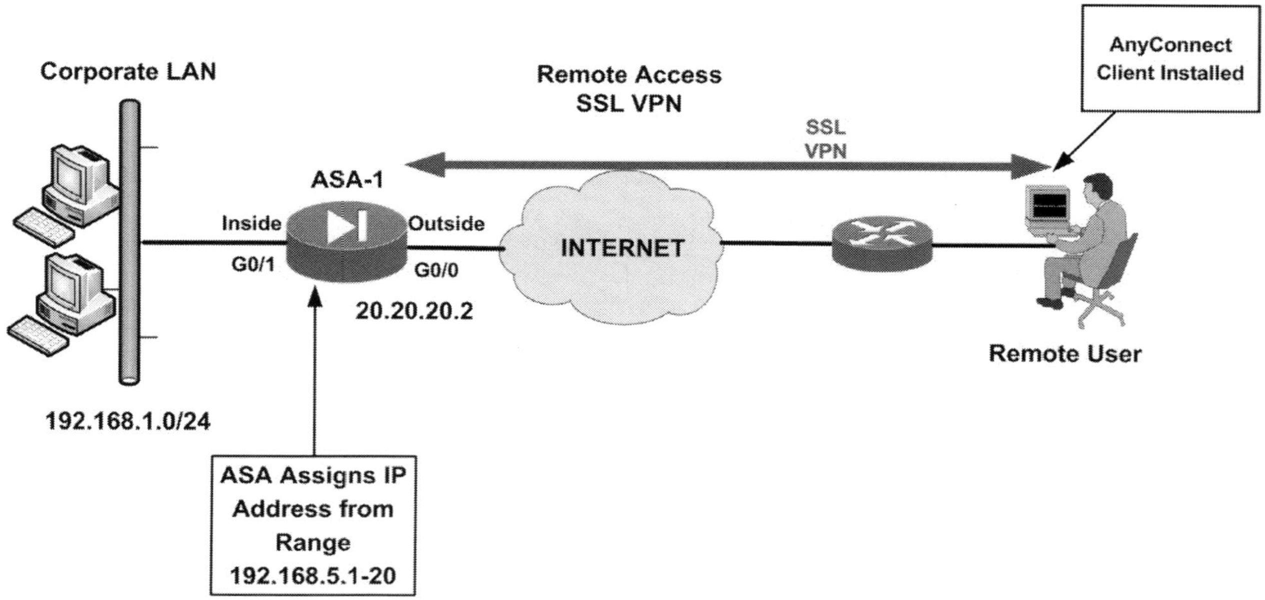

- **STEP1:**

Transfer the Anyconnect PKG file to flash on the ASA. First you need to download one of the **.pkg** files from Cisco website. An example Windows client file has the format "**anyconnect-win-x.x.xxxx-k9.pkg**".

To copy the PKG file to ASA flash:

ASA# copy {tftp|ftp|scp}://*[ip address]/anyconnect-win-x.x.xxxx-k9.pkg* **disk0:**

Assume we have downloaded the Anyconnect client file on our computer with IP address 192.168.1.1. We will use a TFTP server on our PC to transfer the file to ASA.

ASA# copy tftp://192.168.1.1/anyconnect-win-3.1.04072-k9.pkg disk0:

Address or name of remote host [192.168.1.1]?
Source filename [anyconnect-win-3.1.04072-k9.pkg]?
Destination filename [anyconnect-win-3.1.04072-k9.pkg]?
Accessing tftp://192.168.1.1/anyconnect-win-3.1.04072-k9.pkg...!!!!!!

- **STEP2:**

Identify the PKG image file on flash by telling the ASA where the image file is located. Also, enable the webvpn Anyconnect service on the outside ASA interface.

ASA# configure terminal
ASA(config)# webvpn
ASA(config-webvpn)# anyconnect image disk0:/anyconnect-win-3.1.04072-k9.pkg 1
ASA(config-webvpn)# enable outside ← enable ssl webvpn on outside interface
ASA(config-webvpn)# anyconnect enable ← enable anyconnect service
ASA(config-webvpn)# exit

Note: The number 1 at the end of the package file is the file order. It is used when you have more than one images stored on the ASA flash (e.g Anyconnect client images for Windows and MAC).

- STEP3:

Exempt the SSL WebVPN traffic from Access List checks on the outside interface. By default, WebVPN traffic is not exempted from Access List checks after terminated on the outside interface; once the traffic is decrypted, it is checked by the inbound ACL applied on outside interface. You must either include **permit** statements for the decrypted traffic in the ACL, or use the "**sysopt connection permit-vpn**".

ASA(config)# sysopt connection permit-vpn

- STEP4:

This step is optional but it is really helpful. All SSL VPN communication between remote users and ASA works with secure HTTPs (port 443). This means that users have to use "**https://[ASA public IP]**" on their browsers. Since most users will forget to use "https://", you can set up port redirection which means that if the user connects to port 80 ("http://"), the ASA will automatically redirect the browser to port 443.

ASA(config)# http redirect outside 80

- STEP5:

Create an IP address pool from which the ASA will assign addresses to remote users. From the diagram above we see that after the remote user gets authenticated, the ASA assigns an IP address to the remote user from a predefined pool 192.168.5.1 up to 192.168.5.20.

ASA(config)# ip local pool VPNpool 192.168.5.1-192.168.5.20 mask 255.255.255.0

- STEP6:

Create a NAT exemption for traffic between the corporate LAN network behind the ASA (192.168.1.0/24) and the remote user's address pool (VPNpool). We do this exemption because the encrypted traffic must not go through a NAT operation. This step is of course required only if we use NAT on the ASA.

Cisco ASA Version Prior to 8.3

ASA(config)# access-list NONAT extended permit ip 192.168.1.0 255.255.255.0 192.168.5.0 255.255.255.0
ASA(config)# nat (inside) 0 access-list NONAT
ASA(config)# nat (inside) 1 0.0.0.0 0.0.0.0
ASA(config)# global (outside) 1 interface ← We assume that we do PAT on the outside interface

Cisco ASA Version 8.3 and later

For ASA 8.3 and later, we need to configure the above NAT exemption as following:

ASA(config)# object network obj-local
ASA(config-network-object)# subnet 192.168.1.0 255.255.255.0
ASA(config-network-object)# exit

ASA(config)# object network obj-vpnpool
ASA(config-network-object)# subnet 192.168.5.0 255.255.255.0
ASA(config-network-object)# exit

ASA(config)# nat (inside,outside) source static obj-local obj-local destination static obj-vpnpool obj-vpnpool no-proxy-arp route-lookup

- STEP7 (Optional):

Similar with the IPSEC VPN client configuration, if you want to allow users to access the Internet and also access the Corporate LAN network at the same time, you must configure a Split-Tunnel Access Control List.

ASA(config)# access-list split-tunnel standard permit 192.168.1.0 255.255.255.0

Traffic from the remote users towards the network specified in the split-tunnel ACL (192.168.1.0/24) will pass through the SSL VPN tunnel. All other traffic from the remote user will go to the Internet. Note that the ACL created here will be used later in VPN Group Policy. Split-Tunneling is not a good security practice because allowing users to concurrently browse the Internet and also be connected to the corporate network at the same time is risky (malware from Internet might sneak in to the corporate network over the VPN tunnel).

- STEP8:

Create a Group Policy for the AnyConnect WebVPN users. The Group Policy allows you to separate different remote access users into groups with different attributes. The Group Policy attributes that can be configured include DNS server addresses, split-tunneling settings, how the client will be downloaded (automatically or after prompting the user), if the Anyconnect client software will remain permanently on the user's computer etc.

The command format is as following:

ASA(config)# group-policy *"policy name"* **internal**

ASA(config)# group-policy *"policy name"* **attributes**

ASA(config-group-policy)# vpn-tunnel-protocol {[ikev1] [ikev2][l2tp-ipsec][ssl-client]}

ASA(config-group-policy)# split-tunnel-policy {tunnelspecified | tunnelall}

ASA(config-group-policy)# split-tunnel-network-list value *"acl-for-split-tunnel"*

ASA(config-group-policy)# webvpn

ASA(config-group-webvpn)# anyconnect keep-installer {installed | none}

ASA(config-group-webvpn)# anyconnect ask {none | enable [default {webvpn | anyconnect} timeout ***value*****]}**

ASA(config-group-webvpn)# anyconnect dpd-interval {[gateway {*seconds* / none}] / [client {*seconds* / none}]}

Let's clarify some of the Group Policy commands shown above:

vpn-tunnel-protocol {[ikev1] [ikev2][l2tp-ipsec][ssl-client][ssl-clientless]} ← **Select the type of VPN tunnel protocol. For Anyconnect SSL VPN you must select "ssl-client"**

split-tunnel-policy {tunnelspecified | tunnelall} ← **Specify whether only selected traffic will pass through the tunnel ("tunnelspecified") or whether ALL remote traffic will pass through the tunnel ("tunnelall").**

split-tunnel-network-list value *"acl-for-split-tunnel"* ← **Specify the Access List for split-tunnel (see Step 7 above)**

anyconnect keep-installer {installed | none} ← **"installed" means that the client remains installed permanently on the user's computer even after disconnection. The default is that the client gets uninstalled after the user disconnects from the Anyconnect session. It is recommended to keep the Anyconnect installed permanently, so select "installed" here.**

anyconnect ask {none | enable [default {webvpn | anyconnect} timeout *value*]} ← **This command has to do with how AnyConnect client will be downloaded to user's computer.**

- anyconnect ask none default webvpn ← **The ASA immediately displays the WebPortal. This is the default configuration.**
- anyconnect ask none default anyconnect ← **Download the AnyConnect client automatically.**
- anyconnect ask enable default anyconnect timeout 20 ← **The user will get a prompt to install the AnyConnect client. If nothing is done within 20 seconds, the client will be downloaded and installed automatically.**

anyconnect dpd-interval {[gateway {*seconds* / none}*]* / [client {*seconds* / none}*]*} ← **This enables Dead Peer Detection (DPD) mechanism which ensures that the ASA (gateway) or the client can quickly detect a condition where the peer is not responding and the connection has failed.**

Let's see the actual configuration commands of group-policy for our specific scenario:

Example:

ASA(config)# group-policy Anyconnect-Policy internal

ASA(config)# group-policy Anyconnect-Policy attributes

ASA(config-group-policy)# vpn-tunnel-protocol ssl-client ssl-clientless ←allow both anyconnect ssl-client and clientless vpn

ASA(config-group-policy)# split-tunnel-policy tunnelspecified

ASA(config-group-policy)# split-tunnel-network-list value split-tunnel

ASA(config-group-policy)# dns-server value 192.168.1.15

ASA(config-group-policy)# webvpn

ASA(config-group-webvpn)# anyconnect keep-installer installed

ASA(config-group-webvpn)# anyconnect ask none default anyconnect

ASA(config-group-webvpn)# anyconnect dpd-interval client 20 ← The client will check for Dead Peer Detection every 20 seconds.

- STEP9:

Create a Tunnel Group. The tunnel group must incorporate the Group Policy configured above. It also binds the Group Policy with the IP address pool that we have already configured for remote users.

The command format is as following:

ASA(config)# tunnel-group *"tunnel name"* **type remote-access**

ASA(config)# tunnel-group *"tunnel name"* **general-attributes**

ASA(config-tunnel-general)# default-group-policy *"group policy name"* ←Assign the Group Policy configured in Step8 above.

ASA(config-tunnel-general)# address-pool *"IP Pool for VPN"* ← Assign the IP address pool configured in Step5 above.

ASA(config-tunnel-general)# exit

ASA(config)# tunnel-group *"tunnel name"* **webvpn-attributes**

ASA(config-tunnel-webvpn)# group-alias *"group_name_alias"* **enable** ← Create an alias name for the tunnel group which will be listed on the log on screen of the Anyconnect client.

ASA(config-tunnel-webvpn)# exit

ASA(config)# webvpn

ASA(config-webvpn)# tunnel-group-list enable ← Enable the listing of the alias name on the log on screen of the AnyConnect client.

Let's see the actual configuration commands of tunnel-group for our specific scenario:

Example:

ASA(config)# tunnel-group telecommuters type remote-access

ASA(config)# tunnel-group telecommuters general-attributes

ASA(config-tunnel-general)# default-group-policy Anyconnect-Policy

ASA(config-tunnel-general)# address-pool VPNpool

ASA(config-tunnel-general)# exit

ASA(config)# tunnel-group telecommuters webvpn-attributes

ASA(config-tunnel-webvpn)# group-alias sslgroup_users enable ← The name ("sslgroup_users") will be shown to the log-in screen of Anyconnect.

ASA(config-tunnel-webvpn)# exit

ASA(config)# webvpn

ASA(config-webvpn)# tunnel-group-list enable ← Allow users to select which tunnel group to connect (useful if you have multiple tunnel groups)

- STEP10:

Create a local user on ASA which will be used for AnyConnect authentication. This user will be allowed to have remote network access.

ASA(config)# username ssluser1 password secretpass

ASA(config)# username ssluser1 attributes ← OPTIONAL

ASA(config-username)# service-type remote-access ← OPTIONAL

7.3.1 Complete Configuration of Basic AnyConnect SSL VPN:

This configuration is based on the network diagram in the section above.

<u>This is for Cisco ASA Versions 8.3 and later (including 9.x)</u>

ASA# configure terminal

ASA(config)# webvpn

ASA(config-webvpn)# anyconnect image disk0:/anyconnect-win-3.1.04072-k9.pkg 1

ASA(config-webvpn)# enable outside

ASA(config-webvpn)# anyconnect enable

ASA(config-webvpn)# exit

ASA(config)# sysopt connection permit-vpn

ASA(config)# http redirect outside 80

ASA(config)# ip local pool VPNpool 192.168.5.1-192.168.5.20 mask 255.255.255.0

ASA(config)# object network obj-local

ASA(config-network-object)# subnet 192.168.1.0 255.255.255.0

ASA(config-network-object)# exit

ASA(config)# object network obj-vpnpool

ASA(config-network-object)# subnet 192.168.5.0 255.255.255.0

ASA(config-network-object)# exit

ASA(config)# nat (inside,outside) source static obj-local obj-local destination static obj-vpnpool obj-vpnpool no-proxy-arp route-lookup

ASA(config)#object network FOR_PAT

ASA(config-obj)#subnet 192.168.1.0 255.255.255.0

ASA(config-obj)#exit

ASA(config)#nat (inside,outside) source dynamic FOR_PAT interface

ASA(config)# access-list split-tunnel standard permit 192.168.1.0 255.255.255.0

ASA(config)# group-policy Anyconnect-Policy internal

ASA(config)# group-policy Anyconnect-Policy attributes

```
ASA(config-group-policy)# vpn-tunnel-protocol ssl-client ssl-clientless
ASA(config-group-policy)# split-tunnel-policy tunnelspecified
ASA(config-group-policy)# split-tunnel-network-list value split-tunnel
ASA(config-group-policy)# dns-server value 192.168.1.15
ASA(config-group-policy)# webvpn
ASA(config-group-webvpn)# anyconnect keep-installer installed
ASA(config-group-webvpn)# anyconnect ask none default anyconnect
ASA(config-group-webvpn)# anyconnect dpd-interval client 20
ASA(config-group-webvpn)# exit
ASA(config-group-policy)# exit

ASA(config)# tunnel-group telecommuters  type remote-access
ASA(config)# tunnel-group telecommuters general-attributes
ASA(config-tunnel-general)# default-group-policy Anyconnect-Policy
ASA(config-tunnel-general)# address-pool VPNpool
ASA(config-tunnel-general)# exit
ASA(config)# tunnel-group telecommuters webvpn-attributes
ASA(config-tunnel-webvpn)# group-alias sslgroup_users enable
ASA(config-tunnel-webvpn)# exit
ASA(config)# webvpn
ASA(config-webvpn)# tunnel-group-list enable
ASA(config-webvpn)# exit
ASA(config)# username ssluser1 password secretpass
ASA(config)# username ssluser1 attributes
ASA(config-username)# service-type remote-access
ASA(config)# wr mem
```

7.3.2 Connection Steps of Basic Anyconnect SSL VPN

1. Connect to ASA on its public outside address: **https://20.20.20.2**

You will get the following screen:

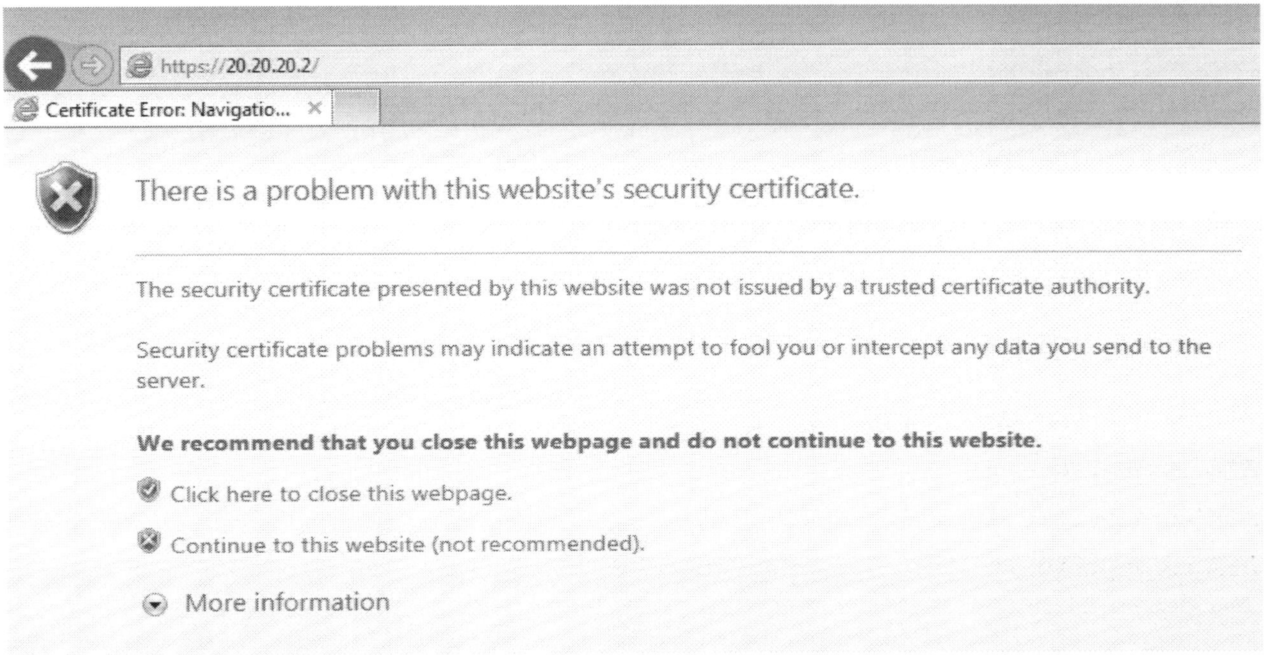

Notice that we get a certificate error. This is because the client does not recognize the SSL Certificate presented by the ASA firewall. The browser of the client does not see a valid certificate signed by a trusted root CA for this connection. In the following sections we will see how to configure certificates to avoid this problem.

If you are on a trusted network with low probability of "man-in-the-middle" attacks, you can click "Continue to this website".

2. Enter your username and password as configured on ASA (Local user: ssluser1)

After you click on "Continue to this Website" from screen above, you will be prompted by the ASA to enter your username and password which corresponds to the local ASA user we have created. Note also that the GROUP name "**sslgroup_users**" corresponds to the group-alias name configured in Step9 of the configuration.

3. Click "Login" on screen above.

After you provide the correct credentials above, the ASA will automatically try to download and install the Anyconnect client to the computer of the user. This automatic downloading and installation is dictated by the command "**anyconnect ask none default anyconnect** "as described in the ASA configuration above. You can change this behavior accordingly (see Step8 above).

By default, the new Anyconnect Secure Mobility Client version 3.1 and above will block your connection because the ASA is untrusted (due to unknown certificate). You will get the following error message.

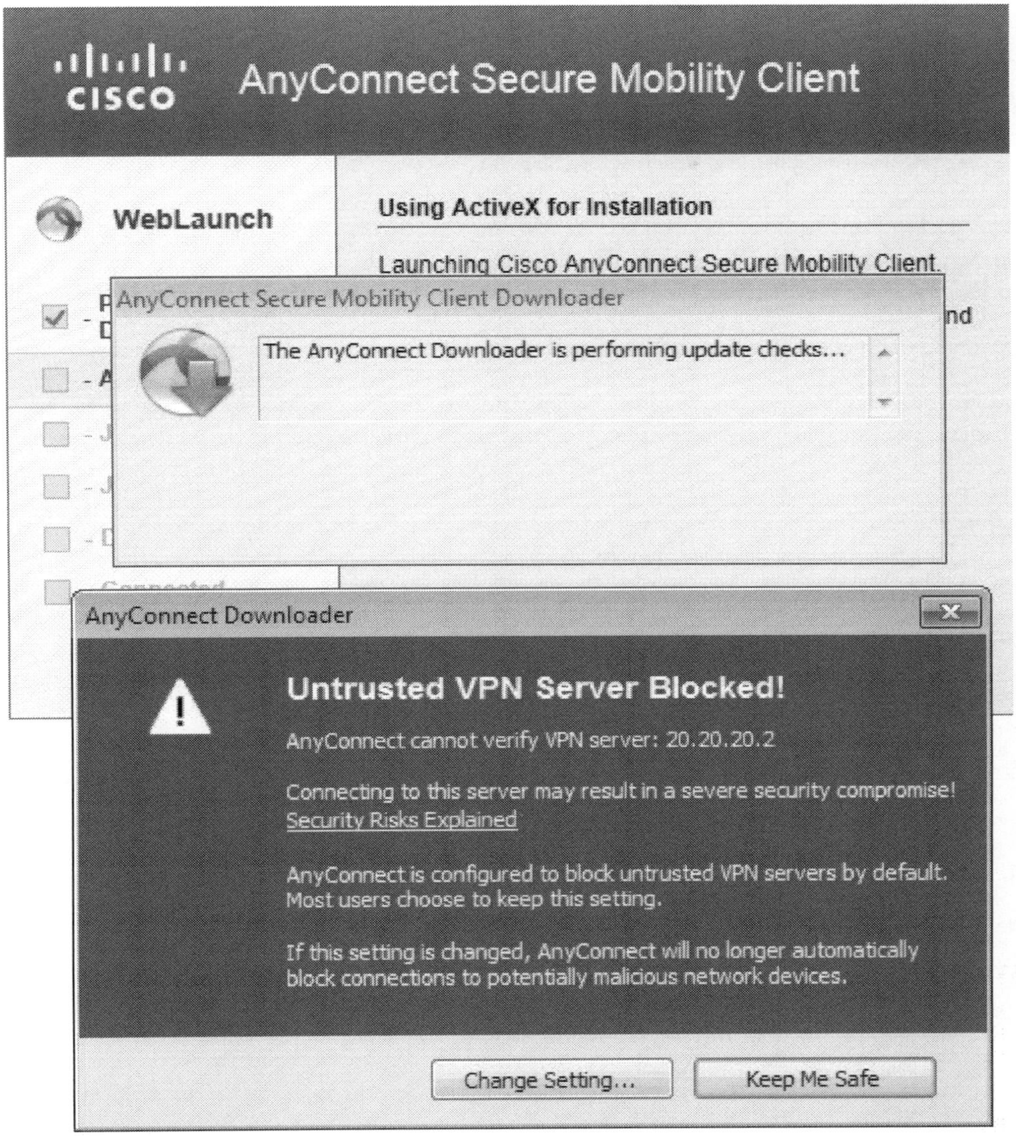

The only way to get rid of this message is to click on "Change Setting" above. If for example you are connected to an open WiFi connection where the probability of being attacked by "Man in the Middle" is higher, you should not try to connect until you get connected to a more trusted network.

4. Click "Change Setting" on screen above.

After clicking "Change Setting" on the warning message above, the installation will continue and depending on the security settings of your browser you will get some more certificate errors and other warning messages. Click to continue again and the installation will proceed as shown below:

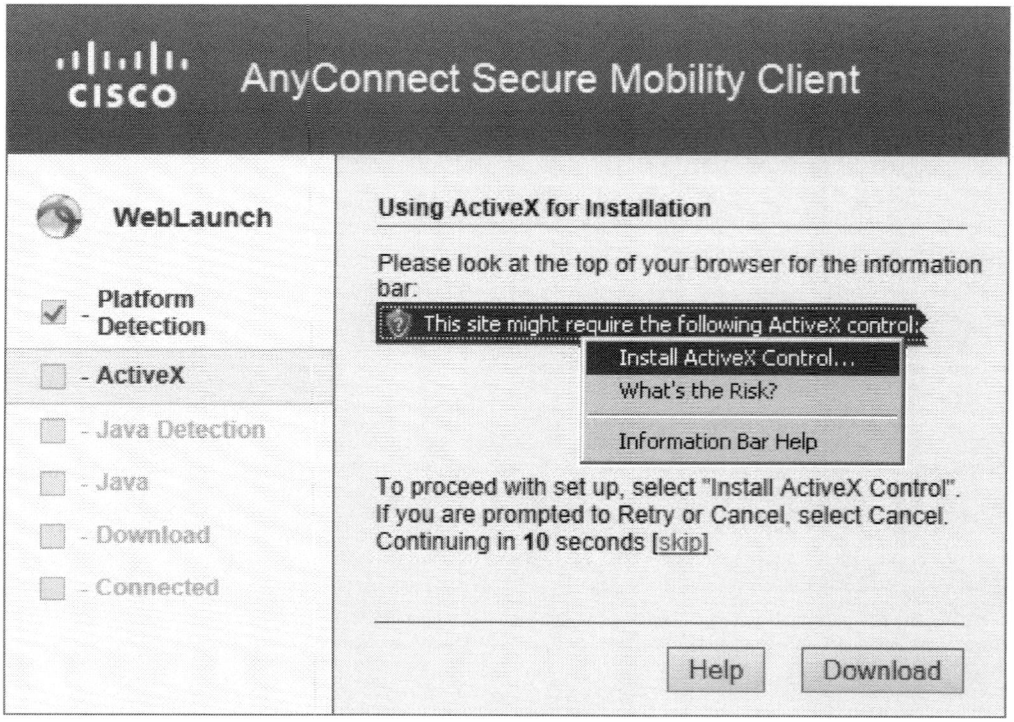

Note that the Anyconnect client is delivered by the ASA to the user using either ActiveX or Java. If one of these methods fail the other one is used.

5. If the automatic Web Installation fails you can do a manual install.

If the installation fails to complete because of the security settings of your browser or computer, you can click on "**Download**" button above in order to manually download the Anyconnect Client and install it. Clicking on the "Download" button above, you will get the following screen:

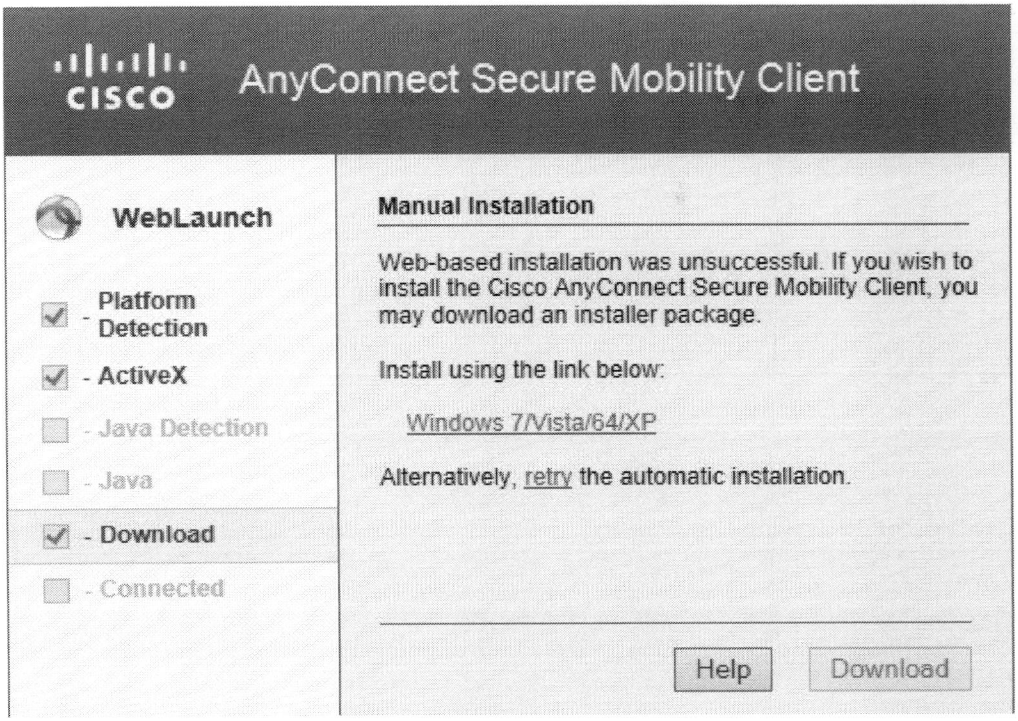

Click on the HyperLink shown above as "**Windows 7/Vista/64/XP**" and the Anyconnect client executable will be downloaded manually from the ASA to your computer. Run this executable in order to install the Anyconnect software to your computer. After installation is finished, you will find the "**Cisco Anyconnect Secure Mobility Client**" under your program files on your Windows machine.

6. Run the Anyconnect client.

Run the Anyconnect application and enter the IP address of the ASA. Click Connect.

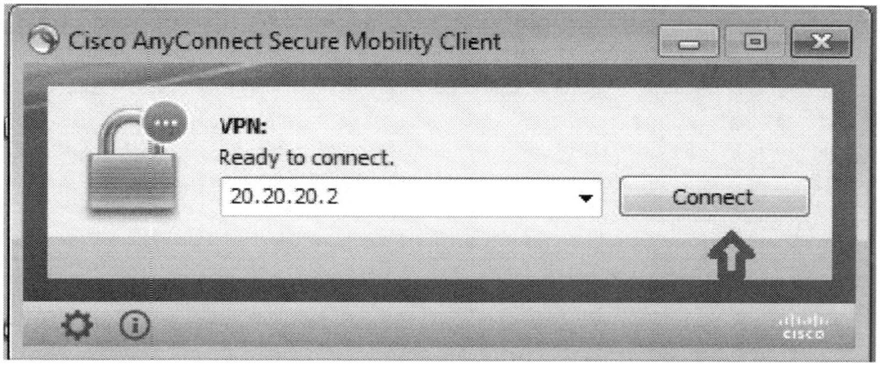

You will get a login screen again. Enter the user credentials as before:

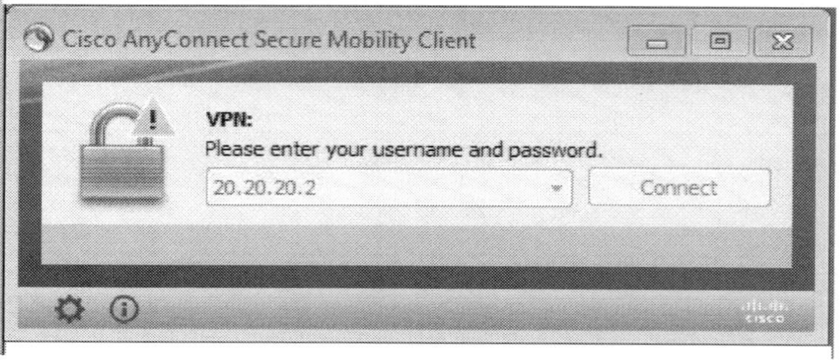

7. Succesful Connection.

If the connection is successful you can see statistics (Bytes sent and received) and the IP address assigned to your client from the VPN Pool configured on the ASA. See screenshot below.

From now on you are fully connected to the remote network. You can now access servers and applications on your corporate LAN.

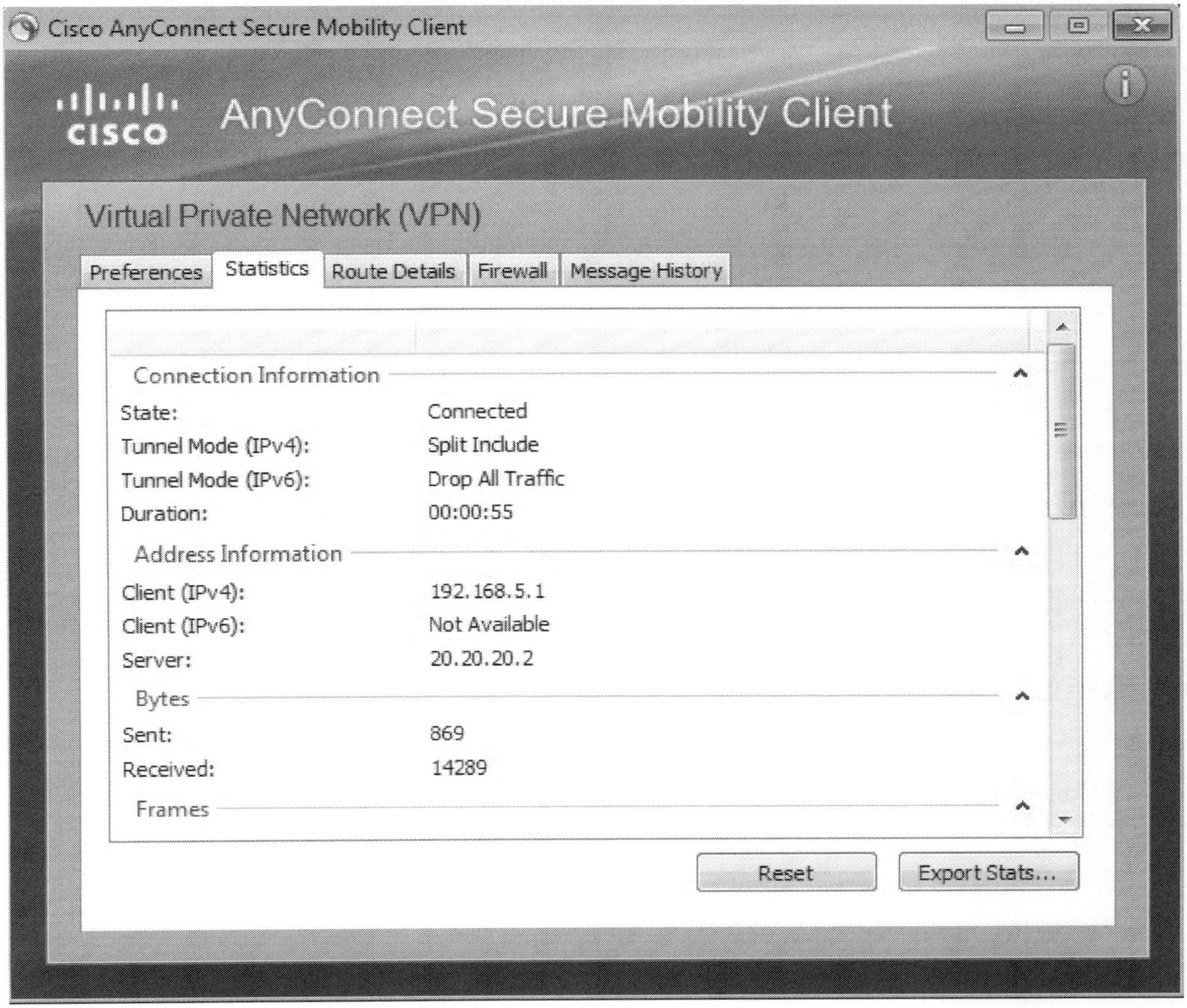

7.4 Anyconnect SSL VPN using Self-Signed ASA Certificate

By default, the ASA security appliance has a self-signed certificate that is regenerated every time the device is rebooted. You can configure the ASA to issue an identity certificate to itself (called self-signed certificate) which remains the same even when the device is rebooted.

On the basic Anyconnect scenario above we have seen that we've received a lot of error messages due to SSL certificate problems. Basically the client does not trust the ASA firewall because the ASA

presents a certificate to the client which is not signed by a trusted CA. One of the easiest ways to avoid these certificate errors is to create a Self-Signed Identity Certificate on the ASA, export this certificate from ASA and install it on the client machines as a trusted CA certificate.
Ofcourse this is not an ideal situation but it's still a viable option for some enterprises. The ideal case would be to purchase an SSL certificate for the ASA (Identity Certificate) from one of the trusted 3rd Party Certificate Authorities out there (such as Verisign, Thawte, Entrust, DigiCert etc). Those trusted root CA certificates are already pre-installed in almost all client computers (windows OS, browsers etc already trust them) so you won't have to install any certificates on the user's computer. However, in the case which we will describe here (where we have self-signed certificate), we will have to install the Identity Certiticate of the ASA to all remote users' computers in order to trust the SSL VPN connection with the ASA and avoid those annoying certificate errors. Ofcourse this is an administration burden if you have many remote users but it can be an easy (and free) option if you don't have too many users.

Below we will see the configuration steps required for creating a self-signed certificate on the ASA.

- **Step1: Configure Domain Name and Clock on the ASA**

Whenever you are working with certificates, it is essential to have correct clock settings on the ASA. Also having an FQDN (Fully Qualified Domain Name) assigned to the ASA device will be helpful for the remote access users to easily identify the certificate presented by the ASA. Let's now create an FQDN and configure correct clock settings.

ASA(config)# clock set 11:40:00 9 Nov 2013
ASA(config)# hostname asafw
asafw(config)# domain-name mycompany.com ← **the FQDN will be asafw.mycompany.com**

It is recommended to configure the ASA with NTP (Network Time Protocol) so that it receives accurate clock from an external source, but for the purposes of our example here we have just set the correct clock locally. Also, the FQDN of the ASA must be registered to a DNS server so that remote users will access the ASA with its FQDN which will be resolved to its public IP address.

IMPORTANT NOTE: Once you generate a self-signed certificate on the ASA using its FQDN, the remote users MUST access the ASA using its FQDN and NOT its public IP address. If a user tries to access the ASA (with the Anyconnect client or with a browser) by IP, then the user will get a certificate error.

- **Step2: Generate RSA key pair**

In PKI (Public Key Infrastructure), you need to generate a public and private key pair. When you generate an RSA key, the ASA will generate two keys (public and private). RSA uses a public key/private key combination. The public key in this pair can be known by anyone and can be distributed widely without issue to encrypt or sign messages.

asafw(config)# crypto key generate rsa label myrsakey modulus 1024 ← **generate an RSA keypair with name "myrsakey" and 1024 bit modulus**

!Verify the key generation

asafw(config)# show crypto key mypubkey rsa

Key pair was generated at: 11:48:23 EEST Nov 9 2013
Key name: myrsakey
Usage: General Purpose Key
Modulus Size (bits): 1024
Key Data:

30819f30 0d06092a 864886f7 0d010101 05000381 8d003081... [output omitted]

- **Step3: Configure a Trust Point for the self-signed certificate**

A "TrustPoint" is a special "container" configuration which includes all the details required to enroll the ASA device with a Certificate Authority (i.e to create a CSR – Certificate Signing Request). Under a TrustPoint configuration we set parameters such as how the ASA will enroll with the CA, what RSA keypair will be used, what will be the DN (Distinguished Name) of the device (configured with the "**subject-name**" command) etc. After creating a certificate for the ASA device, the TrustPoint will be associated with this certificate.

In our example here, the enrollment method defined in the TrustPoint will be "**self**". This means that the ASA will enroll to itself (i.e it will generate a self-signed certificate). In other words, the ASA will act as a CA and sign its own identity certificate.

asafw(config)# crypto ca trustpoint SELF-TP ← **create a trustpoint with name SELF-TP**
asafw(config-ca-trustpoint)# enrollment self ← **ASA will enroll to itself (self-signed cert)**
asafw(config-ca-trustpoint)# fqdn asafw.mycompany.com ←**The certificate will be assigned to this FQDN. This MUST be the same with the CN name below.**
asafw(config-ca-trustpoint)# subject-name CN=asafw.mycompany.com ←**create a DN for this device. CN (Canonical Name) MUST be the same as the FQDN above.**
asafw(config-ca-trustpoint)# keypair myrsakey ← **This trustpoint will use the RSA keypair created in Step 2 above (with label "myrsakey")**
asafw(config-ca-trustpoint)# exit

- <u>Step4: Generate the self-signed certificate</u>

Now we will enroll the ASA to a CA using the settings of the trust-point above. If we don't use "self" enrollment, this command will generate a CSR (Certificate Signing Request) which you have to send it to a 3rd party CA in order to sign a certificate for the device. However, in our scenario here, the command in this step will generate a self-signed certificate for the ASA.

asafw(config)# crypto ca enroll SELF-TP ←**enroll the ASA using the "SELF-TP" trustpoint settings.**

Now the ASA will ask you a few questions as shown below:

% The fully-qualified domain name in the certificate will be: ***asafw.mycompany.com***
% Include the device serial number in the subject name? [yes/no]: ***no***
Generate Self-Signed Certificate? [yes/no]: ***yes***

The self-signed certificate should be generated now. Let's see this certificate:

asafw(config)# show crypto ca certificates

```
Certificate
  Status: Available
  Certificate Serial Number: a2047e52
  Certificate Usage: General Purpose
  Public Key Type: RSA (1024 bits)
  Signature Algorithm: SHA1 with RSA Encryption
  Issuer Name:
    hostname=asafw.mycompany.com
    cn=asafw.mycompany.com
  Subject Name:
    hostname=asafw.mycompany.com
    cn=asafw.mycompany.com
   Validity Date:
    start date: 12:42:19 EEST Nov 9 2013
    end   date: 12:42:19 EEST Nov 7 2023
  Associated Trustpoints: SELF-TP
```

Notice from above that the "**Issuer Name**" (which is the CA) and the "**Subject Name**" (which is the device which will use the certificate) are the same. This is because the ASA acts as a CA to sign its own certificate. Also, this certificate is associated with the "SELF-TP" trustpoint.

- **Step5: Assign the TrustPoint to the outside interface**

The trustpoint above which is associated with the ASA self-signed certificate must be assigned to the outside interface which is going to terminate the SSL access from the clients.

asafw(config)# ssl trust-point SELF-TP outside

- **Step6: Export the self-signed Identity Certificate of the ASA**

As we have said before, we need to export this self-signed certificate of the ASA and import it to the clients as a trusted CA certificate.

asafw(config)# crypto ca export SELF-TP identity-certificate

The PEM encoded identity certificate follows:


```
-----BEGIN CERTIFICATE-----
MIICrTCCAhagAwIBAgIEogR+UjANBgkqhkiG9w0BAQUFADCBmjERMA8GA1UEBxMI
TGF3cmVuY2UxDzANBgNVBAgTBmthbnNhczELMAkGA1UEBhMCVVMxEjAQBgNVBAoT
CW15Y29tcGFueTERMA8GA1UECxMIc2VjdXJpdHkxHDAaBgNVBAMTE2FzYWZ3Lm15
Y29tcGFueS5jb20xIjAgBgkqhkiG9w0BCQIWE2FzYWZ3Lm15Y29tcGFueS5jb20w
HhcNMTMxMTA5MTA0MjE5WhcNMjMxMTA3MTA0MjE5WjCBmjERMA8GA1UEBxMITGF3
cmVuY2UxDzANBgNVBAgTBmthbnNhczELMAkGA1UEBhMCVVMxEjAQBgNVBAoTCW15
Y29tcGFueTERMA8GA1UECxMIc2VjdXJpdHkxHDAaBgNVBAMTE2FzYWZ3Lm15Y29t
cGFueS5jb20xIjAgBgkqhkiG9w0BCQIWE2FzYWZ3Lm15Y29tcGFueS5jb20wgZ8w
DQYJKoZIhvcNAQEBBQADgY0AMIGJAoGBAMyxVvBf0L+E6GQRVjae4GFyQ+1VZGFL
QrJcZAXSFMm4PiR29UUewFfDn6U4r1pIG/mhRS20MCXrmhQGB1QsqtnPK8tWFlTI
tADYzMHvuxeKmZgg5Ssl8ax2p6BUH9zwjoR+M8KlGjueWCffzz5bBJzpQwu8ew8i
oIQhxVCt1jHRAgMBAAEwDQYJKoZIhvcNAQEFBQADgYEAI+7FPaQqgF4udga34Ef8
e68fwgOluEA7j7MexEDLmj+y2DGQ1oeC6WXU28Zy3yT0F3x4H/yM1jzXdlzP70kC
BFMoT6tHTS00q3/7R03PI0BUO3YTh99I3USyj85VqkxrCsBjWF2cNZOYKIPQXzDk
9+Ja8Sil/WrGu3YnVOKQUoU=
-----END CERTIFICATE-----
```


The above command will display on the terminal screen the identity certificate of the ASA in PEM format. From above, copy the certificate text from the terminal (all text including the names ---BEGIN CERTIFICATE---- and ---END CERTIFICATE---) and copy it to a text editor. Save it with extension **.pem** (e.g filename will be **asacert.pem**)

- **Step7: Import the self-signed Identity Certificate of the ASA into the client machine**

By manually importing the ASA self-signed certificate to the user's machine, we make sure that the user will have the actual certificate of the ASA and not a roque certificate which might be presented to the user by a man-in-the-middle attacker.

In our example here I have used a Windows 7 computer for the remote user. We need to import the PEM certificate file from step above into the User Certificate Store of the Windows machine.

- In Windows 7: Open the certificate manager by typing "**certmgr.msc**" on the "search program and files" box (press the bottom left start button of windows).
- Right Click on "Trusted Root Certification Authorities" > All Tasks > Import

- Follow the wizard and import the PEM file created above. Now the user's machine (and hence the Anyconnect client) will trust the **asafw.mycompany.com** with no error warnings about certificates etc.

NOTE: If you are using Firefox or other browser except Internet Explorer, you will need to import the certificate into the browser certificate store as well.

7.5 Anyconnect SSL VPN using Certificates from the Local CA on ASA

On the scenarios above we have seen first a basic Anyconnect SSL VPN configuration without any certificate configuration, and then we have seen a basic Anyconnect SSL VPN with self-signed certificate on ASA. Both of the scenarios above have used basic username/password authentication for the remote users.

Now we will describe a very interesting case which you will not find anywhere else. We will use the Local CA (Certificate Authority) feature of the ASA appliance for issuing signed certificates for both the ASA device and the remote users in order to implement Certificate Based Authentication for SSL VPN. In addition, we will configure also Local user authentication, essentially having a two-factor authentication solution (Certificates + User/Pass).

The ASA's Local CA Server provides the appliance with a basic level of Certificate provisioning functionality. The primary use of the Local CA is to provide registered users the ability to enroll for certificates, which can then be used with features such as SSL VPNs or IKEv2 Remote Access VPNs. See the diagram below for our example.

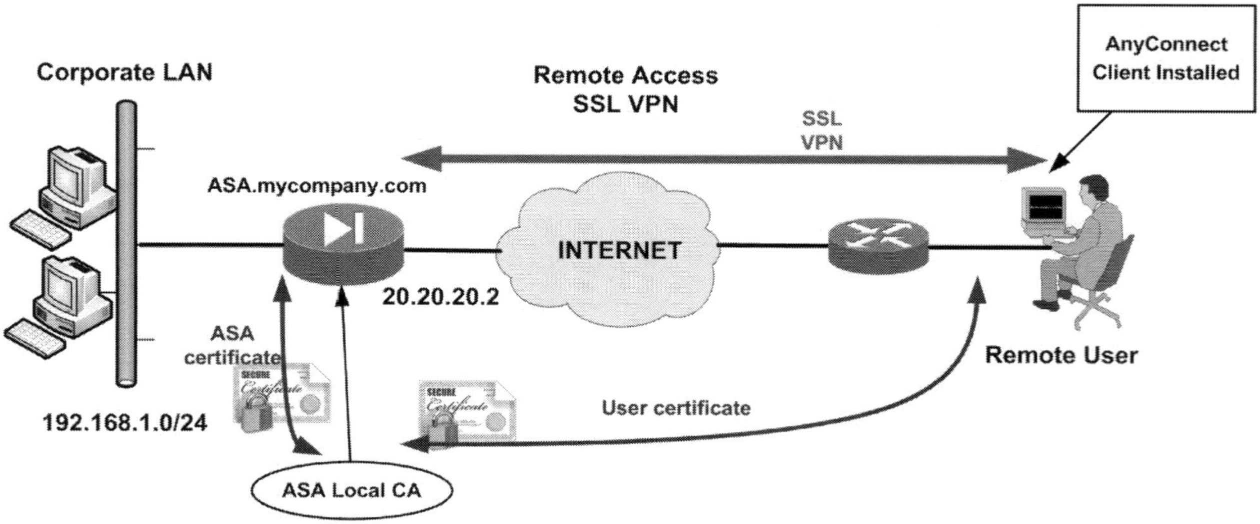

From our diagram above, the Local CA on ASA acts like a basic internal private Certificate Authority server. This private CA can issue certificates to both the ASA device itself and also to remote users.

Please note the following keypoints when configuring a Local CA Server on ASA:

1. When you enable the default Local CA Server on the ASA it will create some default settings like 1024 bit modulus, a CRL Distribution Point URL etc.
2. Enter a strong passphrase to protect the CA's private key.
3. Add a user to the database of the Local CA server and create an OTP (One Time Password) to be used by this user for enrollment to the CA.
4. The URL to be used by the user for enrollment to the CA and for downloading his/her certificate is **https://ASAHostname/+CSCOCA+/enroll.html**
5. User must enroll and download the user certificate from ASA. This certificate must be installed into the certificate store of the user's computer.

By enabling and using the default Local CA Server you get the following default settings:

- 1024 bit modulus for keys and certificates (this can be changed, up to 2048).
- A CRL URL of: http://ASAHostname/+CSCOCA+/asa_ca.crl
- An issuer-name of: cn=FQDN (unless you specify different issuer-name).
- Default storage of CA files in local flash.

So by enabling the Local CA Server on the ASA it is like having a private Certificate Authority server which can be used to generate and sign certificates for the users and for the ASA itself. This functionality can be used to replace the self-signed certificate provisioning which we have discussed in the previous section. That is, instead of generating a self-signed certificate on the ASA and manually importing this certificate to the remote users, now we will enable the users to connect with their browser to a special URL on the ASA and using an OTP (One Time Password) they will download a PKCS12 certificate which will be generated and signed by the Local CA on the ASA. This PKCS12 certificate will contain both the Local CA Certificate and the user Identity Certificate. By double-clicking on this PKCS12 certificate file, Windows machines will automatically import both Certificates (CA and User Certificate) into the computer's certificate store.

The above functionality will provide a trust between remote users and ASA and avoid the SSL certificate errors. However, we will take this one step further: By generating a PKCS12 certificate for the ASA itself and then importing this certificate into a Trustpoint on the ASA, it will be like signing a certificate for the ASA using its Local CA. Therefore now we will have certificates for both the ASA and Users signed by the same trusted private CA (Local CA of ASA) and we can perform Certificate Based Authentication of the users. By enabling also LOCAL AAA (Local User Authentication), we will essentially provide a two-factor authentication scheme (Certificates + User/Pass) for the remote users.

Let's now proceed with the actual configuration and hopefully everything will be clear. Please note that the core Anyconnect SSL VPN configuration is the same as the sections above (basic Anyconnect) so we will reuse several settings from the previous section and will not explain all the configuration for Anyconnect here.

- **STEP1:**

When using certificates it is essential to have correct clock settings on ASA and also have a proper FQDN domain name assigned to the ASA.

ASA(config)# clock set 21:55:00 25 OCT 2013
ASA(config)# hostname ASA
ASA(config)# domain-name mycompany.com ← FQDN will be ASA.mycompany.com

It's even better if you setup NTP on ASA so that the clock will be retrieved from an NTP server.

- **STEP2:**

Enable and configure the Local CA Server on ASA.

ASA(config)# crypto ca server
ASA(config-ca-server)# smtp from-address localca@mycompany.com ←required
ASA(config-ca-server)# subject-name-default CN=ASA, O=mycompany, C=US
ASA(config-ca-server)# lifetime ca-certificate 1095 ← CA Cert lifetime is 1095 days
ASA(config-ca-server)# lifetime certificate 365 ← Certs issued by this CA life 365 days
ASA(config-ca-server)# issuer-name CN=ASALOCALCA, C=US, ST=kansas, L=lawrence, O=mycompany,OU=security ←Distinquished Name of the Local CA
ASA(config-ca-server)# keysize server 1024 ←size of keypair for the Local CA server (can go up to 2048 bits)
ASA(config-ca-server)# no shutdown ← enable the CA server

% Some server settings cannot be changed after CA certificate generation.
% Please enter a passphrase to protect the private key
% or press return to exit
Passphrase: ***[Enter strong password here]***
*Re-enter passphrase: ***********

Keypair generation process begin. Please wait...

Completed generation of the certificate and keypair...

Archiving certificate and keypair to storage... Complete
INFO:
Certificate Server enabled.

ASA(config-ca-server)# exit

To verify that we have a CA certificate in place:

ASA(config)# show crypto ca certificates

CA Certificate
Status: Available
Certificate Serial Number: 01
Certificate Usage: Signature
Public Key Type: RSA (1024 bits)
Signature Algorithm: SHA1 with RSA Encryption
Issuer Name:
cn=ASALOCALCA
c=US
st=kansas
l=lawrence

o=mycompany
ou=security
Subject Name:
cn=ASALOCALCA
c=US
st=kansas
l=lawrence
o=mycompany
ou=security
Validity Date:
start date: 14:00:03 EEST Nov 6 2013
end date: 14:00:03 EEST Nov 5 2016
Associated Trustpoints: ***LOCAL-CA-SERVER***

By enabling the Local CA server on ASA it will automatically create a Trustpoint with name *"**LOCAL-CA-SERVER** "*.

- STEP3:

Add a user in the CA database and authorize it to enroll with the CA Server using an OTP (One Time Password). By adding a user to the CA database, the CA server will sign and generate a certificate for the user in PKCS12 format (when the user enrolls via a browser).

ASA(config)# crypto ca server user-db add remoteuser1 dn CN=remoteuser1 ← create user in CA database and also assign a CN name which must be the same as the username.
ASA(config)# crypto ca server user-db allow remoteuser1 display-otp ← allow the user to enroll and display its enrollment OTP on screen.

Username: ***remoteuser1***
OTP: ***8B5FBD064620843F***
Enrollment Allowed Until: 22:36:09 UTC Mon Oct 28 2013

By using the display-otp keyword above we have chosen to have the one time password shown to the screen instead of via email delivery (you could enable email-delivery of the OTP if needed). Now the remote user needs to enroll with the CA which is easily done using a web browser. The remote user can access the enrollment page at the following URL:

https://ASAhostname/+CSCOCA+/enroll.html

In our scenario above, the actual enrollment URL will be:

https://asa.mycompany.com/+CSCOCA+/enroll.html

The picture below shows a screenshot of the enrollment window for our example above.

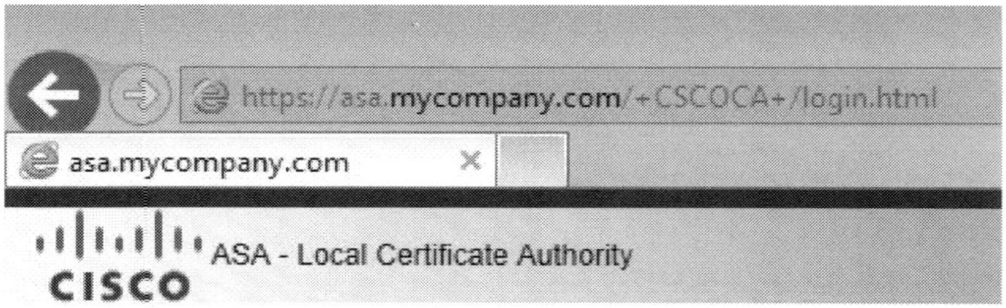

As you can see from above, the Local CA on ASA will ask the remote user to login in order to download its PKCS12 user certificate. Use the username and OTP from above in order to enroll the user to the CA. After clicking "Submit", a certificate with filename "**remoteuser1.p12**" will be generated and downloaded to the user's computer.

On Windows machines, by double-clicking this certificate file a wizard will start to help you import this certificate in the computer's certificate store. **When the wizard asks you to enter the password of the private key, then simply use the OTP password used above**.

This PKCS12 file contains both the user certificate and also the Local CA certificate. The user certificate will be automatically imported in the "**Personal**" certificate store and the CA certitifcate will be imported in the "**Trusted Root Certification Authorities**" store. You can run the "**certmgr.msc**" windows tool to view and manage the certificates.

If you want to verify that the user above has been enrolled successfully:

ASA# show crypto ca server user-db

username: ***remoteuser1***
email: <None>
dn: CN=remoteuser1
allowed: 22:36:09 UTC Mon Oct 28 2013
notified: 1 times
enrollment status: Enrolled*, Certificate valid until 23:28:30 UTC Sat Oct 25 2014,*
Renewal: Allowed

As you can see above, the user "**remoteuser1**" has enrolled succesfuly.

- STEP4:

One of the tasks of this scenario is to implement certificate based authentication for the remote users. This means that the user will authenticate to the ASA using its certificate, and also the ASA will present to the user its own identity certificate for validation. If both certificates are signed by the same trusted CA (i.e the Local CA of the ASA), then authentication will be successful.

In order to issue a certificate to the ASA (identity certificate), we will have to somehow enroll the ASA as a user to its own Local CA. Just like the step above, we can create a user in the CA database which will represent the ASA device. The username must be the hostname of the ASA (in our scenario here the hostname of the ASA device happens to be the name "**asa**"). Then, using a PC we can connect to the enrollment URL on the ASA and enroll this user into the Local CA. This means that the Local CA will sign and generate a PKCS12 certificate which will be downloaded to the PC of the administrator. After that, we will install this certificate in the ASA device (instead of the user's computer as we did in the previous step).

Let's see the commands and procedure below:

ASA(config)# crypto ca server user-db add asa **dn CN=asa.mycompany.com,C=US,ST=kansas,L=lawrence,O=mycompany,OU=security** ← **create user in CA database with name "asa" which is the hostname of ASA device. Also assign a DN.**

ASA(config)# crypto ca server user-db allow asa **display-otp** ← **allow the user "asa" to enroll and display its enrollment OTP on screen.**

Username: ***asa***
OTP: ***E2194722D475A34A***
Enrollment Allowed Until: 23:30:07 UTC Mon Oct 28 2013
Now, just like Step 3 above, visit the enrollment URL:

https://asa.mycompany.com/+CSCOCA+/enroll.html

And enter the credentials of the user (username= **asa** and OTP= ***E2194722D475A34A***)

The CA will generate a PKCS12 certificate for the user "asa". Download this certificate file (**asa.p12**) on your computer.

NOTE: As an administrator of the ASA firewall, you can enroll the user "asa" from the inside network. To do this you must enable webvpn on the inside as shown below:

ASA(config)# webvpn
ASA(config-webvpn)# enable inside

Then you can access the ASA from its inside IP address: https://192.168.1.1/+CSCOCA+/enroll.html

- STEP5:

Now the ASA administrator will have a PKCS12 certificate file ("**asa.p12**") which corresponds to the ASA device. We have to import this certificate into the ASA. We have two options to import a certificate: either using the CLI or using the graphical ASDM firewall management tool.

OPTION 1: Import the ASA Certificate using the CLI

This certificate is in binary format, so you will have to convert it into "**base64**" format (PEM format). I have used a Linux tool called "**openssl**" to convert the file as following:

root@linux:~# openssl base64 -in asa.p12 -out asa.pem

Now the new converted file (**asa.pem**) will be in clear text (a bunch of numbers and letters) which you can open with a text editor.

Now that we have a base64 encoded certificate file from the conversion above, we need to import this certificate into its own Trustpoint on the ASA. This certificate file will contain both an Identity Certificate for the ASA and the CA certificate which generated it.

ASA(config)# crypto ca import TRUSTPOINT1 pkcs12 ***E2194722D475A34A***

Enter the base 64 encoded pkcs12.
End with the word "quit" on a line by itself:

MIILYgIBAzCCCxwGCSqGSIb3DQEHAaCCCw0EggsJMIILBTCCCwEGCSqGSIb3DQEH
AaCCCvIEggruMIIK6jCCA3oGCyqGSIb3DQEMCgECoIICpTCCAqEwGwYKKoZIhvcN
AQwBAzANBAjq+defy7CBcQIBAQSCAoAtyKQtN7PirF5+1OkzdKPrO7cWFYb10jD7
i5wlBDGzuxrZ2Lf604v+Tg8b6xRMuHn+YAcuqvJSyQx0yAa63UM0byrdaBAbsK6m...[Output Omitted]
quit

INFO: Import PKCS12 operation completed successfully

The command above asks the ASA to import a pkcs12 certificate (with password *E2194722D475A34A* which is the OTP generated when we enrolled the user "asa") into a Trustpoint with name "TRUSTPOINT1".

The firewall will wait for you to paste the base64 certificate. Open the "asa.pem" file with a text editor and just copy/paste the certificate into the terminal window on the ASA. Type in "**quit**" on a line by itself. This procedure imports the certificate into the ASA device.

OPTION 2: Import the ASA Certificate using the graphical ASDM

You can connect to the ASA using its graphical management tool (ASDM) in order to import the "asa.p12" certificate without having to convert it to base64 format.

Under the ASDM environment, go to:

Configuration > Remote Access VPN > Certificate Management > Identity Certificates

Click on "Add" button to get the following screen:

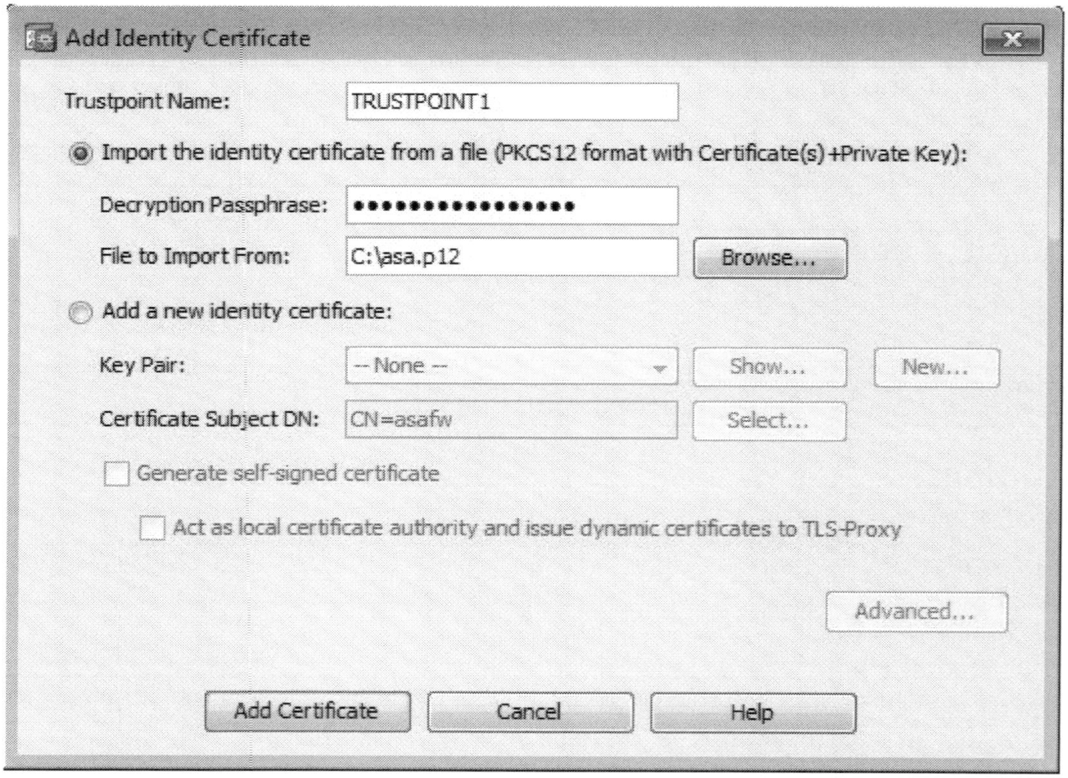

Change the Trustpoint Name to a unique name "TRUSTPOINT1" and for the "Decryption Passphrase" use the OTP we have generated before (i.e *E2194722D475A34A)*. Also select the certificate file to import "**asa.p12**". Clicking on "Add Certificate" will import the PKCS12 certificate without having to convert it to base64 format.

- **STEP6:**

We need to use the Trustpoint created above for SSL certificate validation on the outside ASA interface. Also, we need to allow ssl client connections to be validated by this Trustpoint using the "client-types" command.

ASA(config)# crypto ca trustpoint LOCAL-CA-SERVER
ASA(config-ca-trustpoint)# no client-types **←First disable ssl client validation by the default LOCAL-CA-SERVER trustpoint.**
ASA(config-ca-trustpoint)# exit

ASA(config)# crypto ca trustpoint TRUSTPOINT1
ASA(config-ca-trustpoint)# client-types ssl **←Enable ssl client validation by this trustpoint.**
ASA(config-ca-trustpoint)# exit

ASA(config)# ssl trust-point TRUSTPOINT1 outside **←Apply this Trustpoint on outside interface in order to be used for SSL certificate validation and authentication.**

- **STEP7:**

Configure the rest of Anyconnect settings as we have already done on the previous sections (Basic Anyconnect configuration). That is, configure Group Policy, Tunnel Group, VPN pool, NAT exemption etc. We will not explain these here again.

- **STEP8:**

Enable both Local username authentication as well as certificate authentication.

ASA(config)# username remoteuser1 password *secretpass* **←create a local user with same username as the one created in CA database (Step3).**

ASA(config)# tunnel-group telecommuters webvpn-attributes
ASA(config-tunnel-webvpn)# authentication aaa certificate **←enable both aaa local authentication together with certificate authentication.**

If you have followed every step above, remote users will be able to use Anyconnect for remote access SSL VPN and be authenticated with both certificates and username/password.

To verify the above use the following:

ASA(config)# show vpn-sessiondb detail anyconnect

Session Type: AnyConnect Detailed

*Username : **remoteuser1** Index : 7*
Assigned IP : 192.168.5.1 Public IP : 195.14.24.12
Protocol : AnyConnect-Parent SSL-Tunnel DTLS-Tunnel
License : AnyConnect Premium
Encryption : RC4 AES128 Hashing : SHA1
Bytes Tx : 12202 Bytes Rx : 9616
Pkts Tx : 18 Pkts Rx : 53
Pkts Tx Drop : 0 Pkts Rx Drop : 0
Group Policy : Anyconnect-Policy Tunnel Group : telecommuters
[output omitted]

AnyConnect-Parent:
Tunnel ID : 7.1
Public IP : 195.14.24.12
Encryption : RC4 Hashing : SHA1
Encapsulation: TLSv1.0 TCP Dst Port : 443
Auth Mode : Certificate and userPassword
Idle Time Out: 30 Minutes Idle TO Left : 26 Minutes
Client Type : AnyConnect

As you can see from the output above, the Authentication Mode used is both **Certificate** and **userPassword**.

This concludes our Local CA example here.

Please note that to avoid problems with the specific scenario above, it is better to have the Anyconnect client software pre-installed on the remote user's machine instead of having the users download the Anyconnect image on demand.

7.6 Anyconnect SSL VPN using 3rd Party CA

In the previous section we have discussed SSL VPN with certificates issued from the Local CA server that can be enabled on the ASA device. The Local CA on ASA provides basic functionality and may not be suited for large scale certificate management. Many enterprises prefer to have their own private CA server to issue certificates or even prefer to purchase certificates from external commercial Certificate Authority companies.

In this section we will describe how to configure the Cisco ASA to use certificates from 3rd Party CA for SSL VPN with Anyconnect. The 3rd Party CA can be either a private CA controlled by your enterprise or an external commercial CA. The configuration on ASA is the same in either case (private CA or commercial CA).

We will use a scenario in which we have a private Microsoft CA in our network controlled by our I.T department. We will generate a **Certificate Signing Request** (**CSR**) on ASA and then we will manually import a digital certificate from the CA into the ASA to be used for SSL VPN.

Using a Microsoft Certificate Authority server is a popular option used by many enterprises. Another option for private CA could be the "**openssl**" package in Linux OS.
The actual configuration of the Microsoft CA is outside of the scope of this book. We will see only the ASA configuration below:

A summary of the steps required are shown below:

ASA Steps

- Generate RSA keypair on ASA.
- Generate a Certificate Signing Request (CSR) on ASA.
- Export the CSR and send it to the private CA to be signed. The CA will generate an Identity Certificate for the ASA.
- Import the signed Identity Certificate to the ASA.
- Import the certificate of your CA to the ASA.

NOTE: In order to have a complete Certificate Chain present in the ASA, you must have both an Identity Certificate AND a CA certificate installed in the same Trustpoint on ASA.

Steps for Remote Access Users

- Create a CSR for the user.
- Sign the CSR with your CA server. This will generate a user Certificate.
- Import the User Certificate to the client computer.
- Import the certificate of your CA to the client.

Let's see the ASA steps below:

- STEP1:

You must have correct clock settings and also a valid FQDN for the ASA which must be registered in a DNS server. Then generate an RSA keypair (public and private key for the ASA).

ASA(config)#hostname asafw
asafw(config)#domain-name testcompany.com ←FQDN will be asafw.testcompany.com

asafw(config)# crypto key generate rsa label myrsakey modulus 2048 ←generate rsa key

The above will generate an RSA keypair (2048 bits) with label name "myrsakey".

- STEP2:

Now we need to generate a CSR from the ASA. First create a Trustpoint in which we will define how the ASA will enroll with the CA and several other parameters for the CSR.

asafw(config)# crypto ca trustpoint Trustpoint1

asafw(config-ca-trustpoint)# enrollment terminal ← we will manually enroll to the CA

asafw(config-ca-trustpoint)# fqdn asafw.testcompany.com ←FQDN to be included in cert

asafw(config-ca-trustpoint)# subject-name CN=asafw.testcompany.com, C=US, ST=kansas, L=lawrence, O=testcompany, OU=security ← specify full DN of the ASA device. CN=FQDN

asafw(config-ca-trustpoint)# keypair myrsakey ←Use RSA keypair generated in Step1
asafw(config-ca-trustpoint)#exit
asafw(config)#

NOTE: the Canonical Name (CN) above MUST be the same as the FQDN of the device otherwise you will get error messages.

asafw(config)# crypto ca enroll Trustpoint1 ←generate a CSR using the settings in Trustpoint1

After you execute the enrollment command above you will be asked some questions from the ASA:

% Start certificate enrollment ..
% The subject name in the certificate will be: CN=asafw.testcompany.com,C=US,ST=kansas, L=lawrence,O=testcompany,OU=security
% The fully-qualified domain name in the certificate will be: asafw.testcompany.com
% Include the device serial number in the subject name? [yes/no]: ***no***
Display Certificate Request to terminal? [yes/no]: ***yes***

Certificate Request follows:

-----BEGIN CERTIFICATE REQUEST-----
MIIBoDCCAQkCAQAwLTESMBAGA1UEAxMJY2lzY28uY29tMRcwFQYJKoZIhvcNAQkC
FghjaXNjb2FzYTCBnzANBgkqhkiG9w0BAQEFAAOBjQAwgYkCgYEAyIu44MPUPEp8
oSqftEp5jfLkGoU81QvGJBQU/HpDNu9MKM/c92DvfZnArGRHW8hMH9+7DsPNAWRz
ZbeErkQC9bo37gnCHJhH9Omlu05OfoywTsuTpCYVQl4RoGA/yKnz+3eIPdNZ6TxH
7cL6yWoNbPJRKqHsAcGzZjbGJMiQc0cCAwEAAaAzMDEGCSqGSIb3DQEJDjEkMCIw
CwYDVR0PBAQDAgWgMBMGA1UdEQQMMAqCCGNpc2NvYXNhMA0GCSqGSIb3DQEBBAUA
A4GBADGuCPqsBGj1ANl64qF6WU+Rey/Yuo/bf61Fb1MmhOqWp3g+cpY2b9X5ZfmS
oZQkIJFIyoQs1TEPc8FK3Tuhi6djMvCKIXyLDgC0YstlKQD7Pk2te462b9QG/sgJ
0Wx7A+nx8U+g1Ao/BTxbluhAvpsUHA+rey3LL6Y3JIVNIsUG
-----END CERTIFICATE REQUEST-----

Redisplay enrollment request? [yes/no]: ***no***

Now copy the Certificate Request from the CLI terminal as shown above and paste it into a text file. This file is the CSR of the ASA. You need to send this file to the administrator of your company's CA server (or to an external commercial CA) in order to sign it and generate the Identity Certificate for the ASA.

- **STEP3:**

At this step we assume that you have received a signed certificate from the CA. It would be better if the format of the certificate is **base64** so you can open it with a text editor and copy/paste the certificate to the ASA via the CLI terminal (you can use also the ASDM for this task).

After you receive a signed Identity Certificate from the CA server, you need to import this certificate into the Trustpoint we have created above ("Trustpoint1"). Just copy/paste the certificate in CLI terminal after you execute the command below.

asafw(config)# crypto ca import Trustpoint1 certificate ←**Import certificate in Trustpoint1**

% The fully-qualified domain name in the certificate will be: asafw.testcompany.com
Enter the base 64 encoded certificate.
End with the word "quit" on a line by itself

-----BEGIN CERTIFICATE-----
XyeelEEawIBAgIBATANBgkqhkiG9w0BAQUFADAcMRowGAYDVQQDExFBU0Ez
Mi0yNS5nbmF4Lm5ldDAeFw0xMzA4MzEwNDAxMDFaFw0xNjA4MzAwNDAxMDFaMBwxGjAYBgNVB
AMTEUFTQTMyLTI1LmduYXgubmV0MIGfMA0GCSqGSIb3DQEBAQUAA4GN
Su772Aa=.......[output omitted]
-----END CERTIFICATE-----
quit ← **You must type "quit" in a new line**
INFO: Certificate successfully imported

- **STEP4:**

As we have said before, we must have a combination of both the Identity Certificate and the CA Certificate imported in the same Trustpoint in ASA in order to have a completed certificate chain. In Step3 above we have imported the Identity Certificate. In the Step here we must import the CA certificate in the same Trustpoint.

Now in order to get the CA certificate file, it depends on the CA you are using. For a Microsoft CA server, you can connect to the Web GUI of the server with a browser (usually the URL is **http://serverIP/certsrv**) and select the option "**Retrieve the CA Certificate**". Download the CA Certificate as Base64 format. Open it with a text editor and copy the certificate to clipboard.

Now we need to import this CA certificate to the ASA:

asafw(config)# crypto ca authenticate Trustpoint1 ← **the "authenticate" command is used to import a CA certificate into the trustpoint.**

Enter the base 64 encoded CA certificate.
End with the word "quit" on a line by itself

*** Here Paste the certificate you have copied from the text file above ***

-----BEGIN CERTIFICATE-----
MIICETCCAXqgAwIBAgIBATANBgkqhkiG9w0BAQUFADAcMRowGAYDVQQDExFBU0Ez
aBQwDQYJKoZIhvcNAQEFBQADgYEAQWo8tCdi1z/INM2oIicsX0d/Ufu2TrUP++L+
6jIepdUecXqA41n1QTRAMVETg7DdGZYqA/ZEmEOruo/8J7cszJfd+OoxVFNW7d2k
xo8ugSSir4i2EuHMt7GuhO0L6L3/UAv58AWL6ItcUMpYlrLA/E6DbH8kf/GVNJlR
y5XIevg=....[output omitted]
-----END CERTIFICATE-----
quit
INFO: Certificate has the following attributes:
Fingerprint: dee02adb d3a770e4 4afb4f5e e62ed70d

Do you accept this certificate? [yes/no]: ***yes***

Trustpoint CA certificate accepted.
% Certificate successfully imported
Trustpoint "Trustpoint1" is now authenticated.

<u>Verification:</u>

asafw(config)# show crypto ca certificates

! This is the Identity Certificate of the ASA
Certificate
Status: Available
Certificate Serial Number: 01
Certificate Usage: General Purpose
Public Key Type: RSA (2048 bits)
Signature Algorithm: SHA1 with RSA Encryption
Issuer Name:
ea=admin@testcompany.com
cn=internalrootca
ou=security
o=testcompany
l=lawrence
st=kansas
c=US
Subject Name:
hostname=asafw.testcompany.com
cn=asafw.testcompany.com
c=US
st=kansas
l=lawrence
o=testcompany
ou=security

Validity Date:
start date: 23:05:19 EEST Nov 5 2013
end date: 23:05:19 EEST Nov 5 2014
Associated Trustpoints: Trustpoint1

! This is the CA Certificate (Issuer Name and Subject Name are the same)
CA Certificate
Status: Available
Certificate Serial Number: 00adfc7eaf667ed187
Certificate Usage: General Purpose
Public Key Type: RSA (2048 bits)
Signature Algorithm: SHA1 with RSA Encryption
Issuer Name:
ea=admin@testcompany.com
cn=internalrootca
ou=security
o=testcompany
l=lawrence
st=kansas
c=US
Subject Name:
ea=admin@testcompany.com
cn=internalrootca
ou=security
o=testcompany
l=lawrence
st=kansas
c=US
Validity Date:
start date: 22:07:13 EEST Nov 5 2013
end date: 22:07:13 EEST Nov 3 2023
Associated Trustpoints: Trustpoint1

- **STEP5:**

So far we have created the Trustpoint1 which contains two certificates (Identity + CA certificates). This Trustpoint will be used for SSL validation and authentication on the outside ASA interface.

asafw(config)# ssl trust-point Trustpoint1 outside ←use Trustpoint1 to validate SSL certificates on outside interface

- **STEP6:**

Now if you want you can enable certificate authentication or both AAA and certificate authentication.
asafw(config)# tunnel-group telecommuters webvpn-attributes
asafw(config-tunnel-webvpn)# authentication aaa certificate

- **STEP7:**

For the remote user, you must generate a User certificate using your CA server and import it into the certificate store of the user's computer. Also, you must import the CA certificate to the user's machine as Trusted Root CA. After completing this step you will create a certificate trust between the remote user and ASA.

7.7 IKEv2 Remote Access VPN with Anyconnect

Cisco has already announced the end-of-life of its native IPSec VPN client software but it is now integrating the IPSec support in its **Anyconnect client** (version **3.x** and above). In the past we had two different remote access clients, one for IPSec and one for SSL VPN. Now we have a single remote access client solution which supports both IPSec as well as SSL remote access VPNs. This new solution is called "**Cisco AnyConnect Secure Mobility Client**".

In this section we will discuss the configuration of Remote Access VPN using IKEv2 IPSEC. The client which will be connecting to the ASA is Anyconnect version 3.x (and above) and will use IKEv2 IPSEC instead of SSL.

In the diagram shown below, a remote user wants to connect to the ASA using IKEv2 VPN and wants to access the hosts 192.168.1.101 & 192.168.1.102 on the corporate LAN.

Remember that the configuration of IKEv2 remote-access is a mixture of the IKEv2 generic configuration that we've covered in the site-to-site exercise before and the existing AnyConnect/SSL configuration so it leverages most of the existing configuration commands that you might already be familiar with (that's why you will not find too much explanation on the commands below)

Prerequisites

- Just like the SSL VPN we have seen before, make sure that you have an Anyconnect image copied on the ASA flash. It is generally a file with .pkg extension with various operating system names included in its filename. For example, anyconnect-**win**-3.1.04059-k9.pkg; anyconnect-**macosx**-i386-3.1.04059-k9.pkg. Here **Win** represents Windows based machines and macosx refers to the **MAC** operating systems.
- You must have an XML profile which will be used to define gateway hostname, gateway ip address and Connection Protocol (IPSEC in our case here). More on this later.

- You must configure an Identity Certificate on the ASA (either a self-signed certificate or obtain a certificate from an external CA, or even use the Local CA as we have seen before).

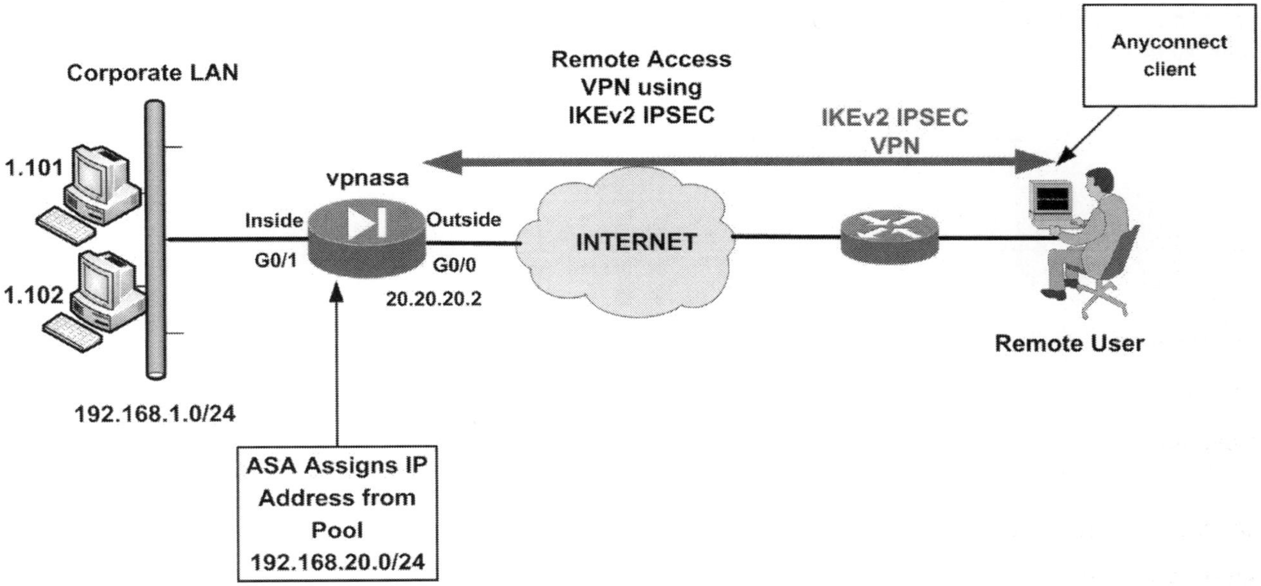

Let's start with the ASA configuration below:

- <u>Step1: Configure IKEv2 Policies and IPSec Proposals</u>

Note that you can reuse these from the site-to-site IKEv2 exercise before.

vpnasa(config)# crypto ikev2 policy 1
vpnasa(config-ikev2-policy)# encryption aes
vpnasa(config-ikev2-policy)# integrity sha
vpnasa(config-ikev2-policy)# group 5 2
vpnasa(config-ikev2-policy)# prf sha
vpnasa(config-ikev2-policy)# lifetime seconds 86400
vpnasa(config-ikev2-policy)# exit
vpnasa(config)#

vpnasa(config)# crypto ipsec ikev2 ipsec-proposal AES-3DES
vpnasa(config-ipsec-proposal)# protocol esp encryption aes 3des
vpnasa(config-ipsec-proposal)# protocol esp integrity sha-1 md5
vpnasa(config-ipsec-proposal)# exit

- <u>Step2: Configure Dynamic Crypto Map referencing the IKEv2 IPSec Policies</u>

vpnasa(config)# crypto dynamic-map DYN_MAP 10 set ikev2 ipsec-proposal AES-3DES ← IPSec Proposal configured above
vpnasa(config)# crypto map OUTSIDE_MAP 10 ipsec-isakmp dynamic DYN_MAP ← Attach the dynamic crypto map on a static map
vpnasa(config)# crypto map OUTSIDE_MAP interface outside

- <u>Step3: Configure IP Pool to assign addresses to remote users</u>

vpnasa(config)# ip local pool vpn-pool 192.168.20.1-192.168.20.254 mask 255.255.255.0

- <u>Step4: Configure Identity certificate trust point</u>

Here we need to configure an Identity Certificate for the ASA. For simplicity we will generate a self-signed certificate trust-point and set it as the IKEv2 remote-access trust-point.

vpnasa(config)# crypto key generate rsa label rsakeys modulus 1024

Keypair generation process begin. Please wait...

vpnasa(config)# crypto ca trustpoint SELF-TP
vpnasa(config-ca-trustpoint)# enrollment self
vpnasa(config-ca-trustpoint)# fqdn vpnasa.mycompany.com
vpnasa(config-ca-trustpoint)# subject-name CN=vpnasa.mycompany.com
vpnasa(config-ca-trustpoint)# keypair rsakeys
vpnasa(config-ca-trustpoint)# exit

vpnasa(config)# crypto ca enroll SELF-TP

Now you will get some questions from the ASA as shown below:

% The fully-qualified domain name in the certificate will be: vpnasa.mycompany.com
% Include the device serial number in the subject name? [yes/no]: ***no***
% Generate Self-Signed Certificate? [yes/no]: ***yes***

Once done with certificate configuration, verify that the certificate is enabled and valid.

vpnasa(config)# show crypto ca certificates

Certificate
Status: Available
Certificate Serial Number: 26239652
Certificate Usage: General Purpose
Public Key Type: RSA (1024 bits)
Signature Algorithm: SHA1 with RSA Encryption

Issuer Name:
hostname=vpnasa.mycompany.com
cn=vpnasa.mycompany.com
Subject Name:
hostname=vpnasa.mycompany.com
cn=vpnasa.mycompany.com
Validity Date:
start date: 19:25:21 EEST Nov 27 2013
end   date: 19:25:21 EEST Nov 25 2023
Associated Trustpoints: SELF-TP

vpnasa(config)# crypto ikev2 remote-access trustpoint SELF-TP ←Set the trust-point configured above as the remote access trustpoint for ikev2

vpnasa(config)# crypto ikev2 enable outside client-services port 443←enable client-services. Client services enable software updates, profiles, localization, etc.

vpnasa(config)# ssl trust-point SELF-TP outside ←client-services run over SSL, so specify also the trustpoint to be used for ssl as well.

- **Step5: Enable and configure the Anyconnect client on the ASA under Webvpn**

The following commands were used also in the SSL VPN Anyconnect configuration so no explanation will be provided here.

vpnasa(config)# webvpn
vpnasa(config-webvpn)# anyconnect image disk0:/anyconnect-win-3.1.04072-k9.pkg
vpnasa(config-webvpn)# anyconnect enable
vpnasa(config-webvpn)# enable outside
vpnasa(config-webvpn)# tunnel-group-list enable
vpnasa(config-webvpn)# exit

- **Step6: Configure a Group Policy and allow IKEv2 as a vpn tunnel protocol**

vpnasa(config)# group-policy Anyconnect-Policy internal
vpnasa(config)# group-policy Anyconnect-Policy attributes
vpnasa(config-group-policy)# vpn-tunnel-protocol ikev2 ssl-client
vpnasa(config-group-policy)# webvpn
vpnasa(config-group-webvpn)#anyconnect keep-installer installed
vpnasa(config-group-webvpn)#anyconnect dpd-interval client 20
vpnasa(config-group-webvpn)#anyconnect ask none default anyconnect
vpnasa(config-group-webvpn)#exit
vpnasa(config-group-policy)#exit
vpnasa(config)#

- **Step7: Configure a Tunnel Group**

vpnasa(config)# tunnel-group telecommuters type remote-access
vpnasa(config)# tunnel-group telecommuters general-attributes
vpnasa(config-tunnel-general)# address-pool vpn-pool
vpnasa(config-tunnel-general)# default-group-policy Anyconnect-Policy
vpnasa(config-tunnel-general)# exit

vpnasa(config)# tunnel-group telecommuters webvpn-attributes
vpnasa(config-tunnel-webvpn)# group-alias ikev2vpn_users enable

- **Step8: Create Local users for authentication**

vpnasa(config)# username ikev2user password *secretpass*

- **Step9: Create an XML profile for Anyconnect and copy it to ASA flash**

This step is important here. In the previous sections for SSL VPN we haven't talked about the Anyconnect XML profile because it was not mandatory. However, for IKEv2 IPSEC VPN with Anyconnect you must configure an XML profile which will change the Protocol to be used by Anyconnect client to IPSec from SSL (SSL is the default). This XML profile must be copied to the Flash of the ASA and also must be copied to the remote user's computer.

You can create the XML profile file manually with a text editor or you can use the ASDM to generate one. A simple XML profile with filename "**ikev2profile.xml**" has been created and is shown below:

```
<?xml version="1.0" encoding="UTF-8"?>
<AnyConnectProfile xmlns="http://schemas.xmlsoap.org/encoding/">
        <ClientInitialization>
        <WindowsVPNEstablishment>AllowRemoteUsers</WindowsVPNEstablishment>
        <WindowsLogonEnforcement>SingleLogon</WindowsLogonEnforcement>
        </ClientInitialization>
 <ServerList>
   <HostEntry>
    <HostName> vpnasa</HostName>  //Specify the Hostname here
    <HostAddress>vpnasa.mycompany.com</HostAddress>  //FQDN of VPN Gateway
    <PrimaryProtocol>IPsec</PrimaryProtocol>  //Select IPSEC Protocol instead of SSL.
   </HostEntry>
 </ServerList>
</AnyConnectProfile>
```

Notice above that we have specified the "PrimaryProtocol" as "IPsec".

Transfer the XML file above to ASA flash (using TFTP for example):

vpnasa(config)#show flash

.....
103 527 Nov 19 2013 17:20:24 ikev2profile.xml
......

Also, this XML profile must be copied to the computer of the remote user. For Windows 7 computers the profile above must be copied to the following path:

C:\ProgramData\Cisco\Cisco AnyConnect Secure Mobility Client\Profile

Normally the profile above is downloaded automatically to the computer of the remote user when the user connects to the ASA with Anyconnect for the first time. However, if you use IKEv2 the user will not be able to connect at first place, so the profile won't be downloaded. Hence you must copy it manually to the user's machine.

- **Step10: Bind the XML profile above to the WebVPN Group Policy**

vpnasa(config)# webvpn
vpnasa(config-webvpn)# anyconnect profiles ikev2profile **disk0:/ikev2profile.xml** ←specify the location and filename of the XML profile
vpnasa(config-webvpn)# exit

vpnasa(config)# group-policy Anyconnect-Policy attributes
vpnasa(config-group-policy)# webvpn
vpnasa(config-group-webvpn)# anyconnect profiles value ikev2profile **type user** ←assign the XML profile to the appropriate group policy

- **Step11: Export the self-signed Identity Certificate of the ASA**

As we have seen in the SSL VPN using self-signed certificate before, we can export the certificate of the ASA and import it to the clients as a trusted CA certificate.

vpnasa(config)# crypto ca export SELF-TP identity-certificate

See the steps in the section about SSL VPN using self-signed certificate for the procedure to import the certificate to the user's computer.

Verification

As shown on the screenshot below, the Anyconnect client is connected using IKEv2/IPSEC protocol.

Also, you can see all the details using:

vpnasa(config)# show vpn-sessiondb detail anyconnect

Session Type: AnyConnect Detailed

Username : ikev2user Index : 2
Assigned IP : 192.168.20.1 Public IP : 212.31.50.12
***Protocol : IKEv2 IPsecOverNatT** AnyConnect-Parent*
License : AnyConnect Premium
Encryption : AES128 Hashing : none SHA1

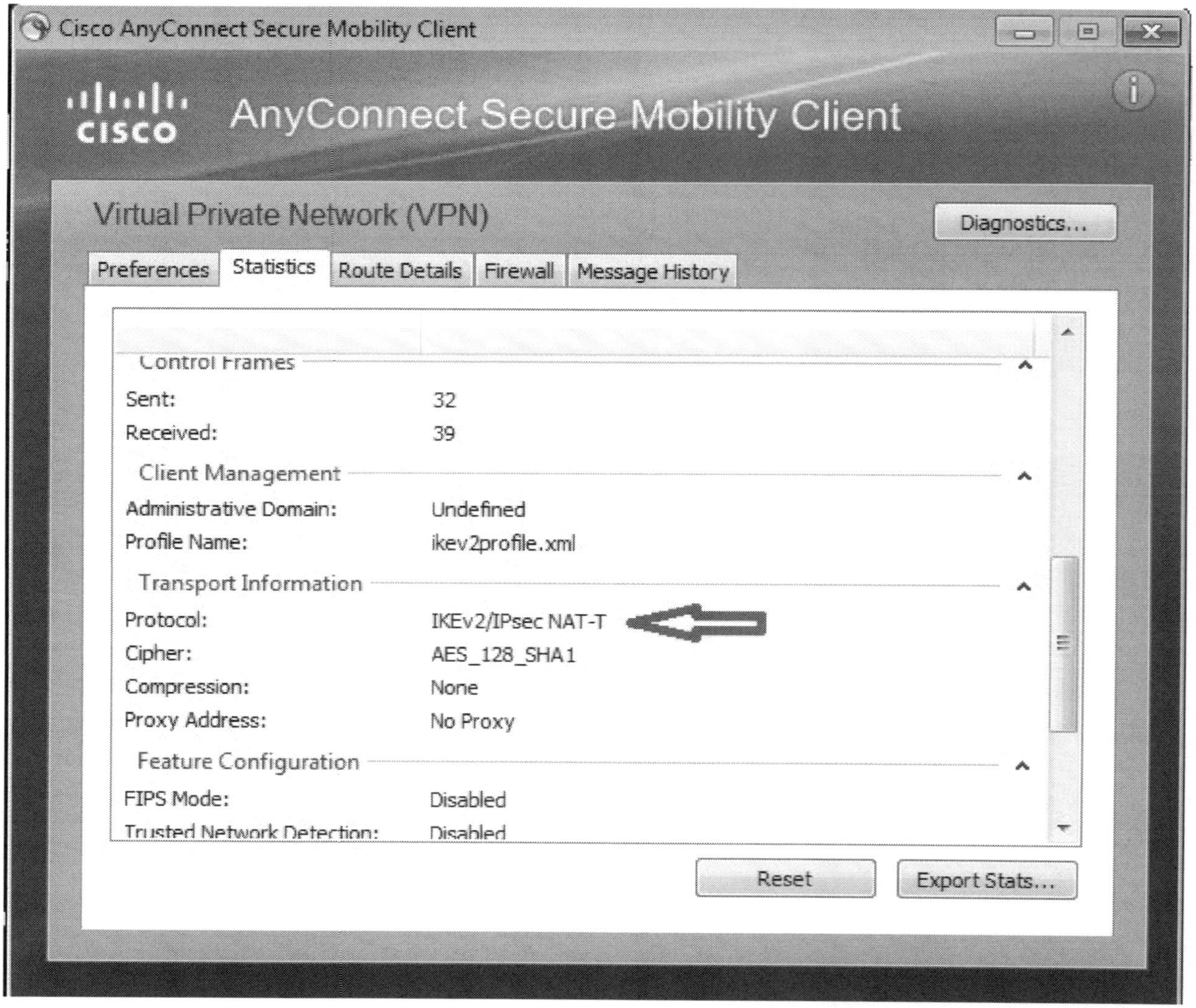

Chapter 8 Configuring Firewall Failover

The Cisco ASA Firewall is a critical component of any network infrastructure and usually several essential enterprise services depend on the availability of the Firewall appliance. Firewall redundancy is therefore a must in many network topologies.

In this Chapter we will describe stateful failover in Active/Standby mode which is the most popular configuration in most networks. ASA supports also Active/Active failover mode which however requires special configuration using multiple firewall contexts. Also, Active/Active failover does not support VPN, which is another limitation of this redundancy mode.

8.1 ASA Models Supporting Failover

At the time of writing this book, support for **Active/Standby (AS)** or **Active/Active (AA)** failover is as following:

- Older ASA 5500 Models:
    - 5505 → Does not support failover
    - 5510 Base License → Does not support failover
    - 5510 Security Plus License → Supports both AS and AA failover
    - All other models (5520, 5540, 5550, 5580) → Support both AS and AA failover

- Next Generation ASA 5500-X Models:
    - 5512-X Base License → Does not support failover
    - 5512-X Security Plus License → Supports both AS and AA failover
    - All other models (5515-X, 5525-X, 5545-X, 5555-X, 5585-X) → Support both AS and AA failover

8.2 Understanding Active/Standby Failover

In an Active/Standby (A/S) mode of operation, one of the firewall units in the failover pair is assigned the active role, handling all traffic and security functions. The other firewall unit in the pair remains in standby mode waiting to automatically take over all the traffic in the event of a failure.

The stateful failover feature passes connection state information from the active to the standby unit. After failover occurs, the same connection information is available at the standby unit, which automatically becomes active without any user traffic disconnection. The stateful connection information that is synchronized between active and standby units include global pool addresses and status, connection and translation information and status, TCP/UDP states, the translation table for NAT, the ARP table and many other details.

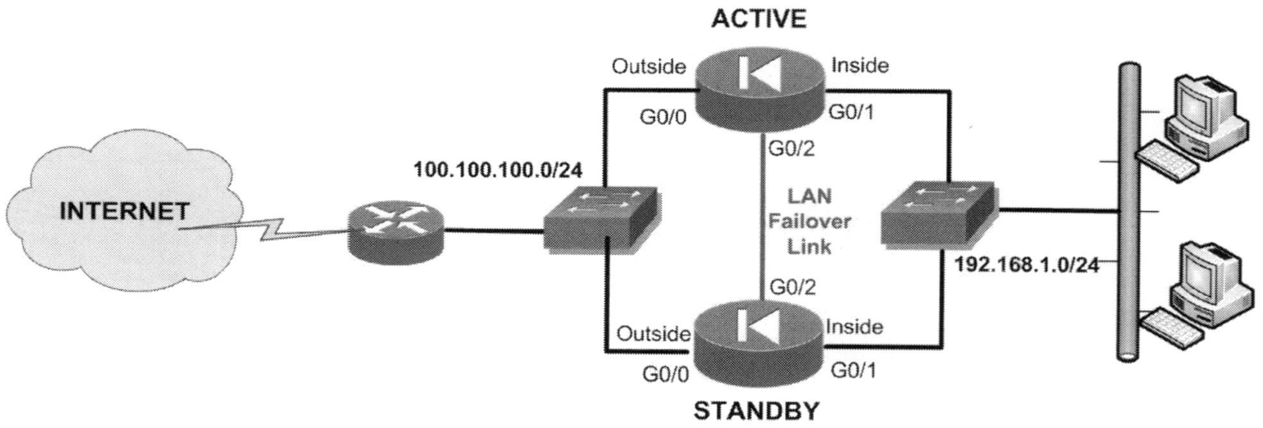

The network topology above shows a firewall failover pair in an Active/Standby setup. The "inside" interfaces are connected to the same internal switch and the "outside" interfaces to the same external switch. Also, a cross-over network cable is required between the two appliances as a LAN Failover Link. During normal operation, all traffic passes through the ACTIVE unit which controls all inbound and outbound communication. In the event of a failure of the active firewall (e.g interface failure, whole appliance failure etc), the STANDBY unit takes over by receiving the IP addresses of the ACTIVE unit so that traffic will continue to flow without interruption. All the connection state information is synchronized through the LAN Failover Link so that the STANDBY firewall unit has knowledge of the established flows when it takes over the traffic.

Failover Requirements:

There are several hardware and software requirements for the two firewall units in order to work in a failover configuration:

- Must be of the same platform model.
- Must have same hardware configuration (number and types of interfaces).
- Must be in the same operating mode (routed or transparent, single or multiple context).
- Must have same amount of Flash and RAM memory.
- Must have the same licensed features (e.g type of encryption supported, number of contexts, number of VPN peers supported etc).
- Proper Licensing. As we've described before, the ASA 5510 and ASA 5512-X must be running a "Security Plus" license in order to support failover. All the other higher models support both Active/Standby and Active/Active modes without any special license needed.

LAN Failover Link:

As shown on our example network schematic above, there is a dedicated LAN Failover Link between the two firewall appliances. This is a requirement for stateful failover configuration. A dedicated Ethernet interface is recommended to be reserved as a LAN Failover Link. This link can be either a cross-over or straight Ethernet cable connected directly between the two appliances.

In the next section we will discuss all technical details for configuring Stateful Active/Standby failover.

8.3 Configuring Active/Standby Failover

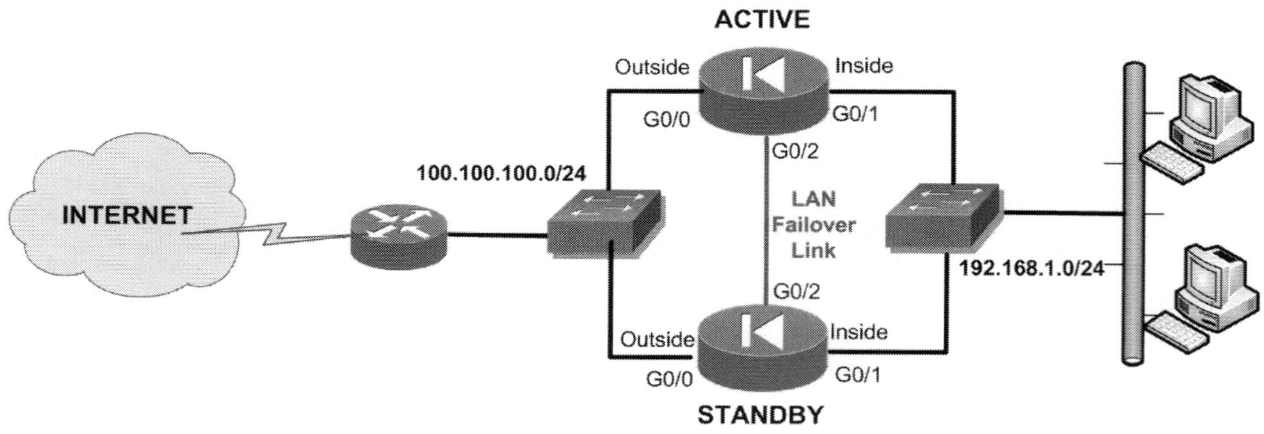

Returning to our example failover network topology, we will discuss the step-by-step process of configuring two ASA Firewalls in Active/Standby Stateful Failover setup.

- **STEP 1: Prepare the Primary (Active) Firewall**

Select one of the Firewall appliances to be the ACTIVE unit. Attach a network cable for each interface you plan to use on the Active Firewall unit and connect it to the appropriate switches. The Standby Firewall **must be disconnected** for now. Set the Active firewall interfaces to fixed speed and duplex mode. For example, use the commands **speed 100** and **duplex full** under Interface Configuration mode. Also, enable the PortFast feature on the switch ports connecting the Firewall interfaces.

Reserve **two** IP addresses for each Firewall network interface and decide which one will be assigned for the Active and which for the Standby unit. The two IP addresses for each interface must be in the same subnet. For example, in our network diagram above, assume that for the Inside interfaces we will use 192.168.1.1/24 for the ACTIVE firewall, and 192.168.1.2/24 for the STANDBY firewall. Also, for the Outside Interfaces we will use 100.100.100.1/24 for the ACTIVE and 100.100.100.2/24 for the STANDBY. Select also a private network subnet that will be used for the point-to-point Dedicated LAN Failover Link (Interface G0/2 in our example above). Assume that we will use 192.168.99.0/24.

- **STEP 2: Configure the LAN Failover Link on the Primary (Active) Firewall**

In our example topology, we will use the dedicated Gigabit Ethernet G0/2 as a LAN Stateful Failover Link. The command format for configuring the Failover link is the following:

ASA(config)# failover lan unit {*primary* / *secondary*} ←Set the unit as primary

ASA(config)# failover lan interface "*Failover Name*" "*Physical Interface*" ←Assign a physical interface as Failover link

ASA(config)# failover link "*Failover Name*" "*Physical Interface*" ←Enable the same Failover Link to be used for Stateful Failover as well.

ASA(config)# failover interface ip "*Failover Name*" "*ip_address*" "*netmask*" standby "*standby_ip_address*" ←Assign IP address to Active and Standby Failover interfaces

ASA(config)# failover ←Enable the failover mechanism

Example (for Primary Firewall):

ACTIVE-ASA(config)# interface GigabitEthernet0/2
ACTIVE-ASA(config-if)# no shut
ACTIVE-ASA(config)# failover lan unit primary
ACTIVE-ASA(config)# failover lan interface FAILOVER GigabitEthernet0/2
ACTIVE-ASA(config)# failover link FAILOVER GigabitEthernet0/2
ACTIVE-ASA(config)# failover interface ip FAILOVER 192.168.99.1 255.255.255.0 standby 192.168.99.2
ACTIVE-ASA(config)# failover

- **STEP 3: Configure Interface IP addresses on the Primary (Active) Firewall**

Each firewall interface in a failover pair must have two IP addresses assigned, one as the active address and another one as a standby address. Before configuring anything on the secondary firewall, we need to configure IP addresses on the Primary unit. The command format is:

ASA(config)# interface {*Physical or Logical Interface*}
ASA(config-if)# ip address "*Active Unit IP*" "*netmask*" standby "*Standby Unit IP*"

Example (for Primary Firewall):

ACTIVE-ASA(config)# interface GigabitEthernet0/1
ACTIVE-ASA(config-if)# nameif inside
ACTIVE-ASA(config-if)# security-level 100
ACTIVE-ASA(config-if)# ip address 192.168.1.1 255.255.255.0 standby 192.168.1.2
ACTIVE-ASA(config)# interface GigabitEthernet0/0
ACTIVE-ASA(config-if)# nameif outside
ACTIVE-ASA(config-if)# security-level 0
ACTIVE-ASA(config-if)# ip address 100.100.100.1 255.255.255.0 standby 100.100.100.2

- STEP 4: Configure Monitoring on Interfaces of Primary (Active) Firewall

One of the events that triggers the Failover mechanism is the failure of a Firewall Interface. We need to specify which Interfaces we want the appliance to monitor in order to switch over to the Standby unit when that Interface fails. In our example above we want to monitor both Inside and Outside firewall interfaces.

The command format is:
ASA(config)# monitor-interface *"Interface Name"*

Example (for Primary Firewall):

ACTIVE-ASA(config)# monitor-interface inside
ACTIVE-ASA(config)# monitor-interface outside

If either the "inside" or "outside" interfaces fail, the Active firewall will switch over to the Standby unit. You can exclude interfaces attached to less critical networks from affecting your failover mechanism by using the **no monitor-interface {*interface name*}** command.

- STEP 5: Configure the LAN Failover Link on the Secondary (Standby) Firewall

After the Primary security appliance is configured, we now need to configure the Secondary Unit. The only configuration required for the secondary appliance is the LAN Failover Link. Power on the secondary appliance and connect its interfaces to the appropriate switches. DO NOT connect the LAN Failover Link between the two firewalls yet. Connect with a console cable and setup the following commands:

Example (for Secondary Firewall):

ASA(config)# interface GigabitEthernet0/2
ASA(config-if)# no shut
ASA(config)# failover lan unit **secondary**
ASA(config)# failover lan interface FAILOVER GigabitEthernet0/2
ASA(config)# failover link FAILOVER GigabitEthernet0/2
ASA(config)# failover interface ip FAILOVER **192.168.99.1 255.255.255.0 standby 192.168.99.2**
ASA(config)# failover

Notice that the only configuration difference we have with the Primary unit is the "**secondary**" keyword. Also, although we are configuring the Secondary unit, the IP address configuration for the failover interface must be the same as that of the Primary unit.

- STEP 6: Reboot the Secondary (Standby) Firewall

Use the **write memory** command to save the configuration of the Secondary Firewall. Connect the LAN Failover Link between the two Firewall appliances and use the **reload** command to reboot the secondary security appliance.

After the Secondary unit boots up, the Primary firewall configuration is replicated to the Secondary firewall. The following messages will appear on the Primary firewall:

Beginning Configuration Replication: Sending to Mate ←This denotes the start of the synchronization
End Configuration Replication to Mate ←This denotes the completion of synchronization

You need to enter the **write memory** command on the active firewall unit to save all the replicated configuration on both the active and standby units.

From now on, any additional configuration must be done only on the Primary Firewall unit, since it will be automatically replicated to the Secondary unit. The **write memory** command on the Primary firewall will save the configuration on both units.

Finally, use the **show failover** command to verify that the failover mechanism works as expected.

Chapter 9 Advanced Features of Device Configuration

9.1 Configuring Clock and NTP Support

The Cisco ASA appliance retains clock settings in memory via a battery on the device motherboard. Even if the device is turned off, the clock is retained in memory. Configuring accurate time settings on the appliance is important for logging purposes since syslog messages can contain a time stamp according to the device clock time setting. If you want the syslog messages to include a time-stamp value, you must first configure the clock (using **clock set** command) and then enable time-stamps using **logging timestamp** command (more on syslog configuration in later sections). Having a time-stamp value on log messages is important for event tracing and forensic purposes when a security incident occurs.

Another important reason for setting the correct time on the ASA firewall is when you use PKI (Public Key Infrastructure) with digital certificates for authentication of IPSEC or SSL VPN peers. The ASA firewall uses the local appliance clock to make sure that a Digital Certificate has not expired. When using PKI digital certificates, set the firewall clock to UTC time zone.

9.1.1 Configure Clock Settings:

To configure the clock settings of the ASA appliance, use the **clock set** command as shown below:

ciscoasa# clock set *hh:mm:ss [day month | month day] year*

Example:

ciscoasa# clock set 18:30:00 Apr 10 2013

To verify the correct clock on the appliance, use the **show clock** command.

9.1.2 Configure Time Zone and Daylight Saving Time:

To configure the time zone and the summer daylight saving time use the commands below:

ciscoasa# config t

ciscoasa(config)# clock timezone *[zone name] [offset hours from UTC]*

ciscoasa(config)# clock summer-time *[zone name]* recurring *[week weekday month hh:mm week weekday month hh:mm] [offset]*

Example:

ciscoasa(config)# clock timezone MST -7

ciscoasa(config)# clock summer-time MST recurring 1 Sunday April 2:00 last Sunday October 2:00

9.1.3 Configure Network Time Protocol (NTP):

If there is an NTP server in the network that provides accurate clock settings, then you can configure the firewall to synchronize its time with the NTP server. Both an authenticated and non-authenticated NTP is supported:

Non-Authenticated NTP:

ciscoasa(config)# ntp server *[ip address of NTP]* source *[interface name]*

Example:

ciscoasa(config)# ntp server 10.1.23.45 source inside

Authenticated NTP:

ciscoasa(config)# ntp authenticate

ciscoasa(config)# ntp authentication-key *[key ID]* md5 *[ntp key]*

ciscoasa(config)# ntp trusted-key *[key ID]*

ciscoasa(config)# ntp server *[ip address of NTP]* key *[key ID]* source *[intf name]*

Example:

ciscoasa(config)# ntp authenticate

ciscoasa(config)# ntp authentication-key *32* **md5** *secretkey1234*

ciscoasa(config)# ntp trusted-key *32*

ciscoasa(config)# ntp server ***10.1.2.3*** **key** *32* **source inside**

9.2 Configuring Logging (Syslog)

The Cisco ASA security appliance generates syslog messages for various events such as security alerts, resource depletion, traffic logs etc. You can configure what type of logging information (Logging Levels) will be generated by the firewall. Also, you can configure where the security appliance will send syslog messages as we will see below. Before configuring anything else, use "**logging enable**" first to enable the firewall to generate syslog messages.

Configure Where the ASA will sent Syslog Messages:

Cisco ASA can send log messages to seven different destinations, either local or remote.

1. **Logging to SSH or Telnet session**:

If you want to monitor log messages while you are connected to the ASA via Telnet or SSH, use the "**logging monitor [logging level]**" command.

Then enable logging to the current terminal session using "**terminal monitor"** command.

2. **Logging to Internal Buffer**:

There is a configurable internal log buffer memory where the security appliance can send syslog messages. Use the "**logging buffered [logging level]**" command to instruct the ASA to store log messages to its internal buffer. Use the "**logging buffer-size [bytes]**" to set the internal log buffer size in bytes. The default is 4KB. The following command sets the log buffer to 16KB: **logging buffer-size 16384.** To display the internal log buffer messages use the "**show logging**" command.

3. **Logging to Console**:

If you want to monitor syslog messages while you are connected to the ASA via the console port, use the "**logging console [logging level]**" command. You should be very careful with this logging option since the console is a slow-speed connection (9600 bps) and will degrade system performance if the ASA generates a lot of log messages.

4. **Logging to E-mail Address**:

The "**logging mail [logging level]**" command sends syslog messages to an email address.

Example:

ASA(config)# logging enable

ASA(config)# logging mail critical

ASA(config)# logging from-address ciscosecurityappliance@example.com

ASA(config)# logging recipient-address admin@example.com

5. **Logging to Adaptive Security Device Manager (ASDM)**:

The ASDM is the Graphical User Interface application to manage an ASA firewall. You can configure the appliance to send syslog messages to the ASDM GUI using "**logging asdm [logging level]**".

6. **Logging to External Syslog Server**:

This is a great logging option since you can store and archive syslog messages for a longer period compared with the other options. Use the "**logging host [interface name] [syslog IP]**" to send log messages to an external syslog host. Use also the "**logging trap [logging level]**" command to specify the logging level.

Example:

ASA(config)# logging enable

ASA(config)# logging host inside 192.168.1.30

ASA(config)# logging trap errors

7. **Logging to SNMP Network Management System**:

If you have an NMS system in your network which collects SNMP alerts, you can send syslog messages as traps to the SNMP NMS system. Use the "**logging history [logging level]**" command.

Example:

ASA(config)# logging enable

ASA(config)# snmp-server host inside 10.1.1.100 trap community *communityname*

ASA(config)# snmp-server enable traps syslog

ASA(config)# logging history warnings

Configuring Logging Levels:

There are 8 configurable Logging Levels (0 to 7). For each command described above for the logging destination options, you should specify also a **logging level** after each command. Each logging level defines how much and what type of information will be logged by the appliance. The eight Logging Levels are:

0 – Emergencies: Generate System unusable messages.

1 – Alerts: Take immediate action messages.

2- Critical: Generate Critical condition messages.

3 – Errors: Generate Error messages.

4 – Warnings: Generate Warning messages.

5 – Notifications: Generate normal but significant condition messages.

6 – Informational: Generate information messages.

7 – Debugging: Generate debug messages and log FTP and WWW commands.

For each Logging Level that you configure, all lower number levels are enabled as well. For example if you enable Logging Level 4 (Warnings), then Logging Levels 0,1,2,3 are also enabled.

Example:

ASA(config)# logging enable

ASA(config)# logging timestamp ← attach timestamp to log messages

ASA(config)# logging buffer-size 8096 ← set log buffer to 8KB

ASA(config)# logging buffered warnings ← send syslog warning messages to log buffer

ASA(config)# logging asdm errors ← send syslog error messages to ASDM

Customize Syslog Output:

Sometimes there are unwanted syslog messages that flood the security appliance logs. You can block these unwanted syslog messages from appearing in the logs by using the "**no logging message [syslog_id]**" command. For example, assume the ASA is flooded with a syslog message id 710005 (NetBIOS traffic). To block the output of this syslog message configure the following:

ASA(config)# no logging message 710005

Displaying Syslog Settings:

To display the current syslog settings (Logging Levels, log destinations etc) and to also monitor the Internal Log Buffer messages, use the "**show logging**" command.

9.3 Configuring Device Access Authentication Using Local Username/Password

In this section we will examine how to configure the security appliance to require authentication for administrator users when they try to connect to the ASA firewall for management. You can configure usernames and passwords locally on the ASA or have an external AAA server (RADIUS or TACACS) which will hold the username/passwords database. In this section we will discuss only Local authentication. The next Chapter will describe Authentication using an external AAA server.

Authentication can be configured for all management access connections, i.e. **Telnet, SSH, Serial, and HTTP**. Also, the "**Enable**" option can be used to request a username and password before accessing Privileged Mode for Serial, Telnet, and SSH connections.

Configure Authentication using the Local username database:

- **Step1: First Configure a Local username/password pair:**

ASA(config)# username *[name of user]* **password** *[user password]*

- **Step2: Then Configure the ASA firewall to request authentication from LOCAL User Database**

ASA(config)# aaa authentication *[serial|telnet|ssh|http|enable]* console LOCAL

Example:

ASA(config)# username *admin* password *cisco123*

ASA(config)# aaa authentication serial **console LOCAL**

ASA(config)# aaa authentication telnet **console LOCAL**

ASA(config)# aaa authentication ssh **console LOCAL**

ASA(config)# aaa authentication enable **console LOCAL**

NOTE: The "**console**" keyword in the commands above does not refer to the console cable that we use for serial access.

- serial **Parameter:** Causes the user to be prompted continually by default until that user successfully logs in with the correct username/password specified in the configuration. You can limit the maximum failed attempts as we will see below. The **serial** option is for users connecting with the serial console cable.
- telnet **Parameter:** Causes the user to be prompted continually by default until that user successfully logs in. You can limit the maximum failed attempts as we will see below. The telnet option requests a username/password for users connecting with telnet before the first command-line prompt.
- ssh **Parameter:** Allows three tries before stopping access attempts. The **ssh** option requests a username and password for users connecting with ssh before the first command-line prompt.
- enable **Parameter:** Allows three tries before stopping access attempts. The **enable** option requests a username and password before accessing privileged mode for Serial, Telnet, and SSH connections.

Configure Maximum Failed Attempts:

For Serial and Telnet connections, the ASA firewall will continually ask the user for username/password until the correct authentication is entered. This is a security problem since an attacker may use Brute Force attack to gain access to the appliance. It is strongly suggested to configure a limit on the maximum failed attempts, as shown below:

ASA(config)# aaa local authentication attempts max-fail *[fail-attempts number]*

Example:

ASA(config)# aaa local authentication attempts max-fail 5

Also:

Use the command "**show aaa local user**" to see if a specific user is locked out.

Use the command "**clear aaa local user lockout all**" to clear the lockout status.

Configure HTTPs Access for GUI Management with ASDM

To use ASDM, you need to enable the HTTPS server, and allow HTTPS connections to the ASA. HTTPs access is enabled as part of the factory default configuration. This section describes how to manually configure ASDM access.

To configure HTTPs access for ASDM, perform the following commands:

ASA(config)# asdm image disk0:/asdm-647.bin ← Location of ASDM image on the ASA

ASA(config)# http server enable ← Enable the http server on the device

ASA(config)# http 10.10.10.0 255.255.255.0 inside ← Tell the device which IP addresses are allowed to connect with HTTP (ASDM)

ASA(config)#username admin password *adminpass* ← configure user/pass

9.4 Configuring a Master Passphrase

There are several configuration features on Cisco ASA that require some sort of password or secret-key that you need to enter. Some examples include:

- VPN pre-shared keys (either for site-to-site IPSEC VPN or for Remote Access).
- AAA server secret key when communicating with a RADIUS server.
- Routing Protocols keys (for OSPF, EIGRP).
- Secret key for failover communication.
- Password to communicate with a Log Server.
- VPN Load Balancing key
- Etc

All the above might be hidden when you view the running configuration (by executing "show run") however they are NOT encrypted inside the configuration file. For example, if you copy the configuration to an external TFTP Server, all the above passwords and secret-keys will be shown as clear text in the configuration file.
Moreover, when you execute the command "**more system:running-config**" you will also be able to view the running configuration with all passwords as plain text.

If you want to store all the above passwords in encrypted format in the configuration file, you can use the "Master Passphrase" feature. The master passphrase provides a key that is used to universally encrypt or mask all passwords, without changing their functionality. This feature is available from ASA version 8.3(1) and above.

Configuration of Master Passphrase

- **Step 1: Create the Master Passphrase. This must be between 8-128 characters. Do not use backspace or double quote.**

ASA(config)# key config-key password-encryption
New key: ***verystrongkey***
Confirm key: ***verystrongkey***

The above creates the Master Passphrase. Next we need to enable AES password encryption for all passwords:

- **Step2: Enable Password Encryption and save the configuration**

ASA(config)# password encryption aes
ASA(config)# write mem

NOTES:

- If you want to remove the master passphrase use "**no key config-key password-encryption [current passphrase]"**
- If you have lost the master passphrase, you must erase the configuration and reboot the ASA: "**write erase**" and then "**reload**".

Chapter 10 Authentication Authorization Accounting

Authentication Authorization Accounting (AAA) is a suit of control mechanisms that are used by network devices to control user access to the network. Authentication is the most common mechanism and is used to verify who the user is. Authorization is used to control what the user can do in the network, and Accounting is used to report what the user did in the network (audit-trail). In this Chapter we will focus mostly on Authentication using an External AAA Server.

In the previous Chapter we've described Authentication using the Local User database of the ASA. In this Chapter we will describe Authentication using an External AAA Server, such as the Cisco Access Control Server (ACS). That is, we will see how to configure the ASA firewall to Authenticate users utilizing an external AAA server.

For the Cisco ASA appliance we have three types of Authentication:

1. Authentication of users when accessing the security appliance itself (Device Access Authentication).
2. Authentication of users when accessing HTTP, HTTPs, Telnet and FTP services through the security appliance. This is called also cut-through proxy.
3. Authentication of users from remote access through an IPSEC or SSL VPN tunnel (Tunnel Access Authentication).

10.1 Device Access Authentication using External AAA Server

Next we will describe how to control Administrative access to the appliance using an external AAA Server. As mentioned above, an example of AAA Server is the Cisco Secure ACS Server (Access Control Server) which supports both RADIUS and TACACS+ Authentication Protocols. "AAA" servers provide a centralized solution for offering authentication services to all of your network devices (ASA Firewalls, Routers, Switches etc). Basically the biggest advantage of a centralized AAA server is that you can keep a central database of username/passwords so that you don't have to configure Local Usernames/Passwords on EACH of your network devices, thus minimizing administration effort and enhancing overall authentication security.

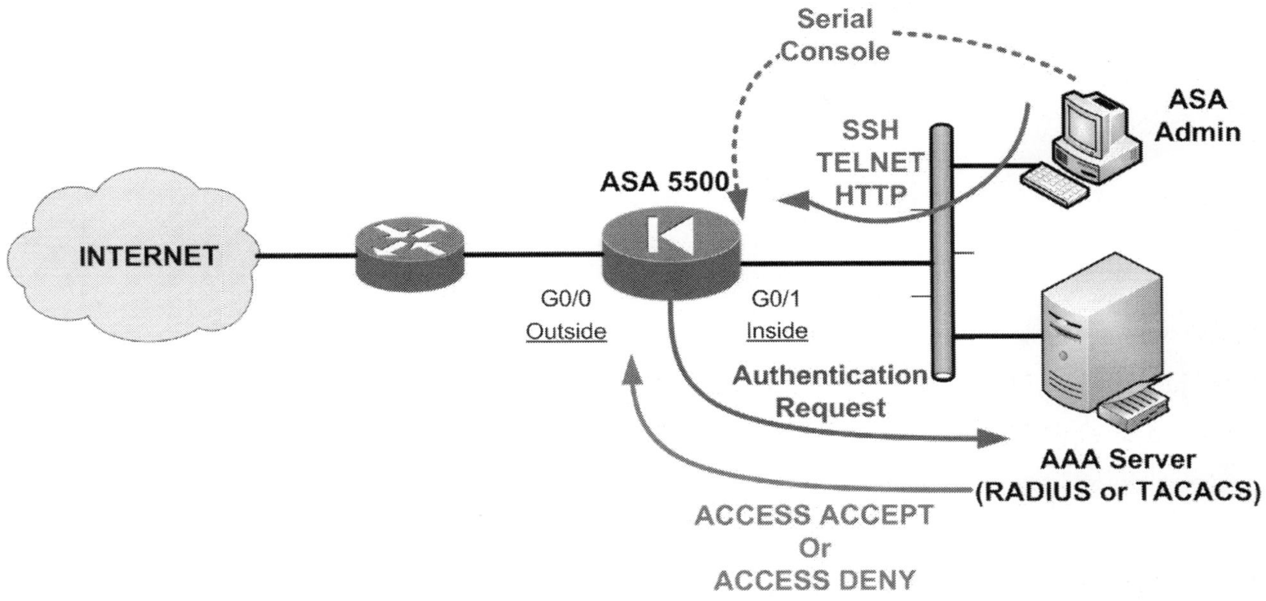

In the diagram above, the ASA Admin workstation can access the firewall using Serial Console cable, or through the network using SSH, TELNET, HTTP. Before allowing access, the ASA will prompt the admin user for his/her credentials. The username/password credentials supplied by the Admin will be sent by the ASA to the AAA Server as an **Authentication request**. If the credentials are valid, the AAA server will reply with "ACCESS ACCEPT" so that the ASA will allow access to the Admin user.

NOTE:

Before the ASA firewall can authenticate a TELNET, SSH, or HTTP access session, you must first configure the security appliance to allow those management protocols using the **telnet**, **ssh**, and **http** commands.

Example:

ASA(config)# ssh 10.1.1.0 255.255.255.0 dmz ← **allow ssh from dmz subnet 10.1.1.0**

ASA(config)# telnet 10.2.2.0 255.255.255.0 inside ← **allow telnet from inside subnet 10.2.2.0**

ASA(config)# http server enable

ASA(config)# http 10.2.2.50 255.255.255.255 inside ← **allow http from inside host 10.2.2.50**

SSH access can be used on all security level interfaces of the ASA (inside, outside, dmz etc). Telnet access is ONLY allowed on the inside interfaces.

10.1.1 Configure Authentication using an external AAA Server:

- **Step1: First specify a AAA server group:**

ASA(config)# aaa-server *[server-tag]* **protocol** *[radius|tacacs+|sdi|nt|ldap|kerberos]*

- **Step2: Then designate an authentication server.**

You need to define the IP address of the AAA server and a pre-shared security key which must be configured also on the AAA server.

ASA(config)# aaa-server *[server-tag] [ASA interface name]* **host** *[IP address of AAA]*

ASA(config-aaa-server-host)# key *[preshared secret key]*

- **Step3: Then Configure the ASA firewall to request authentication from the AAA server**

ASA(config)# aaa authentication *[serial|telnet|ssh|http|enable]* **console** *[server-tag] [LOCAL]*

Example:

ASA(config)# username ***admin*** **password** ***cisco123*** **←** configure LOCAL username/password

ASA(config)# aaa-server ACSSRV **protocol tacacs+ ←** designate tacacs+ as auth. protocol

ASA(config)# aaa-server ACSSRV **(inside) host 10.1.1.1**

ASA(config-aaa-server-host)# key ***sharedsecret***

ASA(config-aaa-server-host)# exit

ASA(config)# aaa authentication serial **console** ACSSRV **LOCAL ←** specify LOCAL as backup

ASA(config)# aaa authentication ssh **console** ACSSRV **LOCAL**

ASA(config)# aaa authentication enable **console** ACSSRV **LOCAL**

ASA(config)# ssh 10.1.1.0 255.255.255.0 inside ← enable ssh access on inside interface

NOTE:

It is strongly recommended to specify LOCAL authentication also in addition to the AAA server-tag. This means that if the AAA server is not available for any reason, the ASA firewall will use the LOCAL username/password as a backup authentication.

10.2 Cut-Through Proxy Authentication for TELNET,FTP,HTTP(s)

The Cut-through proxy feature of the security appliance allows the ASA to transparently verify the identity of users when accessing Telnet, FTP, HTTP and HTTPs services. The firewall first intercepts the Telnet/FTP/HTTP(s) session and authenticates the user identity against a AAA server. If the authentication is successful, the user session is redirected to the destination server. If the destination server has its own authentication, you must enter another username and password. I will not get into many details about the cut-through proxy feature because I have not seen it used very often in real networks, however it might be helpful in some situations (especially for HTTP authentication for example).

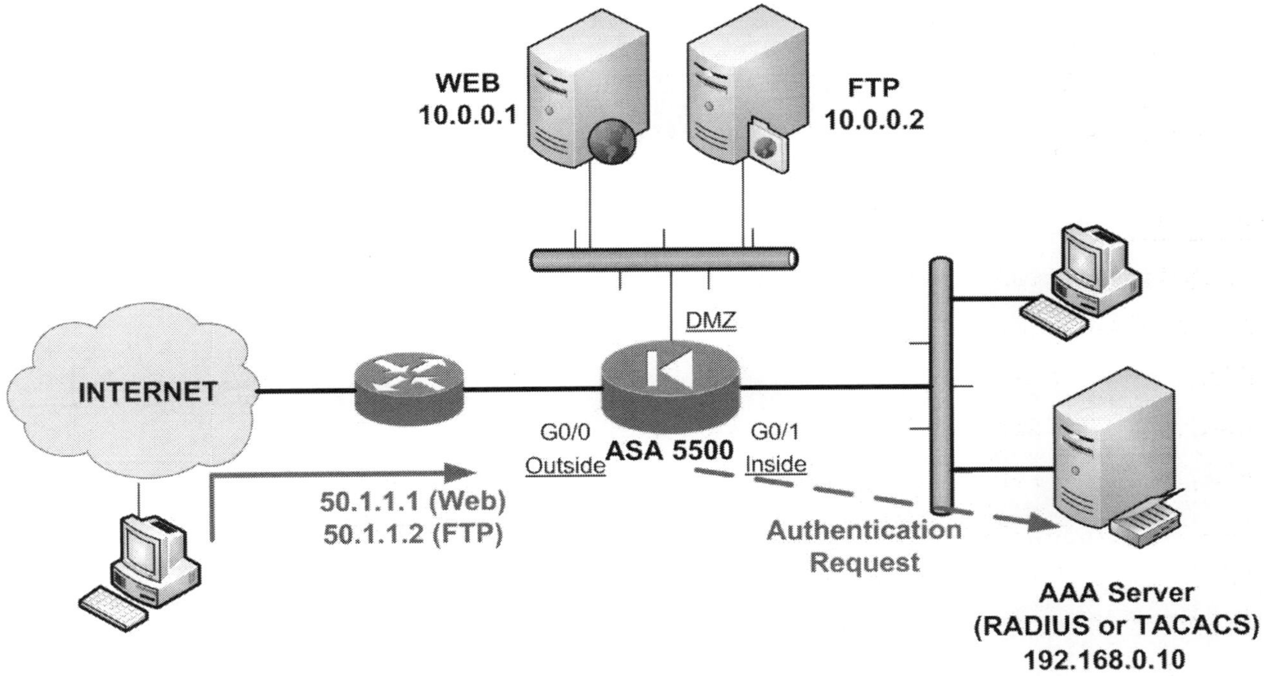

Let's see a scenario for cut-through proxy. From figure above, the Web Server (10.0.01) in DMZ is mapped (static nat) as 50.1.1.1 on the outside. Similarly, the FTP server (10.0.0.2) is mapped as 50.1.1.2 on the outside. When a user on the Internet tries to access either the Web or the FTP server, the ASA will generate an authentication prompt for the user. After the user enters his/her credentials, the ASA will query the AAA server for Authentication. If authentication is successful, the user session will be "cut-through" the security appliance and get redirected to the destination server.

When using cut-through proxy, make sure that the inbound ACL allows the connection first. If the inbound ACL drops the connection from outside, then cut-through proxy authentication will not take place.

10.2.1 Configure cut-through proxy Authentication using an external AAA Server:

- Step1: First specify a AAA server group:

ASA(config)# aaa-server *[server-tag]* **protocol** *[radius/tacacs+]*

- Step2: Then designate an authentication server.

You need to define the IP address of the AAA server and a pre-shared security key which must be configured also on the AAA server.

ASA(config)# aaa-server *[server-tag] [ASA interface name]* **host** *[IP address of AAA]*

ASA(config-aaa-server-host)# key *[preshared secret key]*

- Step3: Configure an ACL that identifies the source and destination IP addresses of traffic that you want to authenticate.

- Step4: Then enable cut-through proxy authentication by specifying which traffic flow to authenticate.

ASA(config)# aaa authentication match *[ACL name] [interface name*] [AAA server-tag]*

**[interface name]* is where the connection originates

Let's see the following example which is based on the network diagram shown above.

Example:

ASA(config)# object network web_server_static

ASA(config-network-object)# host 10.0.0.1 ← Real IP of Web Server

ASA(config-network-object)# nat (DMZ , outside) static 50.1.1.1 ← Mapped IP

ASA(config)# object network ftp_server_static

ASA(config-network-object)# host 10.0.0.2 ← Real IP of FTP Server

ASA(config-network-object)# nat (DMZ , outside) static 50.1.1.2 ← Mapped IP

ASA(config)# access-list OUTSIDE-IN extended permit tcp any host 10.0.0.1 eq 80 ← allow traffic to reach the web server from outside
ASA(config)# access-list OUTSIDE-IN extended permit tcp any host 10.0.0.2 eq 21 ← allow traffic to reach the FTP server from outside
ASA(config)# access-group OUTSIDE-IN in interface outside

ASA(config)# aaa-server ACSSRV **protocol radius** ← designate radius as auth. protocol

ASA(config)# aaa-server ACSSRV **(inside) host 192.168.0.10**

ASA(config-aaa-server-host)# key *sharedsecret*

ASA(config-aaa-server-host)# exit

ASA(config)# access-list 101 permit tcp any host 10.0.0.1 eq www

ASA(config)# access-list 101 permit tcp any host 10.0.0.2 eq ftp

ASA(config)# aaa authentication match 101 outside ACSSRV ← enable cut-through proxy for traffic originating from "outside" and matching ACL 101. Use ACSSRV server for authentication.

Chapter 11 Identity Firewall Configuration

From ASA version **8.4(2)** and later, Cisco introduced a very useful access control feature called the "**Identity Firewall**". With Identity Firewall an ASA device provides more granular access control based on user's identity instead of regular source/destination IP addresses and Port numbers. You can configure access rules and security policies based on user names and user group names rather than through IP addresses.

The ASA applies the security policies based on an association of IP addresses to Windows Active Directory login information. Thus, an Active Directory agent is required to extract the mapping of logged-in users with their IP addresses from the Active Directory server.

To implement an Identity Firewall mechanism you need to have 3 components:

1. **An ASA Firewall with version 8.4(2) and later**.
2. **A Microsoft Active Directory Server**. Supported versions include Windows Server 2003, Windows Server 2008, and Windows Server 2008 R2 servers.
3. **An Active Directory Agent software**. This agent can be installed either on a separate Windows Server (Windows 2003, Windows 2008 or Windows 2008 R2) or on the same server where the Active Directory resides.

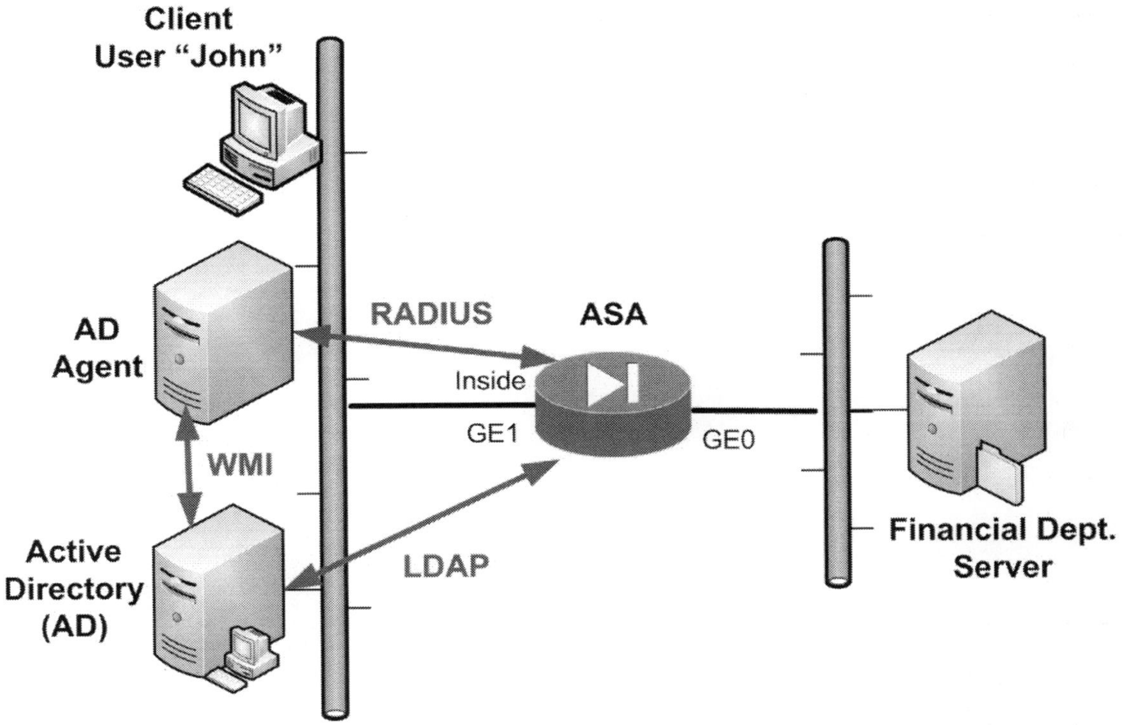

Using the diagram above, let's see a simplistic explanation of how the Identity Firewall works:

- The Active Directory Agent (AD-agent) communicates with the Active Directory Server and retrieves a mapping of logged-in users with their associated IP address. This is done by monitoring the Active Directory server security event log file via WMI for user login and logoff events.
- The ASA firewall sends an LDAP query for the Active Directory groups configured on the AD Server. The ASA consolidates local and Active Directory groups and applies access rules and security policies based on user identity.
- Assume that user "**John**" tries to access a server in the Financial Department through the ASA firewall which is configured with Identity Firewall access control. This means that the ASA has an Access Control List which specifies what user "John" can access on the network. The ASA sends a RADIUS request to the AD-agent asking about the IP address of user "John". If the user is logged-in the AD Domain, the AD-agent will send to the ASA the current IP address that user "John" is assigned. If the ACL on ASA allows user John to access the server in the Financial Department, the ASA will allow the IP address of John's computer (which was retrieved from AD-agent) to access the server.

- The above behavior shows that instead of using the source IP address of John's computer, we have used the actual username "John" to apply access control policies for this Domain User.

11.1 Prerequisites For Identity Firewall

Before configuring the ASA firewall to work as Identity Firewall, you need first to install and setup the other 2 components, the AD Agent and the Active Directory.

11.1.1 AD Agent Configuration

The AD Agent must be installed on a Windows server that is accessible to the ASA. Additionally, you must configure the AD Agent to obtain information from the Active Directory servers and also configure the AD Agent to communicate with the ASA.

For the steps to install and configure the AD Agent, see the ***Installation and Setup Guide for the Active Directory Agent*** (from Cisco website). Before configuring the AD Agent in the ASA, obtain the secret key value that the AD Agent and the ASA use to communicate. This value must match on both the AD Agent and the ASA.

Add the ASA as a client on the AD Agent

Here is how to configure a shared secret key on the AD Agent:

adacfg client create -name *<client-nickname>* **-ip** *<IP-address>[/<prefix-length-for-IP-range>]* **-secret** *<RADIUS-shared-secret>*

Example: (The following command is run on the AD Agent machine)

cd C:\IBF\CLI

adacfg client create -name *ASAFW* -ip *192.168.1.10* -secret *radiussharedsecret*

Add a Domain Controller on the AD Agent

Create all the DCs from which the AD Agent will receive logon-logoff events.

Gather the following information

- DC - Name
- DC - Host name or FQDN
- DC - user (must be a member of domain admin group)
- Password of the above user-ID

adacfg dc create -name *<DC-nickname>* **-host** *<DC-Hostname or FQDN>* **-domain** *<full-AD-Domain>* **-user** *<admin-user>* **-password** *<admin-pass>*

Example: (The following command is run on the AD Agent machine)

cd C:\IBF\CLI

adacfg dc create -name *MAINDC* -host DC1 -domain DC1.company.com –user Administrator –password *adminpass123*

11.1.2 Microsoft Active Directory Configuration

Microsoft Active Directory must be installed on a Windows server and accessible by the ASA. Supported versions include Windows 2003, 2008, and 2008 R2 servers.

Before configuring the Active Directory server on the ASA, create a user account in Active Directory for the ASA.

Additionally, the ASA can send encrypted log in information to the Active Directory server by using SSL enabled over LDAP. SSL must be enabled on the Active Directory server if you want to use SSL over LDAP. See the documentation for Microsft Active Diretory for the steps to enable SSL for Active Directory.

11.2 Configuration of Identity Firewall on ASA

The example configuration that we will describe will be based on the following diagram.

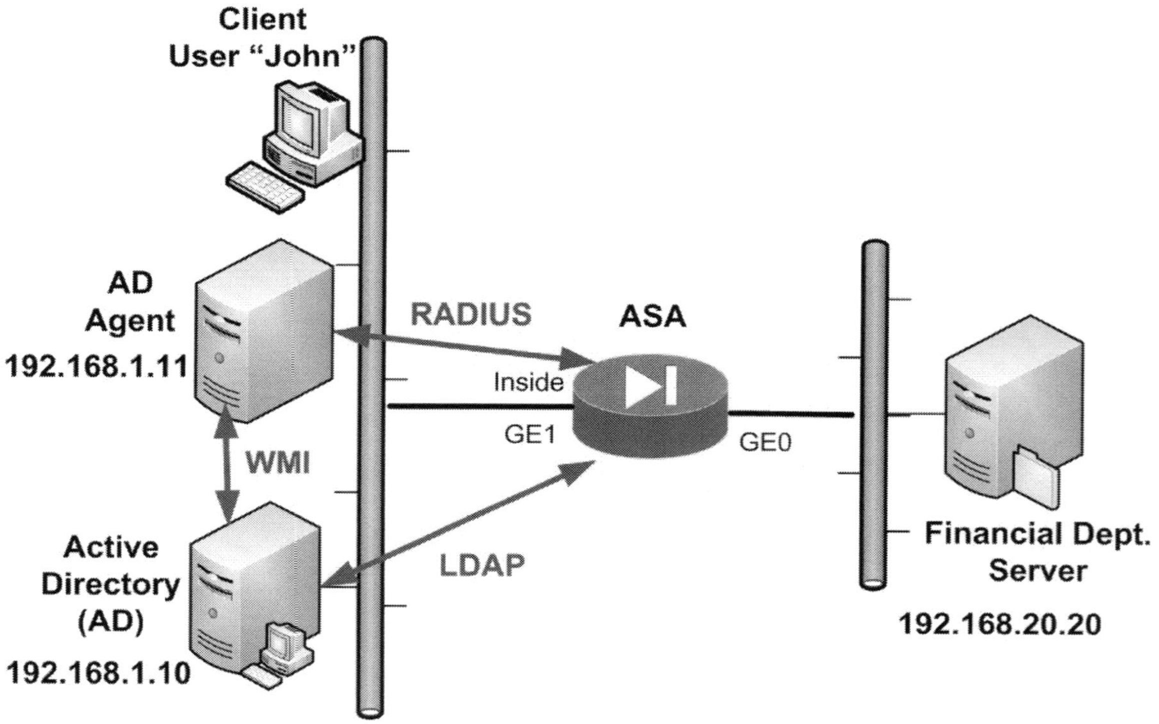

- <u>**Step 1: Configure Communication of ASA with the Active Directory Domain**</u>

As we have described above, the ASA communicates with AD Server (using LDAP) to download User Groups and to accept user identities from specific domains when receiving IP-user mapping from the AD Agent. Therefore we must tell ASA how to communicate with the AD Domain Server.

<u>Example:</u>

ASA(config)# aaa-server ADSRV protocol ldap ← **use LDAP to communicate with AD**

ASA(config-aaa-server-group)#exit

ASA(config)# aaa-server ADSRV (inside) host 192.168.1.10 ← **The AD Server is accessible from the inside interface and has IP address 192.168.1.10**

ASA(config-aaa-server-host)# ldap-base-dn DC=MYDOMAIN,DC=com ← Specifies the Base DN location in the LDAP hierarchy to start searching.

ASA(config-aaa-server-host)# ldap-scope subtree ← Search all levels beneath the Base DN

ASA(config-aaa-server-host)# ldap-login-password *asapass* ← Specify the login password for the account created on AD for the ASA.

ASA(config-aaa-server-host)# ldap-login-dn MYDOMAIN\ASAuser ← Specify the login username for the account created on AD for the ASA.

ASA(config-aaa-server-host)# server-type microsoft ← This is a Microsoft AD Server

ASA(config-aaa-server-host)# ldap-group-base-dn OU=Sample Groups,DC=MYDOMAIN,DC=com ← OPTIONAL. This is the location of the AD Groups

ASA(config-aaa-server-host)# ldap-over-ssl enable ← Allows the ASA to access the Active Directory domain controller over SSL (This is Optional)

ASA(config-aaa-server-host)# server-port 636 ← If ldap-over-ssl is not enabled, the default server-port is 389; if ldap-over-ssl is enabled, the default server-port is 636.

ASA(config-aaa-server-host)# group-search-timeout 300 ← Amount of time before LDAP queries time out (seconds).

ASA(config-aaa-server-host)# exit

- **Step 2: Configure Communication of ASA with the AD Agent**

Periodically or on-demand, the AD Agent monitors the Active Directory server security event log file via WMI for user login and logoff events. The AD Agent maintains a cache of user ID and IP address mappings and notifies the ASA of changes.

The ASA communicates with the AD Agent using the RADIUS protocol, therefore we must configure the ASA device accordingly.

Example:

ASA(config)# aaa-server ADAGENT protocol radius← use RADIUS with AD Agent

ASA(config-aaa-server-group)# ad-agent-mode ← Enable AD Agent mode

ASA(config-aaa-server-group)#exit

ASA(config)# aaa-server ADAGENT (inside) host 192.168.1.11← The AD Agent is accessible from the inside interface and has IP address 192.168.1.11

ASA(config-aaa-server-host)# key *secretradiuskey* ← Specifies the pre-shared key between ASA and the AD Agent

ASA(config-aaa-server-host)# user-identity ad-agent aaa-server ADAGENT← Define the AAA Server Group for the AD Agent

- **Step 3: Configure Identity Firewall Options**

In this step we will enable the Identity Firewall feature (it is disabled by default) and also configure some Identity Firewall options.

ASA(config)# user-identity enable ← Enable the Identity Firewall

ASA(config)# user-identity domain MYDOMAIN aaa-server ADSRV← Associate the Domain name with the LDAP AAA server group we have configured in Step 1.

ASA(config)# user-identity default-domain MYDOMAIN ← Specify the default Domain to be used for all users in the Identity Firewall (except VPN users).

ASA(config)# user-identity logout-probe netbios local-system probe-time minutes 10 retry-interval seconds 10 retry-count 2 user-not-needed ← Enables NetBIOS probing. Enabling this option configures how often the ASA probes the user client IP address to determine whether the client is still active.

- **Step 4: Configure Security Policies which use the Identity Firewall**

Now that we have set up the Identity Firewall feature, its time to utilize it in actual security policies. Any feature that uses Extended Access Lists (ACLs) can take advantage of Identity Firewall. For example, we can now add user identity arguments to extended ACLs in order to permit or deny traffic to certain users in the network.

The following are some examples where we can use Identity Based policy control:

- Access Rules: With identity firewall, you can now control access based on user names.
- Cloud Web Security: You can control which users are sent to the Cloud Web Security proxy server.
- VPN Filter: You can configure the ASA to enforce identity-based access rules on VPN traffic

Example1:

Based on the network diagram above, we will allow access of Domain User "John" to the Financial Department Server (192.168.20.20).

ASA(config)# access-list INACL extended permit ip user MYDOMAIN\john any host 192.168.20.20 ← User "john" from any source IP can access server 192.168.20.20
ASA(config)# access-group INACL in interface inside

From the ACL above, the argument **"user MYDOMAIN\john any"** will match traffic from user "john" coming from "any" source IP address.

Example2:

Assume now that we want to allow a whole group of domain users to access the server. The ACL will be configured as following:

ASA(config)# access-list INACL extended permit ip user-group MYDOMAIN\\ADMINS any host 192.168.20.20 ← User Group "ADMINS" from any source IP can access the server at 192.168.20.20
ASA(config)# access-group INACL in interface inside

Chapter 12 Routing Protocol Support

Firstly you need to know that the ASA appliance is not a full-functioning router. However, it still has a routing table which is used to select the best path to reach a certain destination network. After all, if a packet successfully passes all firewall rules, it needs to be routed by the firewall to its destination.

The Cisco ASA Firewall appliance supports both Static and Dynamic Routing. Three dynamic routing protocols are supported, namely RIP, OSPF, and EIGRP. It is highly recommended to prefer static routing configuration on the ASA firewall, instead of dynamic routing. This is because the usage of dynamic routing protocols might expose your internal network structure to the outside world. If you are not careful with dynamic routing configuration, it is possible to start advertising your internal network subnets to external untrusted networks, thus revealing your hidden networks to the outside world.

However, there are situations where dynamic routing configuration is necessary. Such a case would be a large network in which the ASA firewall is located within the internal network campus or data center. In such a case, you will benefit from using a dynamic routing protocol on the ASA since you will not have to configure tons of static routes, and also you will not run into the risk of revealing any hidden subnets to untrusted networks (since the ASA is located deep inside the campus network).

The following are some routing protocol best practices for the ASA:

- For small networks, use only static routes. Use a default static route pointing to the gateway connected to the outside interface (usually Internet), and also use static routes for internal networks which are more than one hop away (i.e not directly connected).
- Any network that is directly connected on an ASA interface DOES NOT need any static route configuration since the ASA firewall already knows how to reach this network.
- If the ASA is connected on the perimeter of the network (i.e border between trusted and untrusted networks), then configure a default route towards the outside untrusted zone, and then configure specific static routes towards the internal networks.

- If the ASA is located deep inside a large network campus with many internal network routes, then configure a dynamic routing protocol.

12.1 Static Routing

There are three types of static routes:

- Directly Connected Route
- Normal Static Route
- Default Route

Directly Connected Route

The Directly Connected Route is automatically created in the ASA routing table when you configure an IP address on an appliance interface. For example, if you configure the IP address 192.168.1.10/24 on the inside interface of ASA, then a Directly Connected Route of 192.168.1.0 255.255.255.0 will be automatically created.

Normal Static Route and Default Route

For configuring a Normal Static Route and Default Static Route refer to the diagram below.

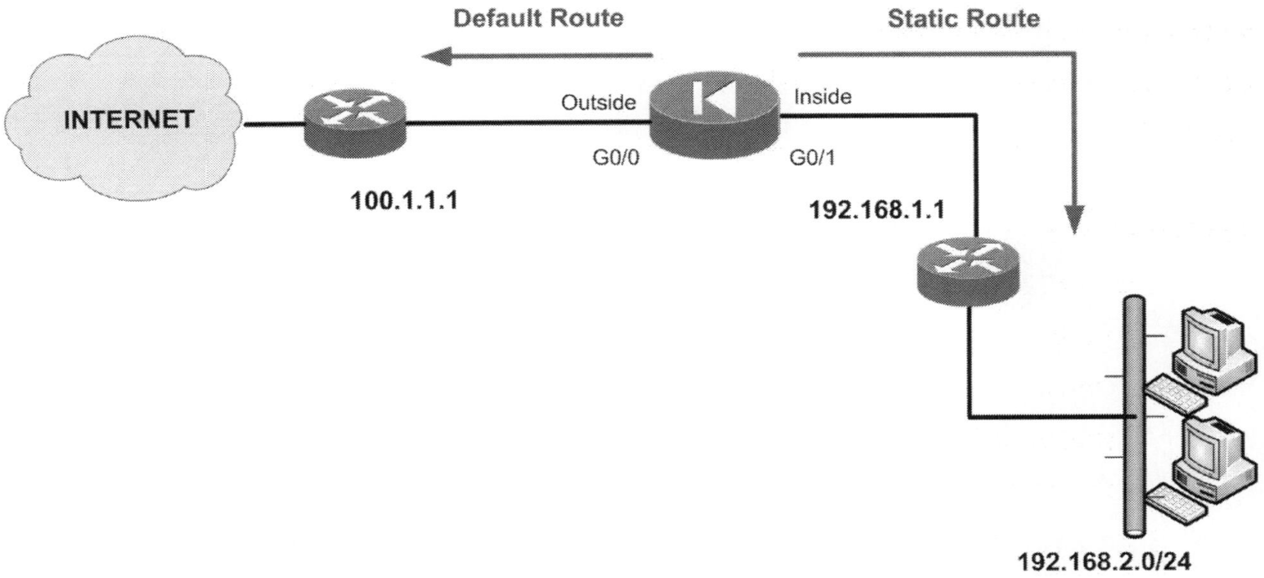

A static route configuration on the ASA is like telling the appliance the following: "To send a packet to the specified network, give it to this router gateway".

Use the **route** command to enter either a static or default route. The command format is:

ASA(config)# route *[interface-name] [destination-network] [netmask] [gateway]*

[interface-name]: This is the ASA interface from which the packet will exit.
[destination-network] [netmask]: This is the destination network/mask we want to reach
[gateway]: Next hop device that ASA will send the packet to.

Let's see an example configuration below (refer to diagram above):

ASA(config)# route outside 0.0.0.0 0.0.0.0 100.1.1.1 ← **Default Route**
ASA(config)# route inside 192.168.2.0 255.255.255.0 192.168.1.1 ← **Static Route. To reach network 192.168.2.0 send the packets to 192.168.1.1**

For the default route (usually towards the Internet), you set both the *destination-network* and *netmask* to 0.0.0.0. All traffic for which the ASA has no route in its routing table will be sent to 100.1.1.1 (the gateway in the default route).

To see what is included in the appliance's routing table, use the "**show route**" command:

ASA# show route

S 0.0.0.0 0.0.0.0 [1/0] via 100.1.1.1, outside ← **Default Static Route**
C 192.168.1.0 255.255.255.0 is directly connected, inside ← **Connected Route**
C 100.1.1.0 255.255.255.0 is directly connected, outside ← **Connected Route**
S 192.168.2.0 255.255.255.0 [1/0] via 192.168.1.1, inside ← **Static Route**

12.1.1 IPv6 Static Routing

Configuring Default IPv6 Static Route

ASA(config)# ipv6 route outside ::/0 3FFE:1100:0:CC00::1 ← **The prefix ::/0 means any IP**

The above will send any traffic (**::/0**) that doesn't match any other route to the default gateway IP which is **3FFE:1100:0:CC00::1**

Configuring Static IPv6 Route

ASA(config)# ipv6 route inside 7fff::0/32 2FFE:1120:0:CC00::2

The IPv6 network **7fff::0/32** is reachable via gateway **2FFE:1120:0:CC00::2**

12.1.2 Static Route Tracking - Dual ISP Redundancy

When you configure a static route on the security appliance, the route remains permanently in the routing table. The only way for the static route to get removed from the routing table is when the associated ASA interface goes physically down. In all other cases, such as for example when the remote default gateway goes down, the ASA will keep sending packets to its gateway router without knowing that it is actually down.

From ASA version 7.2 and later, the **Static Route Tracking** feature was introduced. The ASA tracks the availability of static routes by sending ICMP echo request packets through the primary static route path and waits for replies. If the primary path is down, a secondary path is used. This feature is useful when you want to implement **Dual-ISP redundancy**, as we will see in the scenario below.

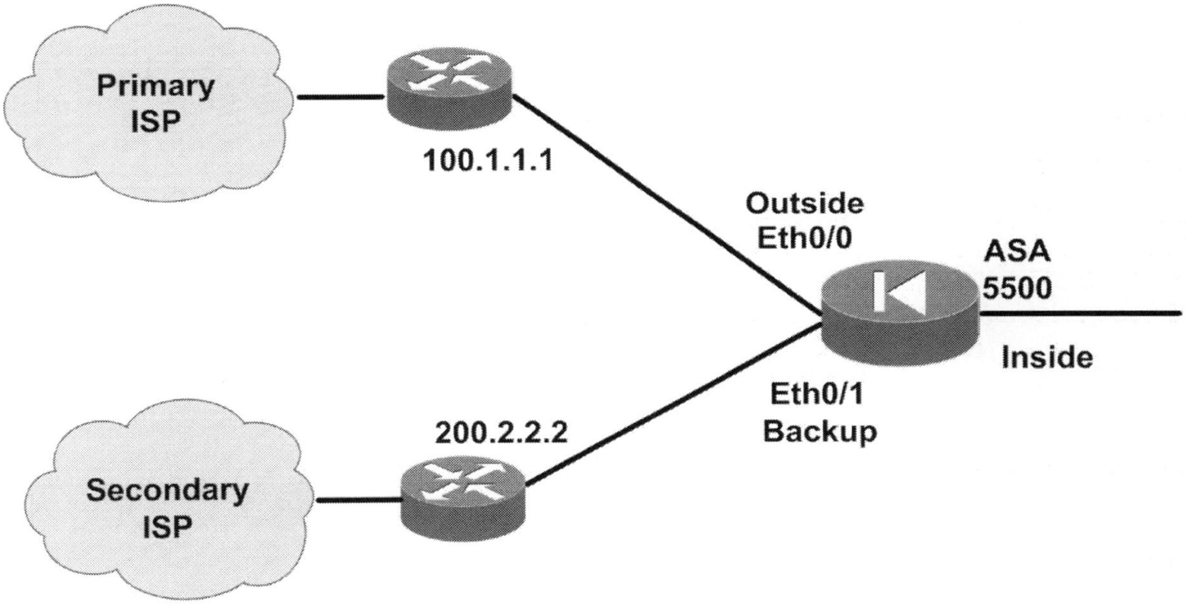

In the network scenario above, interface Eth0/0 (outside) is connected to the Primary ISP and interface Eth0/1 (backup) is connected to the Secondary ISP. Two default static routes will be configured (one for each ISP) which will use the "**track**" feature. The primary ISP path will be tracked using ICMP echo requests. If an echo reply is not received within a predefined period, the secondary static route will be used. Note however that the scenario above is suitable only for outbound communication (that is, from the inside network towards the Internet).

12.1.2.1 Configuring Static Route Tracking

1. Use the "**sla monitor**" command to specify the monitoring protocol (e.g ICMP), the target address to track (e.g ISP gateway router) and the tracking timers.
2. Use the "**sla monitor schedule**" command to schedule the monitoring process (usually the monitoring process is configured to run "**forever**" but duration and start times are configurable).
3. Define the primary static route to be tracked using the "**route**" command with the "**track**" option.
4. Define the backup static route and set its metric higher than the primary static route.

Let's see an example configuration below (related to the diagram shown above)

! Assume we have configured an interface named "outside" and another interface named "backup"
! Configure Port Address Translation (PAT) for internal network towards the Internet.

ASA(config)# object network PAT_PRIMARY

ASA(config-network-object)# subnet 192.168.1.0 255.255.255.0

ASA(config-network-object)# nat (inside,outside) dynamic interface

ASA(config)# object network PAT_BACKUP

ASA(config-network-object)# subnet 192.168.1.0 255.255.255.0

ASA(config-network-object)# nat (inside,backup) dynamic interface

! Now configure Route Tracking using SLA Monitor feature

ASA(config)# sla monitor 100 ← Define SLA_ID 100

ASA(config-sla-monitor)# type echo protocol ipIcmpEcho 100.1.1.1 interface outside

ASA(config-sla-monitor)# timeout 3000 ← Define timeout 3000 milliseconds (3 sec)

ASA(config-sla-monitor)# frequency 5 ← track target 5 times

ASA(config-sla-monitor)# exit

ASA(config)# sla monitor schedule 100 **life forever start-time now** ← Schedule the monitoring process SLA_ID 100 to start now and run forever

ASA(config)# track 10 **rtr** 100 **reachability** ← Associate a Track_ID 10 with the SLA_ID 100

ASA(config)# route outside 0.0.0.0 0.0.0.0 100.1.1.1 1 **track** 10 ← Associate the Track_ID 10 to the primary static route. Define also a metric 1 for this route.

ASA(config)# route backup 0.0.0.0 0.0.0.0 200.2.2.2 254 ← Define the backup static route with a higher route metric of 254

In the scenario above, the firewall appliance will be tracking the primary ISP gateway router (100.1.1.1) . If an echo reply is not received within 3 sec (timeout 3000 milliseconds) and the process is repeated 5 times (frequency 5), the primary default route is considered down and therefore the secondary backup route will be used.

12.2 Dynamic Routing using RIP

RIP is one of the oldest dynamic routing protocols. Although it is not used a lot in modern networks, you still find it in some cases. Cisco ASA version 7.x supports RIP in a limited fashion. The ASA appliance (v7.x) can only accept RIP routes and optionally advertise a default route. However, it cannot receive RIP advertisements from one neighbor and then advertise these routes to another neighbor. From ASA version 8.x however, the security appliance supports full RIP functionality. Both RIPv1 and RIPv2 are supported. However, using RIPv1 is not recommended because it does not support routing updates authentication.

12.2.1 Configuring RIP

Configuration of RIP on the ASA appliance is similar with a Cisco router. RIP is configured using the "**router rip**" Global Configuration command. RIP authentication security is configured under Interface Configuration.

ASA(config)# router rip

ASA(config-router)# network *[network-subnet]* ← network to advertise via RIP

ASA(config-router)# version *[1 / 2]* ← select RIP version

ASA(config-router)# default-information originate ← Inject a default route into the network

ASA(config-router)# passive-interface *[ASA interface name]* ← **disable RIP updates propagation on specified interface**
ASA(config-router)# no auto-summarize ← **disable automatic route summarization**

The "**no auto-summarize**" command works only for RIPv2. It disables automatic route summarization to their network Class boundary. For example if you have a route 10.1.3.0/24 which you want to advertise via RIP, by default it will be advertised as 10.0.0.0/8 by the ASA. Using the "**no auto-summarize**" command, the route will be advertised as 10.1.3.0/24.

Regarding RIP updates authentication, this is configured on a per Interface basis:

ASA(config)# interface *[interface number]*
ASA(config-if)# rip authentication mode *[text | md5]* ← **I suggest to always use md5 auth.**
ASA(config-if)# rip authentication key *[secret key]* **key-id** *[key ID number]* ← **Use the same secret authentication key to all neighbor devices running RIP.** ***[secret key]*** **can be up to 16 characters, and** ***[key ID number]*** **is a number between 0-255**

The diagram below shows an example network topology with an ASA firewall running RIP within a network with other routers.

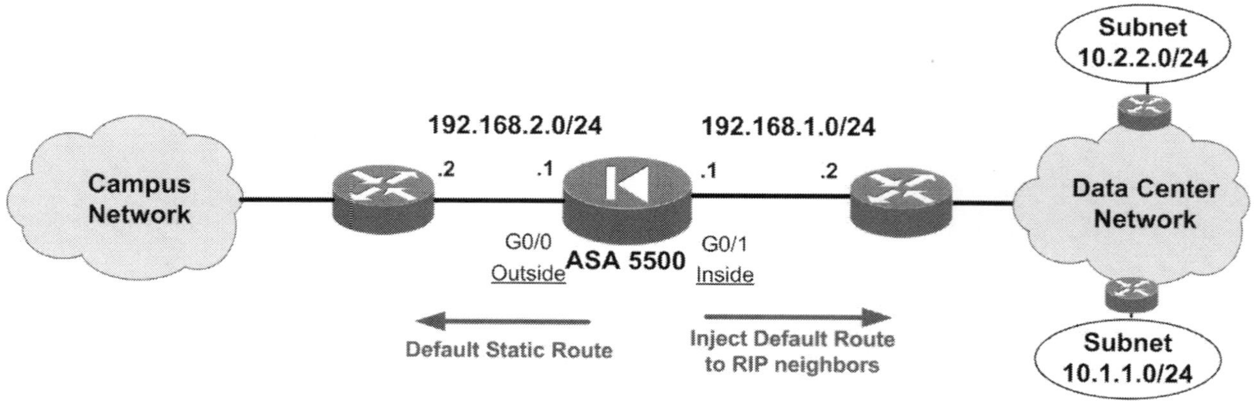

Assume the ASA is located between the Campus Network and the Data Center Network. All router neighbors behind the inside interface are running RIP.

Configuration Example:

ASA(config)# route outside 0.0.0.0 0.0.0.0 192.168.2.2

ASA(config)# router rip

ASA(config-router)# network 192.168.1.0

ASA(config-router)# version 2

ASA(config-router)# default-information originate

ASA(config-router)# exit

ASA(config)# interface GigabitEthernet0/1

ASA(config-if)# rip authentication mode md5

ASA(config-if)# rip authentication key *somesecrethere* key-id 10

12.3 Dynamic Routing using OSPF

OSPF (Open Shortest Path First) is a dynamic routing protocol based on Link States rather than Distance Vectors (such as RIP) for optimal path selection. It is a much better and more scalable routing protocol compared to RIP, that's why is widely used in large Enterprise networks. OSPF can be very complex and one can write a whole book for it. In this section I will keep OSPF discussion as brief as possible, and I will try to discuss features and scenarios that are most commonly used in real networks.

Notes:

1. OSPFv2 supports IPv4 and OSPFv3 supports IPv6.
2. OPSFv3 supports IPv6 in ASA version 9.x and later.

12.3.1 Configuring OSPFv2

OSPF is based on Areas. In brief, to configure OSPF you need to create an OSPF routing process (up to two routing processes can be configured on ASA), specify the IP network addresses associated with the routing process, and then assign area IDs associated with each IP network address. Similarly with RIPv2, we can also configure MD5 authentication for OSPF updates security.

ASA(config)# router ospf *[process ID]* ← **enable the ospf routing process**
ASA(config-router)# network *[IP address] [subnet mask]* **area** *[area ID]* ← **IP network address to advertise via OSPF. This network address must belong in a specific OSPF Area**

Note that "subnet mask" above must be a normal subnet mask (such as 255.255.255.0) and NOT an inverse (wildcard) subnet mask like we use in Cisco routers (such as 0.0.0.255).

To configure OSPF MD5 authentication, you need to enable authentication per Area (within the routing process) and also configure the MD5 authentication key under Interface configuration.

ASA(config)# router ospf *[process ID]*
ASA(config-router)# area *[area ID]* **authentication message-digest** ← **Enable MD5 authentication in the specific Area**
ASA(config-router)# exit
ASA(config)# interface *[interface number]*
ASA(config-if)# ospf authentication message-digest
ASA(config-if)# ospf message-digest-key *[key ID]* **md5** *[secret key]*

We will see two OSPF example scenarios which are commonly used in real implementations. The first example depicts a Cisco ASA within an Enterprise network working as an ABR (Area Border Router), and the second example shows an ASA firewall injecting a default route into the internal network via OSPF.

Scenario 1: ASA working as OSPF ABR

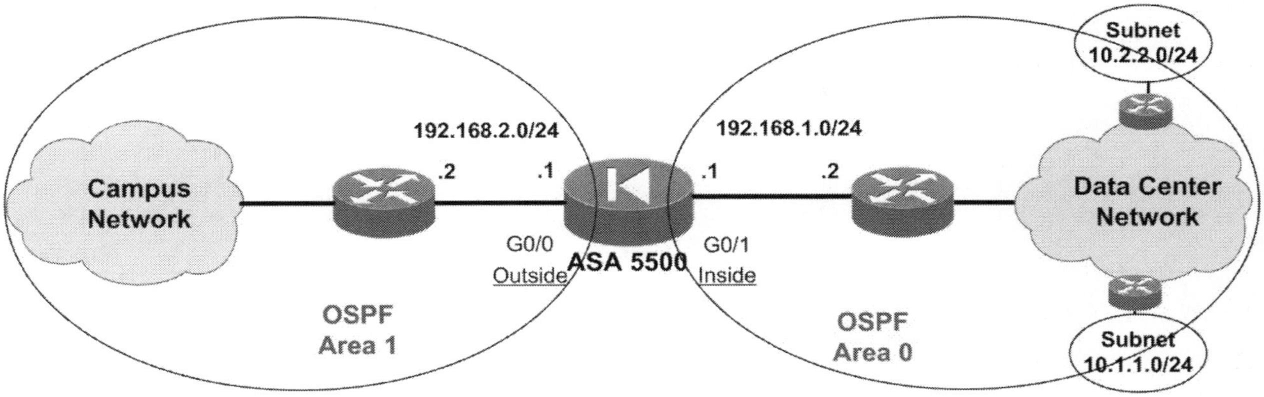

In the example above, the ASA5500 firewall is located between the Data Center and Campus Networks. All routers within the Data Center network are running OSPF in Area 0. On the other hand, all routers in Campus Network are running OSPF in Area 1. The ASA works as Area Border Router. We assume also that there is no NAT configured on the ASA ("**no nat-control**"). Firewall policies can be enforced using Access-Lists on both the Inside and Outside interfaces.

Configuration Example:

ASA(config)# router ospf 10

ASA(config-router)# network 192.168.1.0 255.255.255.0 area 0

ASA(config-router)# network 192.168.2.0 255.255.255.0 area 1

ASA(config-router)# area 0 authentication message-digest

ASA(config-router)# area 1 authentication message-digest

ASA(config-router)# exit

ASA(config)# interface GigabitEthernet0/0

ASA(config-if)# ospf authentication message-digest

ASA(config-if)# ospf message-digest-key 20 md5 *somesecretkey*

ASA(config-if)# exit

ASA(config)# interface GigabitEthernet0/1

ASA(config-if)# ospf authentication message-digest

ASA(config-if)# ospf message-digest-key 20 md5 *somesecretkey*

Scenario 2: ASA Injecting a default route in OSPF network

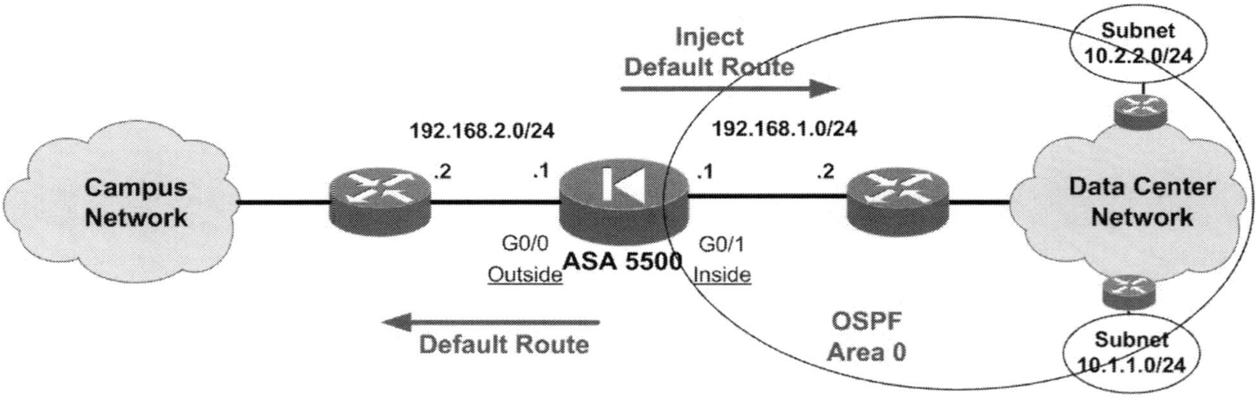

In the example above, the ASA has a default route towards the Campus Network and injects this default route in the inside network (Data Center). This means that all routers within the Data Center network (which will be running OSPF in Area 0) will acquire a default route which will point to their next-hop closest to the ASA.

Configuration Example:

ASA(config)# route outside 0.0.0.0 0.0.0.0 192.168.2.2

ASA(config)# router ospf 10

ASA(config-router)# network 192.168.1.0 255.255.255.0 area 0

ASA(config-router)# default-information originate always ← **Inject default route**

ASA(config-router)# area 0 authentication message-digest

ASA(config-router)# exit

ASA(config)# interface GigabitEthernet0/1

ASA(config-if)# ospf authentication message-digest

ASA(config-if)# ospf message-digest-key 20 md5 *somesecretkey*

ASA(config-if)# exit

12.3.2 Configuring OSPFv3 (ASA Version 9.x and later)

This is a new feature supported on ASA 9.x and later. We will see just the basic configuration which is different than the philosophy used in OPSFv2. Basically you need first to enable an OPSFv3 process and then configure a specific interface to run OSPFv3 (under interface config).

As we've said before, OSPFv3 is used for distributing IPv6 routing information.

ASA(config)# ipv6 router ospf 10 ← First enable an OSPFv3 routing process (10)
ASA(config)# interface GigabitEthernet0/1 ← Run OPSFv3 under this interface
ASA(config-if)# ipv6 ospf 10 **area 0** ← This interface will be running OSPFv3 in Area 0

12.4 Dynamic Routing using EIGRP

EIGRP is the enhanced version of the older IGRP. It is a Cisco proprietary protocol which runs only between Cisco devices. Support for EIGRP on Cisco ASA was included from version 8.0 and later. Although EIGRP is very easy to use and flexible, network designers and administrators hesitate to use it widely since it works only with Cisco equipment, so you are effectively dependent on a single vendor. I have not seen this protocol used a lot on Cisco ASA firewalls, so I will keep the discussion just to the basics. (Note: Currently, EIGRP on Cisco ASA does not support IPv6)

12.4.1 Configuring EIGRP

EIGRP configuration on a Cisco ASA is very similar with a Cisco router. Basically you just enable the EIGRP process by assigning it an AS number, and then configure the IP network ranges that will be advertised by the routing protocol to other EIGRP neighbors.

ASA(config)# router eigrp *[AS Num]* ← enable the EIGRP routing process
ASA(config-router)# network *[IP address] [subnet mask]* ← IP network address to advertise

MD5 authentication for EIGRP updates is configured under Interface config mode as shown below:

ASA(config)# interface *[interface number]*

ASA(config-if)# authentication mode eigrp *[AS-num]* **md5**

ASA(config-if)# authentication key eigrp *[AS-num] [key]* **key-id** *[key ID]*

Note: All neighbor routers must belong in the same AS number and have the same MD5 key. The *[key ID]* is just a number between 0-255

Configuration Example:

ASA(config)# router eigrp 2 ← we are in Autonomous System 2

ASA(config-router)# network 192.168.1.0 255.255.255.0

ASA(config-router)# network 192.168.2.0 255.255.255.0

ASA(config-router)# exit

ASA(config)# interface Ethernet0/2

ASA(config-if)# authentication mode eigrp 2 **md5**

ASA(config-if)# authentication key eigrp 2 ***somesecretkey*** **key-id 20**

This concludes our discussion on routing protocol support.

Chapter 13 Modular Policy Framework Configuration

In this Chapter we will see the key concepts behind Modular Policy Framework (MPF). MPF is quite complex and extensive so I will only describe the basic features of it and the most useful concepts as implemented in real world networks.

13.1 MPF Overview

The Modular Policy Framework provides greater granularity and flexibility in implementing network and security policies with the ASA appliance. The MPF mechanism can be used for example to apply Quality of Service (prioritization) for voice traffic, to rate-limit specific remote access VPN connections, to apply TCP connection limits to specific traffic flows, to apply deep packet (Layer 7) inspection on specific flows of traffic etc.

When configuring MPF, the traffic is first identified (traffic matching) with a Class-Map, then actions are applied to the matched traffic using a Policy-Map, and finally the whole policy is enabled on an interface or globally using a Service-Policy.

As described above, there are three main components of a Modular Policy Framework: A **Class-Map** component, a **Policy-Map** component and a **Service-Policy** component.

- **Class-Map**: This is used to identify a traffic flow that we want to apply policies on. You can create either a Layer3/4 Class Map or a Layer 7 Class Map. In this Chapter we will focus only on Layer3/4 class maps. This type of class map matches traffic based on protocols, ports, IP addresses and other Layer3/4 characteristics of the traffic flow. On the other hand, a Layer7 Class Map matches traffic based on application characteristics (for example a certain URL name in an HTTP traffic flow or even a certain FTP command in an FTP connection).
- **Policy-Map**: After the firewall appliance identifies the traffic flow with a Class-Map, a Policy-Map is used to apply certain actions (or policies) to the selected class of traffic. An example of a policy-map is to limit the maximum number of TCP connections towards a Web Server on the DMZ to a certain number. Another example of a policy-map is to apply

high priority to voice packets between two sites. Similarly with Class-Maps, an administrator can create a Layer3/4 Policy-Map or a Layer 7 Policy-Map.

- **Service-Policy**: The Service-Policy component is used to apply the configured policy framework to an Interface or Globally on the appliance. The ASA appliance supports one Service-Policy per interface and one Globally.

The diagram below illustrates the structure of the Cisco ASA Modular Policy Framework. Keep this structure in mind to help you understand the various configuration examples and scenarios that we will describe later on.

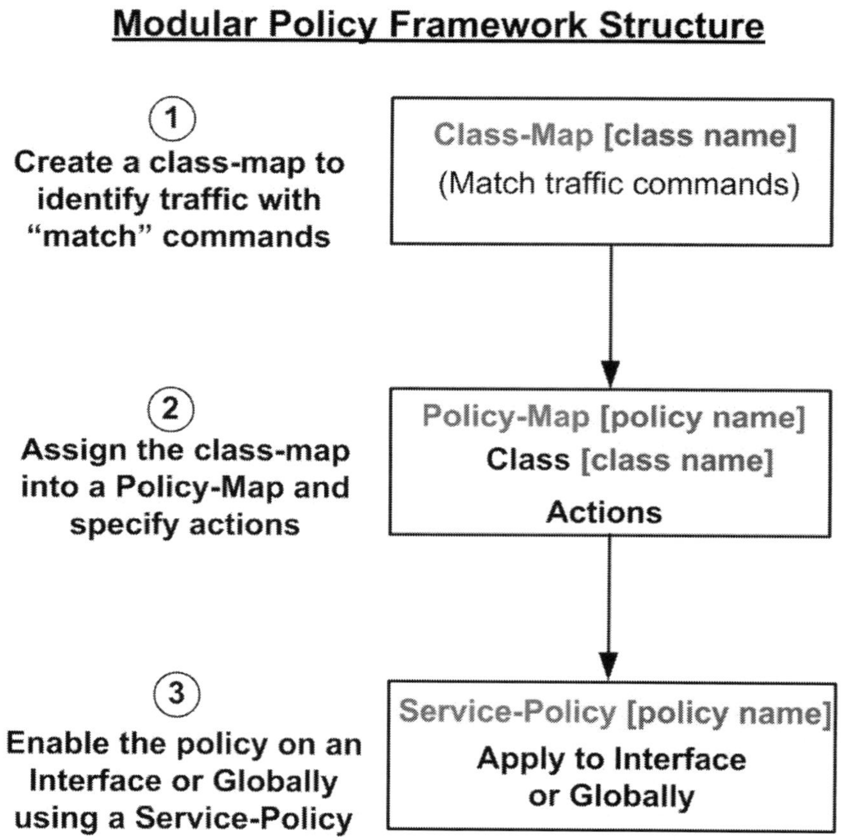

13.1.1 Default Modular Policy Configuration

By default, an out-of-the-box Cisco ASA appliance has a class-map already configured which matches the default-inspection-traffic. You can view this default class-map in the configuration by using the "**show run class-map**" command.

ASA(config)# show run class-map
class-map inspection_default
match default-inspection-traffic

The keyword "**default-inspection-traffic**" is a special name which denotes matching of several default applications and protocols on their default ports, as shown on the table below.

Protocol/Application	Protocol Type (tcp/udp)	Port
CTIQBE (Computer Telephony Interface)	TCP	2748
DNS	UDP	53
FTP	TCP	21
GTP (GPRS Tunneling Protocol) *requires special license	UDP	2123 3386
H323 H225	TCP	1720
H323 RAS	UDP	1718-1719
HTTP	TCP	80
ICMP	N/A	N/A
ILS (LDAP)	TCP	389
IPSec Pass-Through	UDP	500
MGCP (Media Gateway Control Protocol)	UDP	2427,2727
NetBIOS Name Server	UDP	137,138 (source ports)
PPTP	TCP	1723
RADIUS Accounting	UDP	1646
RSH	TCP	514

RTSP	TCP	554
SIP	TCP/UDP	5060
SCCP (Cisco Skinny)	TCP	2000
SMTP-ESMTP	TCP	25
SNMP	UDP	161,162
SQL*Net	TCP	1521
SUN RPC	UDP	111
TFTP	UDP	69
XDMCP	UDP	177

Most of the applications and protocols shown above are inspected by the ASA in its default configuration. For example, an FTP communication through the ASA between an FTP client and server uses a Control connection on port 21 and a Data connection on port 20. Normally a stateful firewall would not allow such a communication to go through because the initial connection is on port 21 and the return FTP data traffic is on a different port (20). Using the "**default-inspection-traffic**" mechanism described above (together with the "inspect" command under Global policy-map configuration), the Cisco ASA will inspect the FTP traffic in order to allow both the control and the data connection flows to pass through with no problems. The rest of the protocols from the Table above either exhibit similar behavior with FTP or generally require some special "handling", therefore they are inspected by the firewall on the application layer for proper communication. For example, the voice signaling protocol H323 has to be inspected on the application layer in order for the firewall to allow the voice RTP (Real Time Protocol) traffic (which works on random range of UDP ports) to pass through the ASA for a successful VoIP communication.

The default policy configuration on a Cisco ASA (out-of-the-box) is the following:

```
class-map inspection_default  ← Create a default class-map
 match default-inspection-traffic

policy-map type inspect dns preset_dns_map
 parameters
 message-length maximum 512
```

policy-map global_policy ← Create a global policy
class inspection_default ← Attach the default class map to the global policy
inspect dns preset_dns_map
inspect ftp
inspect h323 h225
inspect h323 ras
inspect rsh
inspect rtsp
inspect esmtp
inspect sqlnet
inspect skinny
inspect sunrpc
inspect xdmcp
inspect sip
inspect netbios
inspect tftp
inspect ip-options

service-policy global_policy **global** ← Enable the global policy for all traffic

13.2 Modular Policy Framework Configuration

13.2.1 Configuring Class-Maps

As stated above, in this Chapter we will focus only on Layer3/4 Class-Map. This type of class map classifies traffic based on Layer3 or Layer4 attributes, such as IP address, port number, DSCP values etc. The configuration involves two steps: First configure a name for the class-map and then use the "match" command under the class-map configuration mode in order to identify the traffic flow.

ASA(config)# class-map *[class name]* ← assign a name to the class of traffic
ASA(config-cmap)# match access-list *[ACL name]* ←match traffic based on ACL
ASA(config-cmap)# match port *[**tcp/udp**] [**eq** port_no | **range** port port]*←match based on ports
ASA(config-cmap)# match any ←match any traffic
ASA(config-cmap)# match default-inspection-traffic ←match the default ports for the supported applications as we've discussed before.
ASA(config-cmap)# match dscp *[value]* ←match specific dscp value(s) in the IP header. E.g dscp ef means "match expedited forwarding packets" which are usually voice packets.

ASA(config-cmap)# match precedence *[value]* ←match specific precedence value(s) in the IP header. Similar with dscp.
ASA(config-cmap)# match tunnel-group *[tunnel name]*←match specific site-to-site VPN tunnel or even remote access VPN group
ASA(config-cmap)# match flow ip destination-address ←this must be used together with the tunnel-group command above
ASA(config-cmap)# match rtp *[start port-end port]* ←match port range of RTP traffic

Configuration Example for Class-Map

Consider a scenario where we want to apply some specific policies for the traffic reaching our company's Web Server from the Internet. Maybe we need to apply a restriction on the maximum number of simultaneous TCP connections allowed to reach our Web Server. Also, we want to prioritize voice traffic having a DSCP value of "**ef**" (expedited forwarding) that goes through a specific site-to-site IPSec VPN tunnel. We will create two class-maps which will classify the traffic that we described above:

ASA(config)# access-list websrv_traffic permit tcp any host 50.50.50.10 eq 80 ← assume our public web server is host 50.50.50.10
ASA(config)# class-map HTTP_To_Web_Server ← create a class-map for the http traffic
ASA(config-cmap)# match access-list websrv_traffic ←match traffic going to web server

ASA(config)# class-map L2L_Voice_Traffic ←create a class-map for the voice lan-to-lan traffic
ASA(config-cmap)# match tunnel-group SITE_B_VPN ←match IPSec tunnel group SITE_B_VPN
ASA(config-cmap)# match dscp ef ←match EF type traffic (i.e voice)

Keep in mind the configuration snapshot above because we will refer to it later on when we will describe Policy Maps.

13.2.2 Configuring Policy Maps

After classifying the traffic with a class-map, we need to assign this class-map into a Policy-Map which is responsible to apply some actions (policies) on the selected traffic (i.e traffic that matches a "**match**" statement in the class-map). We will focus only on Layer3/4 Policy Maps.

The security appliance supports one Policy-Map per interface and one Global Policy-Map. Also, each Policy-Map can support multiple Class-Maps and multiple actions on traffic. For instance, in the configuration example shown in the previous section for class-maps, we have configured two class-maps, namely "**HTTP_To_Web_Server**" and "**L2L_Voice_Traffic**". We can assign both class-maps into a single Policy-Map and apply actions on them.

To configure a Policy-Map, first configure a name for it, then assign a class-map (using the "**class**" command) and then configure actions for the specific class-map.

ASA(config)# policy-map *[policy name]* ← **assign a name to the policy map**
ASA(config-pmap)# class *[class-map name]* ←**assign a class-map**
ASA(config-pmap-c)# ***[configure actions]*** ←**here configure actions for the specific class-map**
ASA(config-pmap-c)# exit
ASA(config-pmap)# class *[class-map name]* ←**assign a second class-map on the same policy**
ASA(config-pmap-c)# ***[configure actions]*** ←**configure actions for the second class-map**

The available categories of "***actions***" that can be configured on a policy-map are the following:

1. **CSC**: send the traffic to Content Security and Control service module.
2. **IPS**: send the traffic to the Intrusion Prevention System service module.
3. **set connection**: enforce connection limits on traffic.
4. **inspect**: apply protocol inspection services.
5. **police**: apply rate limiting for traffic
6. **shape**: apply traffic shaping
7. **priority**: apply priority for voice traffic (Low Latency Queuing-LLQ)
8. **flow-export**: configure filter for Netflow events

NOTES:

1) For the older ASA models (5500 series), the **CSC** (Content Security and Control) and **IPS** (Intrusion Prevention System) mentioned above are add-on card modules that can be inserted into the ASA firewall chassis to provide specialized security functionality (content inspection, antivirus, antispam, intrusion prevention etc).
2) For the newest ASA models (5500-X series), this specialized security functionality is provided by software modules instead of hardware ones. So in the new 5500-X devices we have an IPS software module and a CX software module. Both of these require additional software licenses to work.

Now, to get a more complete picture of the usage of both class-maps and policy-maps, let's see some configuration examples below in various scenarios. The example scenarios below will cover some of the available "action" categories that can be applied from a policy-map to a class-map.

Configuration Scenario 1: Send traffic to CSC ASA Module for inspection

The CSC module is an SSM card (Security Services Module) that is purchased separately and inserted into the ASA chassis to offer extra functionality such as antivirus, antispam, antispyware etc. This module is available only for the older ASA 5500 models (not the 5500-X models). The CSC module communicates with the ASA firewall via its backplane.

The CSC module can inspect and filter the following protocols (on their default port):

- HTTP traffic on TCP port 80
- POP3 traffic on TCP port 110
- SMTP traffic on TCP port 25
- FTP traffic on TCP port 21

The Cisco ASA appliance can send HTTP, FTP, POP3 and SMTP traffic to the CSC module for inspection and filtering before allowing the traffic to continue to its destination. You can choose to scan traffic for all of these protocols or any combination of them. By default, the ASA does not sent any traffic to the CSC module. You must configure a class-map to identify traffic to be scanned, and then configure a policy-map with the "**csc**" command which will instruct the ASA firewall to send the traffic to CSC module for inspection. Here is how we configure CSC policy:

ASA(config)# policy-map *[policy name]*

ASA(config-pmap)# class *[class name]* **←first identify traffic to be scanned by CSC**

ASA(config-pmap-c)# csc {fail-close | fail-open} ←send traffic to CSC card

fail-close = if CSC card fails, traffic will be dropped

fail-open = if CSC card fails, traffic will be forwarded

Using the CSC module with the ASA

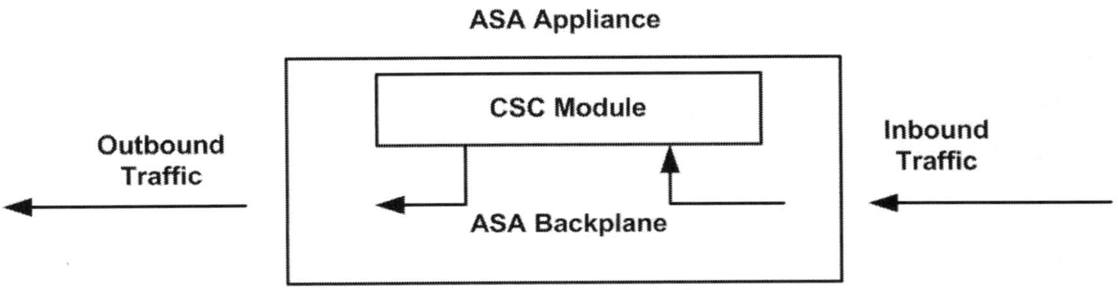

In our example below we want to scan and inspect HTTP and POP3 traffic from our internal network users towards the Internet, and also scan and inspect SMTP traffic coming from the Internet towards our company's mail server located on DMZ.

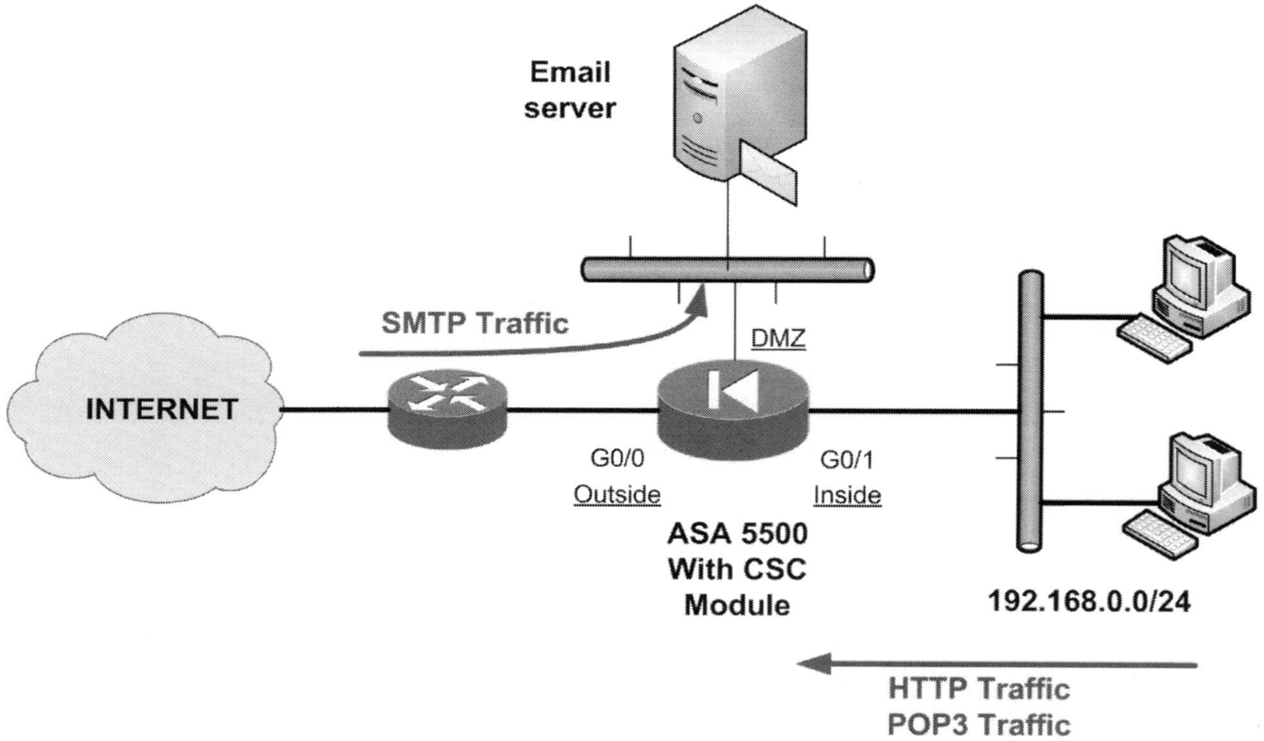

Assume that our SMTP mail server listens on IP address 50.50.50.1 (port 25). The policy will be applied globally, which means it will affect <u>ingress</u> traffic on <u>all interfaces</u>.

ASA(config)# access-list CSC_traffic permit tcp 192.168.0.0 255.255.255.0 any eq 80

ASA(config)# access-list CSC_traffic permit tcp 192.168.0.0 255.255.255.0 any eq 110

ASA(config)# access-list CSC_traffic permit tcp any host 50.50.50.1 eq 25

ASA(config)# class-map CSC_class **← create a class-map for traffic towards CSC**

ASA(config-cmap)# match access-list CSC_traffic ←identify traffic to be inspected

ASA(config-cmap)# exit

ASA(config)# policy-map global_policy **← get into the default global policy**

ASA(config-pmap)# class CSC_class **← attach the CSC class-map in global policy**

ASA(config-pmap-c)# csc fail-open ←send traffic to CSC

ASA(config-pmap-c)# exit

ASA(config-pmap)# exit

ASA(config)# service-policy global_policy **global ←attach the policy globally (this line should be already configured in the default ASA configuration)**

Configuration Scenario 2: Send traffic to IPS Module for inspection

Similarly with a CSC card described above, an Intrusion Prevention System (IPS) module card can also be used in an ASA chassis to provide intrusion detection and prevention functionality. For the older ASA 5500 models, the IPS functionality is offered by an add-on hardware module, whereas for the new ASA 5500-X devices the IPS functionality is offered by a special software module that can be enabled by a license upgrade.

The IPS module is loaded with specialized intrusion detection software which uses "signatures" to identify patterns of malicious traffic in order to block it. Only one module can be used in an ASA though, either a CSC or an IPS module. The IPS module (also called AIP-SSM in 5500 ASA series) can operate in two modes:

- **IPS Inline Mode**: In inline mode, the IPS sits in the traffic path and therefore the traffic is fully intercepted and inspected by the IPS before being sent back to the ASA firewall. The traffic that passes through the IPS is the traffic that matches a class-map configured with the "**ips**" command. In inline mode, the IPS is capable to block attacks by itself..
- **IPS Promiscuous Mode**: In promiscuous mode, the IPS does not intercept traffic that passes through the ASA. Instead, the ASA firewall sends a copy of each packet to the IPS for inspection. If the packet is identified as malicious by the IPS, it issues an alarm or instructs the ASA firewall (using the "shun" command) to block the traffic. In this mode the IPS does not block attacks by itself.

Using the IPS module with the ASA

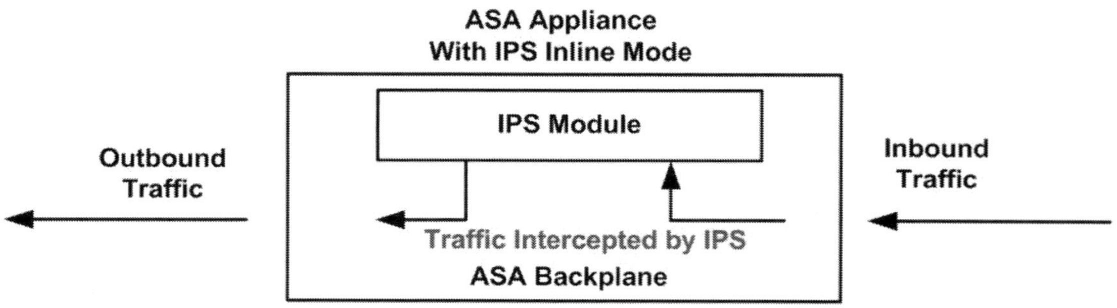

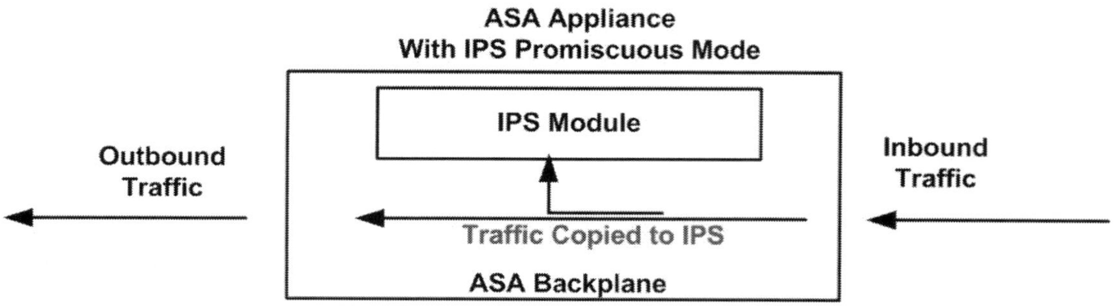

By default, the ASA does not sent any traffic to the IPS module. You must configure a class-map to identify traffic to be inspected by IPS, and then configure a policy-map with the "**ips**" command which will instruct the ASA firewall to send the traffic to IPS module for inspection. Here is how we configure the IPS policy:

ASA(config)# policy-map *[policy name]*
ASA(config-pmap)# class *[class name]* **←first identify traffic to be inspected by IPS**
ASA(config-pmap-c)# ips {inline | promiscuous} {fail-close | fail-open} ←send traffic to IPS

inline = the IPS will be working in inline mode
promiscuous = the IPS will be working in promiscuous mode
fail-close = if IPS card fails, traffic will be dropped
fail-open = if IPS card fails, traffic will be forwarded

Let's see a more complete example below. Assume that we have a DMZ zone with public servers on a class C subnet 50.50.50.0/24. We want all traffic coming from Internet towards our DMZ servers to be inspected by the IPS in inline mode.

ASA(config)# access-list DMZ_traffic permit ip any 50.50.50.0 255.255.255.0

ASA(config)# class-map IPS_class **← create a class-map for traffic towards IPS**
ASA(config-cmap)# match access-list DMZ_traffic ←identify traffic to be inspected
ASA(config-cmap)# exit
ASA(config)# policy-map outside_ips_policy **← create a policy-map for IPS**
ASA(config-pmap)# class IPS_class **← attach the IPS class-map in the IPS policy**
ASA(config-pmap-c)# ips inline fail-open ←send traffic to IPS in inline mode
ASA(config-pmap-c)# exit
ASA(config-pmap)# exit
ASA(config)# service-policy outside_ips_policy **interface outside ←attach the policy on the outside interface**

Configuration Scenario 3: Set Connection Limits Policy

The "**set connection**" command used under a policy-map configuration is used to enforce connection limits for specific traffic flows. When a connection matches the associated match criteria in the class-map, the ASA appliance sets the specified connection limits to the traffic. You can use the "set connection" command to configure the following:

- **conn-max**: Maximum number of simultaneous connections allowed. Can help to protect against Denial of Service attacks.
- **per-client-max**: Maximum number of connections allowed per client. Can help to restrict internal users from opening excessive connections (e.g when using torrent or peer-to-peer)
- **embryonic-conn-max**: Maximum numbers of TCP "half-open" (embryonic) connections allowed. Protects against "SYN" attacks.
- **per-client-embryonic-max**: Maximum number of TCP embryonic allowed per client.

Let's see an example scenario below.

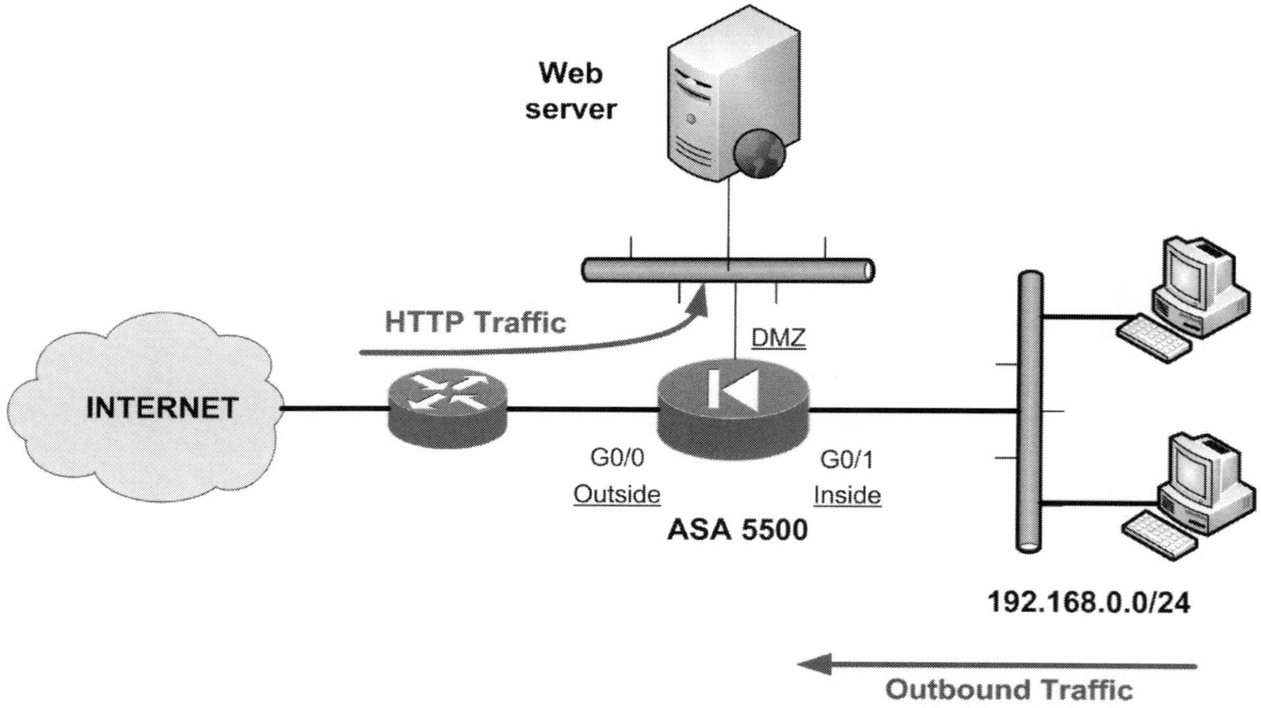

We want to apply connection limit policies for HTTP inbound traffic (from Internet to DMZ Web Server) and also for users' outbound traffic (on a per user basis). Assume that our Web Server listens on public IP address 50.50.50.1.

ASA(config)# access-list HTTP_traffic permit tcp any host 50.50.50.1 eq 80

ASA(config)# access-list outbound_traffic permit ip 192.168.0.0 255.255.255.0 any

ASA(config)# class-map Web_SRV_Class ← create a class-map for DMZ Web Server

ASA(config-cmap)# match access-list HTTP_traffic ←identify HTTP traffic to web srv

ASA(config-cmap)# exit

ASA(config)# class-map Outbound_Class ← create a class-map for Outbound traffic

ASA(config-cmap)# match access-list outbound_traffic ←identify outbound traffic

ASA(config-cmap)# exit

ASA(config)# policy-map Web_SRV_policy ← create a policy-map for Web Server

ASA(config-pmap)# class Web_SRV_Class ← attach the class-map on the policy

ASA(config-pmap-c)# set connection conn-max 3000 ←limit max connections to web srv

ASA(config-pmap-c)# set connection per-client-max 100 ←limit max per client connections to web server to 100

ASA(config-pmap-c)# set connection embryonic-conn-max 1500 ←limit max half-open connections to web server to 1500

ASA(config-pmap-c)# exit

ASA(config-pmap)# exit

ASA(config)# policy-map outbound_policy ← create a policy-map for outbound traffic

ASA(config-pmap)# class Outbound_Class ← attach the class-map on the policy

ASA(config-pmap-c)# set connection per-client-max 70 ←limit max simultaneous connections for each internal user to 70

ASA(config-pmap-c)# exit

ASA(config-pmap)# exit

ASA(config)# service-policy Web_SRV_policy **interface outside** ←attach the Web server policy on the outside interface

ASA(config)# service-policy outbound_policy **interface inside** ←attach the outbound policy on the inside interface

Configuration Scenario 4: Traffic Inspection Policy

An out-of-the-box Cisco ASA firewall has a global default inspection policy which applies inspection policies on several applications and protocols which are matched by the default class map. If you view the running configuration of the ASA (using the "show run" command) you will notice the following default configuration commands:

```
class-map inspection_default
 match default-inspection-traffic
!
policy-map type inspect dns preset_dns_map
 parameters
  message-length maximum 512

policy-map global_policy
 class inspection_default
  inspect dns preset_dns_map
  inspect h323 h225
  inspect h323 ras
  inspect rsh
  inspect rtsp
  inspect sqlnet
  inspect skinny
  inspect sunrpc
  inspect xdmcp
  inspect sip
  inspect netbios
  inspect tftp
  inspect ils
  inspect ftp
  inspect http
!
service-policy global_policy global
```

From the default configuration shown above, you can observe that there is a default class-map (***class-map inspection_default***) and a default policy-map (***policy-map global_policy***). The default policy is applied globally on the appliance (*service-policy* ***global_policy*** *global*).

Notice that we use the "inspect" command to apply application layer inspection on several protocols. We can add or remove protocols from the global policy accordingly. You can go under the ***policy-map global_policy*** > ***class inspection_default*** and type "**inspect ?**" to see which other protocols are supported for inspection. Then you can add more protocols for inspection as needed.

The "inspect" command for each protocol helps the security appliance to do the following:

- Look for common security issues in the application layer and prevent them.
- Look for additional connections that need to be opened (e.g for FTP or voice traffic) and open those connections as well.
- Look for embedded addressing information inside packets that will be translated with NAT.

Configuration Scenario 5: Apply Bandwidth Policy to traffic using the Police Command

The "**police**" command under a policy-map configuration is used to apply rate-limiting to traffic flow. You need to specify the direction of the traffic to be policed, the rate limit bandwidth (in bps) and optionally the burst size and the actions to be taken for conforming or non-conforming burst traffic (we will discuss QoS rate limiting, traffic shaping and priority queuing in another Chapter later in this book).

The "police" mechanism is configured as below:

ASA(config)# policy-map *[policy name]*

ASA(config-pmap)# class *[class name]* **←first identify traffic to be policed**

ASA(config-pmap-c)# police {input|output} *conform-rate-in-bps [burst size in bytes]* **conform-action {drop|transmit} exceed-action {drop|transmit}**

The "**input**" keyword applies traffic limiting to packets entering an interface and the "**output**" keyword applies traffic limiting to packets leaving an interface. The burst size indicates the maximum size in bytes of an instantaneous burst of traffic allowed before the traffic is capped to get it back to the policing rate. A formula to calculate a good maximum burst size, according to the maximum rate limit applied, is the following:

Burst Size = (conform rate in bps)/8 * 1.5

Assume that we want to apply rate limiting to a specific IPSec remote access user group (with name "Remote_VPN") as following:

- Maximum allowed bandwidth of 512kbps
- Burst Size = (512000/8)*1.5 = 96000 bytes

Let's see the configuration snapshot below:

ASA(config)# class-map VPN_Users_Class **← create a class-map for VPN remote users**

ASA(config-cmap)# match tunnel-group Remote_VPN ←identify the VPN tunnel group

ASA(config-cmap)# exit

ASA(config)# policy-map VPN_policy **← create a policy-map for VPN remote access**

ASA(config-pmap)# class VPN_Users_Class **← attach the class-map on the policy**

ASA(config-pmap-c)# police input 512000 96000 conform-action transmit exceed-action drop ←limit the traffic to 512kbps and 96000 bytes of burst size

ASA(config-pmap-c)# police output 512000 96000 conform-action transmit exceed-action drop ←do the same for outgoing traffic

ASA(config-pmap-c)# exit

ASA(config-pmap)# exit

ASA(config)# service-policy VPN_policy **interface outside ←attach the VPN policy on the outside interface**

Configuration Scenario 6: Setting Prioritization for traffic

The last configuration example that we will see here has to do with priority and queuing (more details on QoS and prioritization of traffic in another Chapter later on). We can use the "**priority**" command under the policy-map configuration to enable Low Latency Queuing for traffic that is delay-sensitive (mainly voice). Together with the "**priority**" command we must also use the "**priority-queue**" command in order to enable the priority **queue** on the interface on which we want to apply high priority for traffic. Each interface of the security appliance has two queues: A priority queue which is used to transmit delay-sensitive traffic and a default queue which transmits all other traffic. Priority queuing is applied ONLY on egress traffic (packets that exit from an interface).

The "**priority**" mechanism is configured as following:

ASA(config)# policy-map *[policy name]*

ASA(config-pmap)# class *[class name]* **←first identify traffic to apply priority on**

ASA(config-pmap-c)# priority

ASA(config-pmap-c)# exit

ASA(config-pmap)# exit

ASA(config)# priority-queue ***logical_if_name*** **←enable the priority queue on an interface**

In the following example we will apply high priority for voice traffic that passes through a specific Lan-to-Lan IPSec tunnel between two sites.

ASA(config)# class-map Voice_L2L_Class ← create a class-map for voice VPN traffic
ASA(config-cmap)# match tunnel-group L2L_VPN ←identify the IPSec VPN tunnel
ASA(config-cmap)# match dscp ef ←match the expedited forwarding "ef" voice traffic
ASA(config-cmap)# exit

ASA(config)# policy-map voice_policy ← create a policy-map for VPN voice traffic
ASA(config-pmap)# class Voice_L2L_Class ← attach the class-map on the policy-map
ASA(config-pmap-c)# priority ← apply high priority to voice traffic
ASA(config-pmap-c)# exit
ASA(config-pmap)# exit
ASA(config)# priority-queue outside ←enable the priority queue on the outside interface

13.2.3 Configuring a Service-Policy

So far we have seen the two (out of three) components of a Modular Policy Framework (MPF) configuration. That is, we have described **Class-Maps** and **Policy-Maps**. The third and last component of an MPF is a **service-police**. A service-policy is used to attach the policy-map either Globally or on a specific interface.

- If the policy-map is applied globally, actions are applied to traffic in the ingress direction only.
- If the policy-map is applied to a specific interface, actions are applied to traffic bidirectionally.
- Exception to the above is the Priority Queuing policy which is always applied to traffic on the egress direction.

The service-policy is used as following:

ASA(config)# service-policy {*policy-map name}* **{global | interface** *if_name***}**

So, to apply a service policy with name "**voice_policy**" to the outside interface we would use the following command:

ASA(config)# service-policy voice_policy interface outside

To verify that your policies are being enforced use the "**show service-policy**" command.

Chapter 14 Quality of Service (QoS) Configuration

Although the purpose of a Cisco ASA appliance is to secure the network, it incorporates also some features that enhance traffic flow through the appliance. QoS is one of these features. Some network traffic, such as voice and streaming video, cannot tolerate long latency times. QoS is a feature that lets you give priority to these types of traffic over other types of traffic (such as pure data traffic).

The following QoS features/mechanisms are supported by the ASA appliance:

- **Policing (Rate limiting)** – setting threshold limits to traffic (max). Limits the maximum bandwidth used per flow.
- **Priority Queuing** – If congestion occurs, intelligently identify critical traffic and use Low Latency Queuing for transmitting critical traffic before other traffic. Used for VoIP mainly. Priority Queuing is further divided into Standard and Hierarchical Priority Queuing.
- **Traffic Shaping** - match device and link speeds in order to control packet loss, variable delay, and link saturation. For example, if you have an ASA with FastEthernet links connected to an ADSL line, you can configure the ASA to transmit packets at a fixed slower rate.

NOTE: In order for QOS to be effective in any given network, you must implement it end-to-end on all devices. For known bottleneck devices within a network, it's critical that QoS be enabled on those devices as well.

You can configure each of the QoS features above alone or can you make also a couple of supported combinations of QoS mechanisms. The supported QoS feature combinations per interface are shown below:

- Standard priority queuing (for specific traffic) + Policing (for the rest of the traffic). You cannot configure priority queuing and policing for the same set of traffic.

- Traffic shaping (for all traffic on an interface) + Hierarchical priority queuing (for a subset of traffic).

You cannot configure traffic shaping and standard priority queuing for the same interface; only hierarchical priority queuing is allowed.

NOTES:

- Typically, if you enable traffic shaping, you do not also enable policing for the same traffic, although the ASA does not restrict you from configuring this.
- Priority queuing needs to be used with policing or traffic shaping. The reason is that the Low Latency Queue (LLQ) in Priority Queuing is used only if the ASA links are saturated. In other words, prioritization of packets will not occur unless the link is full. Since ASA interfaces are either 100Mbps or 1Gbps or more, saturating these links isn't something that will happen often. Therefore, by implementing policing or traffic shaping along with LLQ actually makes LLQ kick in at the point the policing or shaping limits are met.

14.1 Traffic Policing

Traffic policing is a feature through which we can define a rule on the ASA which will drop packets if they exceed the defined traffic (bandwidth) limit. With policing, you can specify a class of traffic that you want the policing to take effect.

We have seen the Policing feature in the previous Chapter. To refresh our memory, it is configured as below:

ASA(config)# policy-map *[policy name]*
ASA(config-pmap)# class *[class name]* **←first identify traffic to be policed with a class map**
ASA(config-pmap-c)# police {input|output} *conform-rate-in-bps [burst size in bytes]* **conform-action {drop|transmit} exceed-action {drop|transmit}**

The "**input**" keyword applies traffic limiting to packets entering an interface and the "**output**" keyword applies traffic limiting to packets leaving an interface. The burst size indicates the maximum size in bytes of an instantaneous burst of traffic allowed before the traffic is capped to get it back to the policing rate. A formula to calculate a good maximum burst size, according to the maximum rate limit applied, is the following:

Burst Size = (conform rate in bps)/8 * 1.5

For a maximum allowed bandwidth of 512kbps, then Burst Size = (512000/8)*1.5 = 96000 bytes

Let's see how to configure a basic QoS Traffic Policing scenario:

For example, assume we want to restrict traffic from a host with IP 192.168.10.1 to another host with IP 10.1.1.1. The rate limit should be 512kbps with 92kbytes burst traffic.

Let's see the configuration snapshot below:

!First identify the traffic with an ACL

ASA(config)# access-list policing-acl extended permit ip host 192.168.10.1 host 10.1.1.1

ASA(config)# class-map Rate_Limit_Class **←** create a class-map for the traffic

ASA(config-cmap)# match access-list policing-acl ←attach the ACL created above

ASA(config-cmap)# exit

ASA(config)# policy-map Limit_Policy **←** create a policy-map for rate limiting

ASA(config-pmap)# class Rate_Limit_Class **←** attach the class-map on the policy

ASA(config-pmap-c)# police output 512000 96000 conform-action transmit exceed-action drop ←limit the traffic to 512kbps and 96000 bytes of burst size

ASA(config-pmap-c)# exit

ASA(config-pmap)# exit

ASA(config)# service-policy Limit_Policy **interface outside ←**attach the rate limit policy on the outside interface

14.2 Traffic Shaping

For Traffic Shaping on ASA you must have in mind three important notes:

1. Traffic Shaping is applied only on the outgoing traffic from an interface.
2. For Traffic Shaping you can only use the "**class-default**" class map which is automatically created by the ASA and matches all traffic. In comparison with Policing above, you can't create a custom class-map to match specific traffic.
3. Traffic Shaping is not supported on the new ASA models 5500-X.

Traffic shaping is similar to policing except that shaping will place the packet into a buffer and smoothen the traffic flow to match the limit imposed. On the other hand, policing will drop the packet once the limit has been exceeded.

Basically the configuration of traffic shaping alone is much simpler since only the "class-default" is used. Let's see an example below. Assume the ASA is connected to a cable modem with upstream bandwidth of 1Mbps. We want to shape outgoing traffic from ASA to 1Mbps.

ASA(config)#policy-map QOS-TRAFFIC-OUT ←start with policy map directly
ASA(config-pmap)#class class-default ←Only class-default is allowed
ASA(config-pmap-c)# shape average 1000000 ←Traffic shaping to 1Mbps for all out traffic

ASA(config-pmap-c)#exit
ASA(config-pmap)#exit

ASA(config)# service-policy QOS-TRAFFIC-OUT interface outside ←apply shaping policy to outside interface

Traffic Shaping alone is not used a lot in actual networks. Instead, it is usually combined with Priority Queuing as we will see in the next section.

14.3 Priority Queuing

We have two types of Priority Queuing:

1. **Standard Priority Queuing**: It uses a Low Latency Queue (LLQ) on an interface while all other traffic goes into a "best effort" queue.
2. **Hierarchical Priority Queuing**: Used on interfaces where you enable a Traffic Shaping queue. Basically you have a certain amount of traffic which is traffic shaped, and a subset of this traffic is prioritized.

14.3.1 Standard Priority Queuing

A Standard Priority Queue is used when doing traffic prioritization without traffic shaping. When doing traffic prioritization without traffic shaping, the standard priority queue must be configured explicitly on the interface on which we need to apply priority QoS.

!First enable the standard priority queue on the interface which Priority QoS is required
ASA(config)# priority-queue outside **←Enable priority queue on outside interface**

!Optionally you can configure also the queue limit (default limit is 1024 packets)
ASA(config-priority-queue)# queue-limit 2048

Usually Standard Priority Queuing is configured with Policing, so the examples we will see below take this into consideration.

Scenario 1:

Assume we have a total of 1Mbps of upload bandwidth on the ASA outside interface. We want to reserve 200kbps for voice traffic and the rest 800kbps will be rate-limited (policed).

ASA(config)# priority-queue outside ←first enable standard priority queue on outside
ASA(config-priority-queue)#exit

ASA(config)# class-map voice-traffic
ASA(config-cmap)# match dscp ef ←match voice packets with Expedited Forwarding bit
ASA(config-cmap)#exit

ASA(config)#policy-map QOS
ASA(config-pmap)# class voice-traffic
ASA(config-pmap-c)# priority ←enable priority QoS for voice class.
ASA(config-pmap-c)#exit
ASA(config-pmap)# class class-default←rest of traffic policed at 800kbps
ASA(config-pmap-c)# police output 800000 conform-action transmit exceed-action drop
ASA(config-pmap-c)#exit
ASA(config-pmap)#exit
ASA(config)# service-policy QOS interface outside← apply policy on outside interface

Note from above that you don't set a bandwidth value for the voice traffic. Since you know that the link bandwidth is 1Mbps and you rate-limit the rest of the traffic at 800kbps, this means that voice traffic will have 200kbps reserved.

Also, on the example above we assumed that voice traffic is already marked with "**dscp ef**" which is the usual case with voice packets.

Scenario 2:

This is a scenario that you will find frequently in actual networks. You have two sites connected with Site-to-Site IPSec VPN between two ASA firewalls. In addition to normal data traffic inside the VPN tunnel between the two sites, we have also voice traffic generated by an IP Telephony system (VoIP phones etc). So we want to give priority to voice traffic which is passed inside the VPN tunnel (see diagram below).

We will see the configuration on ASA1 (for ASA2 the configuration will be similar). Assume that the site-to-site VPN is already configured on ASA1 with a tunnel-group name of "**200.200.200.1**".

The total upload bandwidth on the ASA outside interface is 1Mbps. We want to reserve 400kbps total for the VPN traffic and 600 kbps for the rest of the traffic (non-tunnel traffic). For the 400kbps VPN traffic we want to reserve 100kbps for voice and the rest for the other VPN traffic.

So, the bandwidth requirements are summarized below:

Total Upload Link Bandwidth: 1Mbps		
Total VPN Tunnel Traffic: 400kbps		**Total non-tunnel Traffic:** 600kbps
Voice VPN Traffic: 100kbps	**Rest of VPN traffic:** 300kbps	

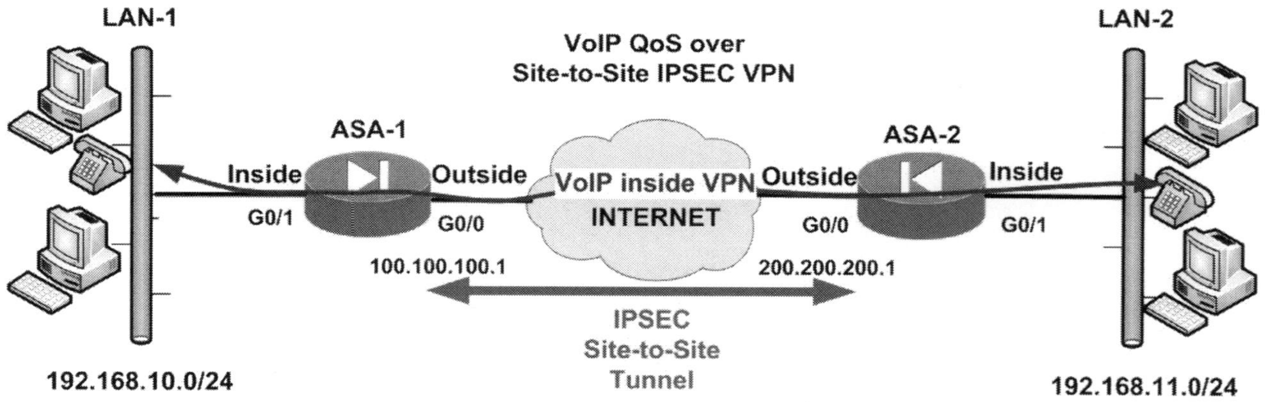

Assume we have the following tunnel-group configured:

ASA(config)# tunnel-group 200.200.200.1 type ipsec-l2l

!Enable priority queue on outside
ASA(config)# priority-queue outside
ASA(config-priority-queue)#exit

```
ASA(config)# class-map voice-vpn-traffic
ASA(config-cmap)# match tunnel-group 200.200.200.1←match packets inside this tunnel
ASA(config-cmap)# match dscp ef ←which also have EF bit set (i.e voice inside vpn tunnel)
ASA(config-cmap)#exit

ASA(config)# class-map rest-vpn-traffic
ASA(config-cmap)# match tunnel-group 200.200.200.1←match packets inside this tunnel
ASA(config-cmap)# match flow ip destination-address ←match flows going to each IP addr
ASA(config-cmap)#exit

ASA(config)#policy-map QOS
ASA(config-pmap)# class voice-vpn-traffic
ASA(config-pmap-c)# priority ←enable priority QoS for voice inside vpn class of traffic.
ASA(config-pmap-c)#exit
ASA(config-pmap)# class rest-vpn-traffic←rate-limit 300kbps for rest of traffic inside vpn
ASA(config-pmap-c)# police output 300000 conform-action transmit exceed-action drop
ASA(config-pmap-c)#exit
ASA(config-pmap)# class class-default←all non-tunnel traffic policed at 600kbps
ASA(config-pmap-c)# police output 600000 conform-action transmit exceed-action drop
ASA(config-pmap-c)#exit
ASA(config-pmap)#exit
ASA(config)# service-policy QOS interface outside← apply policy on outside interface
```

14.3.2 Hierarchical Priority Queuing

When doing traffic prioritization together with traffic shaping, the ASA uses the Hierarchical Priority Queue. In such a case, there is no need to explicitly configure the hierarchical priority queue on the outside interface (like we did for the standard priority queue before).

In Hierarchical Priority Queuing you need to use nested policy maps. One policy map will be configured for the priority traffic and this policy map will be used inside another policy map which will enforce traffic shaping.

Let's see a couple of scenarios below:

Scenario 1:

Consider again the network diagram we have seen in the previous section (Scenario2 in Standard Priority Queue). Assume we have a total of 1Mbps of upload bandwidth on the ASA outside interface. Also we have a VPN tunnel between the two ASAs. We want to give priority to VPN traffic between the two sites. Because encryption occurs before prioritization, we need to classify traffic based on the VPN tunnel endpoints (i.e traffic between outside IP addresses of 100.100.100.1 and 200.200.200.1).

Let's see configuration on ASA1:

!First Classify IPSEC traffic between the tunnel endpoints with an ACL
ASA(config)# access-list VPN-TRAFFIC extended permit udp host 100.100.100.1 host 200.200.200.1 eq isakmp
ASA(config)# access-list VPN-TRAFFIC extended permit esp host 100.100.100.1 host 200.200.200.1

ASA(config)# class-map vpn-traffic
ASA(config-cmap)# match access-list VPN-TRAFFIC←match vpn traffic ACL from above
ASA(config-cmap)#exit

ASA(config)# policy-map PRIORITY ←this policy map will be nested next
ASA(config-pmap)# class vpn-traffic
ASA(config-pmap-c)#priority ←prioritize VPN traffic
ASA(config-pmap-c)#exit
ASA(config-pmap)#exit

ASA(config)# policy-map QOS
ASA(config-pmap)# class class-default
ASA(config-pmap-c)#shape average 992000←shape just a little below link bandwidth
ASA(config-pmap-c)#service-policy PRIORITY←nested policy map
ASA(config-pmap-c)#exit
ASA(config-pmap)#exit

ASA(config)#service-policy QOS interface outside

NOTES: From the configuration above, notice the nested policies. First we have defined the PRIORITY policy which is then used inside another policy (QOS policy). Also, the link bandwidth is 1Mbps but we are shaping traffic a little bit below (992kbps) which from my experience works better in prioritization. This means that when the link bandwidth is saturated (around 992kbps) then shaping and priority queue will kick in and priority traffic will be transmitted first. Remember that in Hierarchical Queuing we are prioritizing a subset of the shaped traffic.

Scenario 2:

This is similar with the above but we are going to match VoIP traffic inside the VPN.

NOTE: When using Hierarchical Priority Queuing for encrypted VPN traffic you can match packets only based on DSCP value. Packet matching based on tunnel group name (as we did in the previous section on Standard Priority Queuing) is not supported.

ASA(config)# class-map voice-traffic
ASA(config-cmap)# match dscp ef←match voice traffic (tunnel matching not supported)
ASA(config-cmap)#exit

```
ASA(config)# policy-map PRIORITY ←this policy map will be nested next
ASA(config-pmap)# class voice-traffic
ASA(config-pmap-c)#priority ←prioritize voice traffic
ASA(config-pmap-c)#exit
ASA(config-pmap)#exit

ASA(config)# policy-map QOS
ASA(config-pmap)# class class-default
ASA(config-pmap-c)#shape average 992000←shape just a little below link bandwidth
ASA(config-pmap-c)#service-policy PRIORITY←nested policy map
ASA(config-pmap-c)#exit
ASA(config-pmap)#exit

ASA(config)#service-policy QOS interface outside
```

Chapter 15 Cisco ASA 5505 Overview

This Chapter is dedicated to the Cisco ASA 5505 firewall appliance which has some Hardware, Licensing and Configuration differences compared with the other models. The ASA 5505 provides a high-performance and flexible upgrade from the older PIX 501 and PIX 506E appliances and is designed for small offices or remote branches. Below we will provide an overview of the ASA5505 appliance and also describe the basic differences of this model compared with the other ASA devices.

15.1 ASA 5505 Hardware and Licensing

15.1.1 Hardware Ports and VLANs

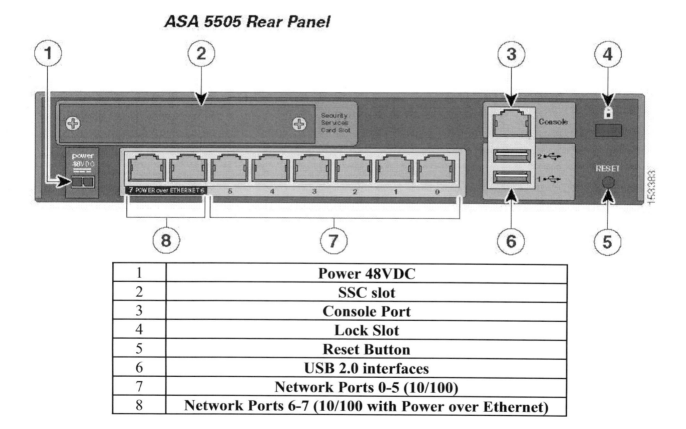

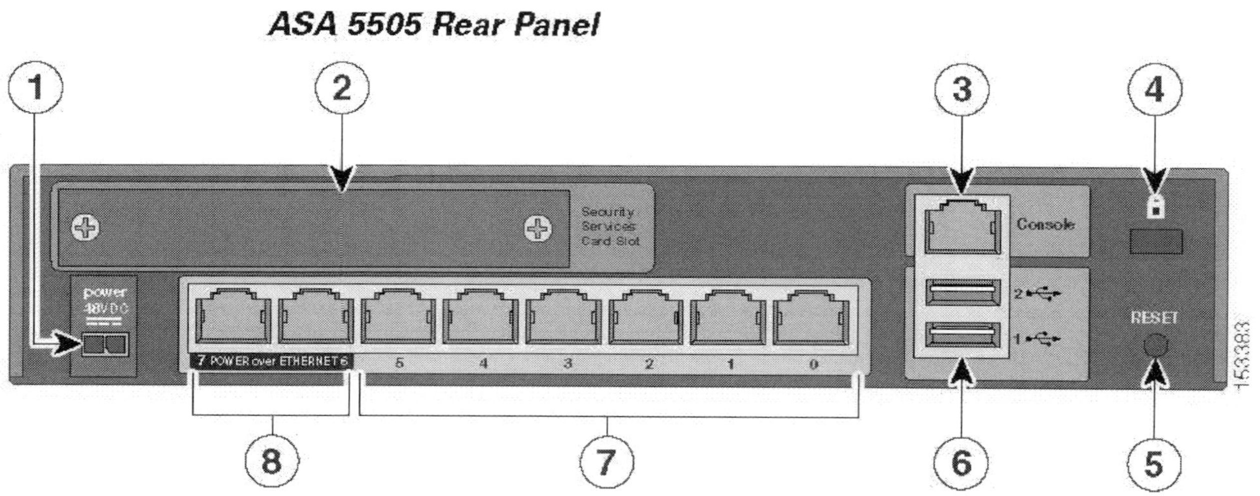

1	**Power 48VDC**
2	**SSC slot**
3	**Console Port**
4	**Lock Slot**
5	**Reset Button**
6	**USB 2.0 interfaces**
7	**Network Ports 0-5 (10/100)**
8	**Network Ports 6-7 (10/100 with Power over Ethernet)**

Unlike the other Cisco ASA models, the ASA 5505 has a built-in 8-port 10/100 switch as shown on the figure above.

Starting from right to left, we have Ethernet0/0 up to Ethernet0/7. The last two Ports 6 and 7 are also Power over Ethernet Ports (PoE), which means that in addition to normal computers, you can also connect IP Phones (or other PoE devices) which will be powered by the firewall PoE ports. The eight network interfaces of the ASA 5505 work only as Layer 2 ports, which is the difference of the 5505 from the other ASA models. This means that you cannot configure a Layer 3 IP address directly on each interface. Instead, you have to assign the interface port in a VLAN, and then configure all Firewall Interface parameters under the **interface VLAN** command.

You can divide the eight physical ports into groups, called VLANs, that function as separate networks. This enables you to improve the security of your business because devices in different VLANs can only communicate with each other by passing the traffic through the firewall appliance where relevant security policies can be enforced. Devices in the same VLAN can communicate between them without Firewall control. Your license determines how many active VLANs you can have on the ASA 5505.

The ASA 5505 comes preconfigured with two VLANs: VLAN1 and VLAN2. By default, Ethernet switch port 0 (Ethernet 0/0) is allocated to VLAN2. All other switch ports are allocated by default to VLAN1.

The factory Default configuration of the network interfaces uses port Ethernet0/0 as the Outside untrusted interface (connecting to Internet), and the rest of the interfaces (0/1 to 0/7) are configured as the trusted Inside interfaces connecting to internal hosts. Two Switch Vlan Interfaces (SVI) exist by default (**Interface Vlan 1** and **Interface Vlan 2**) which can be used to assign the Layer 3 IP addresses and other interface settings for the **Outside** zone (Ethernet 0/0) and for the **Inside** zone (Ethernet0/1 to 0/7). The default configuration of the Cisco ASA 5505 will be explained in the next section.

15.1.2 Licensing

Although the ASA 5505 comes preconfigured with two VLANs, you can create as many as 20 VLANs, depending on your license. For example, you could create VLANs for the Inside, Outside, and DMZ network segments. There are two license options for the ASA 5505:

- **Base License**
- **Security Plus License**

Base License

With the Base License, you can configure up to 3 VLANs, thus segmenting your network into three security zones (Inside, Outside, DMZ). However there is a communication restriction between VLANs (zones). Communication between the DMZ VLAN and the Inside VLAN is restricted: the Inside VLAN is permitted to send traffic to the DMZ VLAN, but the DMZ VLAN is not permitted to send traffic to the Inside VLAN. Also, you cannot configure firewall failover redundancy with the Base License. These limitations are removed with the Security Plus license.

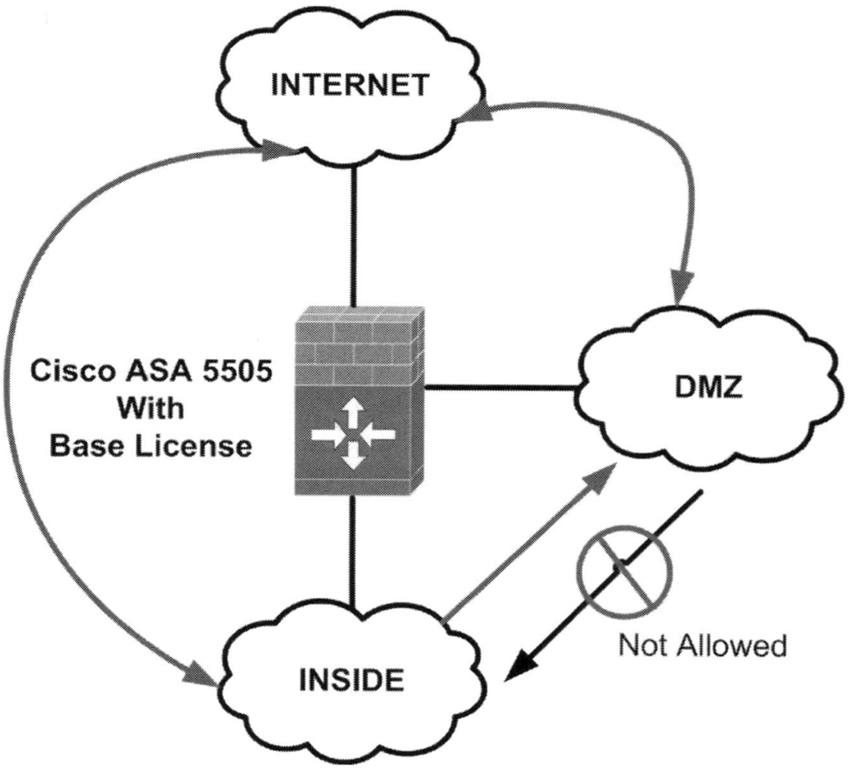

To configure a DMZ VLAN on a Base License use the following commands:

asa5505(config)# interface Vlan 3
asa5505(config-if)# no forward interface vlan 1
asa5505(config-if)# nameif DMZ
asa5505(config-if)# security-level 50
asa5505(config-if)# ip address 10.2.2.1 255.255.255.0

asa5505(config)# interface Vlan 1
asa5505(config-if)# nameif inside
asa5505(config-if)# security-level 100
asa5505(config-if)# ip address 192.168.1.1 255.255.255.0

asa5505(config)# interface Vlan 2
asa5505(config-if)# nameif outside
asa5505(config-if)# security-level 0
asa5505(config-if)# ip address 100.100.100.1 255.255.255.0

Security Plus License

This license removes all restrictions of the Base license. Up to 20 VLANs can be configured (ports can be configured as Trunk ports thus supporting multiple VLANs per port). Also there are no communication restrictions between VLANs. This license supports also Active/Standby (non stateful) firewall failover redundancy and Backup ISP Connectivity (Dual ISP connection).

15.2 ASA 5505 Default Configuration

The ASA 5505 is factory configured in such a way as to work right away out of the box. The Internet Outside Interface (Ethernet 0/0) is configured to obtain IP address automatically from the ISP, and the Inside Interfaces (Ethernet 0/1 to 0/7) are configured to provide IP addresses to internal hosts dynamically (DHCP). Specifically, the default ASA 5505 configuration includes the following:

- An inside VLAN 1 interface that includes the Ethernet 0/1 through 0/7 switch ports. The VLAN 1 IP address and mask are 192.168.1.1 and 255.255.255.0.
- An outside VLAN 2 interface that includes the Ethernet 0/0 switch port. VLAN 2 derives its IP address using DHCP (from the ISP).
- The default route is also derived from DHCP.
- All inside IP addresses are translated when accessing the outside using interface PAT.

- By default, inside users can access the outside, and outside users are prevented from accessing the inside.
- The DHCP server is enabled on the security appliance, so a PC connecting to the VLAN 1 interface receives an address between 192.168.1.5 and 192.168.1.254.
- The HTTP server is enabled for ASDM and is accessible to users on the 192.168.1.0 network.

Restore the default factory configuration using the **configure factory-default** command.

The Default Configuration consists of the following commands.

interface Ethernet 0/0
  switchport access vlan 2 ← **This assigns Ethernet0/0 to Vlan 2**
  no shutdown

interface Ethernet 0/1
  switchport access vlan 1 ← **This assigns Ethernet0/1 to Vlan 1**
  no shutdown

interface Ethernet 0/2
  switchport access vlan 1
  no shutdown

interface Ethernet 0/3
  switchport access vlan 1
  no shutdown

interface Ethernet 0/4
  switchport access vlan 1
  no shutdown

interface Ethernet 0/5
  switchport access vlan 1
  no shutdown

interface Ethernet 0/6
  switchport access vlan 1
  no shutdown

interface Ethernet 0/7
  switchport access vlan 1
  no shutdown

interface vlan2 ← **Configure all interface parameters under "interface Vlan [*number*]"**
  nameif outside
  no shutdown
  ip address dhcp setroute ←**Receive IP dynamically using DHCP from the ISP**

```
interface vlan1
  nameif inside
  ip address 192.168.1.1 255.255.255.0
  security-level 100
  no shutdown
object network obj_any
subnet 0 0
nat (inside,outside) dynamic interface

http server enable
http 192.168.1.0 255.255.255.0 inside
```
← **Allow ASDM access from inside network**

```
dhcpd address 192.168.1.5-192.168.1.254 inside
dhcpd auto_config outside
```
← **Obtain IP address dynamically from the ISP**

```
dhcpd enable inside
```
← **Assign IP addresses dynamically to internal PCs**

```
logging asdm informational
```

<u>Allow ICMP for testing</u>

If you want to allow ICMP for testing purposes, you need to enable icmp inspection as shown below:

```
policy-map global_policy
class inspection_default
inspect icmp
```

Chapter 16 Complete Configuration Examples

16.1 ASA 5505 Configuration Examples

16.1.1 ASA 5505 Basic Internet Access with DHCP

The ASA 5505 (the smallest ASA model) is ideal for small businesses or small branch offices with approximately 50 internal users (recommended maximum). This model comes with 8 port 10/100 switch, with port Ethernet0/0 used for the Public/Outside zone and ports Ethernet0/1 up to 0/7 for the Inside zone. The difference of this model compared with the rest ASA models is that its network ports are pure Layer 2 switch ports. This means you cannot configure IP addresses directly on the physical interfaces. Instead, you have to assign the interface port in a VLAN, and then configure all Firewall Interface parameters using the **interface VLAN** command.

In this scenario the 5505 is used for basic internet access using PAT, with a static Public IP address on the outside (100.1.1.2). The Firewall will act also as a DHCP server for assigning IP addresses to inside hosts.

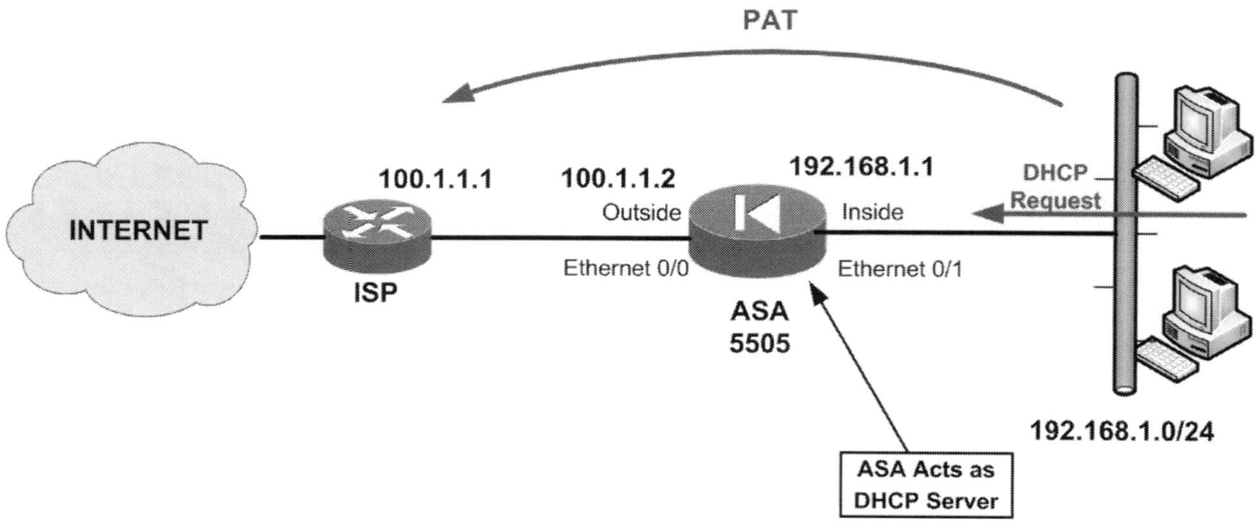

Let's see the complete configuration below. The commands with Bold are important.

```
ASA-5505# show run
: Saved
:
!
hostname ASA-5505
domain-name test.com
enable password xxxxxxxxxxxxxxxx encrypted
names
!
! Vlan 1 is assigned by default for all ports Ethernet0/1 to 0/7 which belong to the inside zone.
interface Vlan1
 nameif inside
 security-level 100
 ip address 192.168.1.1 255.255.255.0
!
! Vlan 2 is assigned to port Ethernet0/0 which belongs to the outside zone.
interface Vlan2
 nameif outside
 security-level 0
 ip address 100.1.1.2 255.255.255.252
!
! Assign Eth0/0 to vlan 2.
interface Ethernet0/0
 switchport access vlan 2
!
! By default, Eth0/1 to 0/7 are assigned to vlan 1. No need to change anything.
interface Ethernet0/1
!
interface Ethernet0/2
!
interface Ethernet0/3
!
interface Ethernet0/4
!
interface Ethernet0/5
!
interface Ethernet0/6
!
interface Ethernet0/7
!
ftp mode passive
dns server-group DefaultDNS
 domain-name test.com

! Create an ACL on the outside that will allow only echo-reply for troubleshooting purposes. Use a
!deny all with log at the end to monitor any attacks coming from outside.
access-list outside_in extended permit icmp any any echo-reply
access-list outside_in extended deny ip any any log
```

```
pager lines 24
logging asdm informational
mtu inside 1500
mtu outside 1500
icmp unreachable rate-limit 1 burst-size 1
no asdm history enable
arp timeout 14400
! Do PAT using the outside interface address
object network internal_lan
   subnet 192.168.1.0 255.255.255.0
   nat (inside,outside) dynamic interface

!Apply the ACL created above to the outside interface.
access-group outside_in in interface outside
route outside 0.0.0.0 0.0.0.0 100.1.1.1 1
timeout xlate 3:00:00
timeout conn 1:00:00 half-closed 0:10:00 udp 0:02:00 icmp 0:00:02
timeout sunrpc 0:10:00 h323 0:05:00 h225 1:00:00 mgcp 0:05:00 mgcp-pat 0:05:00
timeout sip 0:30:00 sip_media 0:02:00 sip-invite 0:03:00 sip-disconnect 0:02:00
timeout uauth 0:05:00 absolute
! Configure Local authentication for firewall management (For accessing the Firewall you need to
!use the username/password configured later).
aaa authentication serial console LOCAL
aaa authentication telnet console LOCAL
aaa authentication ssh console LOCAL
no snmp-server location
no snmp-server contact
snmp-server enable traps snmp authentication linkup linkdown coldstart
! Allow internal hosts to telnet to the device
telnet 192.168.1.0 255.255.255.0 inside
telnet timeout 5
! Allow an external management host to ssh from outside for firewall management
ssh 100.100.100.1 255.255.255.255 outside
ssh timeout 5
console timeout 0
! Assign a DNS server to internal hosts
dhcpd dns 200.200.200.1
!
! Assign IP addresses to internal hosts
dhcpd address 192.168.1.10-192.168.1.40 inside
dhcpd enable inside
!
!Create a Local username and password with administrator privileges
username admin password secretpass privilege 15

![other commands omitted]....
```

16.1.2 ASA 5505 with Dynamic IP Address and DMZ Host

This is an extension scenario of the previous one. The Cisco ASA 5505 receives an outside IP address dynamically from the ISP and has three security zones (Inside, Outside, DMZ). The Inside zone network shall be able to access the Internet and DMZ, and also Internet hosts shall be able to access the DMZ Web Server. This scenario can work with both Base License and Security Plus License. However, with a Security Plus license the DMZ public server (whatever that be – FTP, Email, Web etc) will be able to initiate traffic also to the Inside network zone (with the proper configuration). Instead of having a web server on DMZ, you can use this scenario also to host a Web Camera, a DVR, or a WiFi Router in the DMZ zone.

Since we have three security zones, we must create also three VLANs. VLAN1 (Inside) will be assigned to ports Ethernet0/2 up to 0/7, VLAN2 (Outside) will be assigned to port Ethernet 0/0, and VLAN3 (DMZ) will be assigned to Ethernet 0/1.

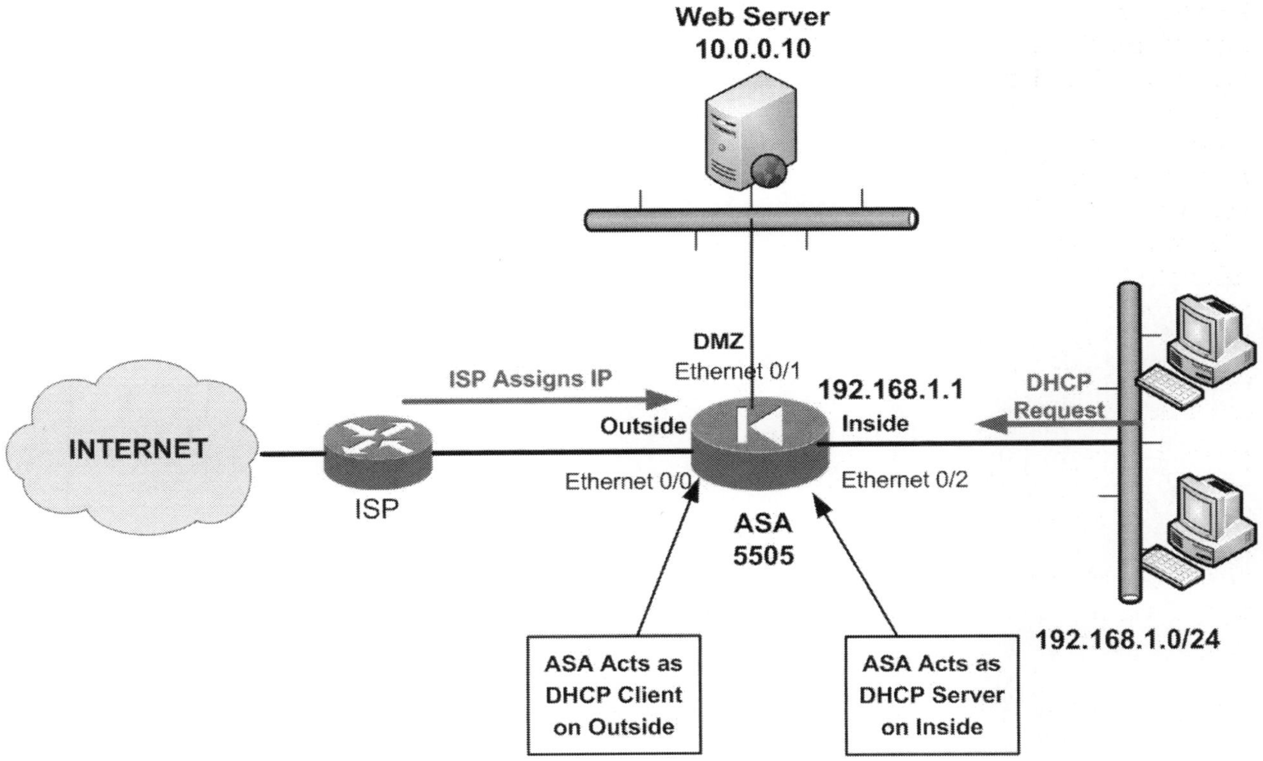

Let's see the complete configuration below. The commands with Bold are important.

```
ASA-5505# show run
: Saved
:
!
hostname ASA-5505
domain-name test.com
enable password xxxxxxxxxxxxxxxx encrypted
names
!
interface Vlan1
 nameif inside
 security-level 100
 ip address 192.168.1.1 255.255.255.0
!
interface Vlan2
 nameif outside
 security-level 0
! Get outside address and default gateway from ISP
 ip address dhcp setroute
!
interface Vlan3
! Use the following command ONLY if you have a BASE LICENSE
 no forward interface vlan 1
 nameif DMZ
 security-level 50
 ip address 10.0.0.1 255.255.255.0
!

! Assign Eth0/0 to vlan 2.
interface Ethernet0/0
 switchport access vlan 2
!
! Assign Eth0/1 to vlan 3.
interface Ethernet0/1
 switchport access vlan 3

! The rest are by default assigned to vlan 1. No need to change anything.
!
interface Ethernet0/2
!
interface Ethernet0/3
!
interface Ethernet0/4
!
interface Ethernet0/5
!
```

```
interface Ethernet0/6
!
interface Ethernet0/7
!
ftp mode passive
dns server-group DefaultDNS
 domain-name test.com

! Create an ACL on the outside that will allow access to the DMZ Web Server.
access-list outside_in extended permit tcp any host 10.0.0.10 eq 80
access-list outside_in extended deny ip any any log
pager lines 24
logging asdm informational
mtu inside 1500
mtu outside 1500
mtu DMZ 1500
no asdm history enable
arp timeout 14400

!Do PAT on the outside and DMZ interfaces for the inside network
object network internal_lan_outside
   subnet 192.168.1.0 255.255.255.0
   nat (inside,outside) dynamic interface

object network internal_lan_dmz
   subnet 192.168.1.0 255.255.255.0
   nat (inside,DMZ) dynamic interface

! Create a static redirection for port 80 towards the DMZ web server
object network web_server_static
   host 10.0.0.10
   nat (DMZ,outside) static interface service tcp 80 80

! Do PAT on the outside for the DMZ web server. This will allow Web Server access to Internet.
object network dmz_to_outside
   subnet 10.0.0.0 255.255.255.0
   nat (DMZ,outside) dynamic interface

access-group outside_in in interface outside
timeout xlate 3:00:00
timeout conn 1:00:00 half-closed 0:10:00 udp 0:02:00 icmp 0:00:02
timeout sunrpc 0:10:00 h323 0:05:00 h225 1:00:00 mgcp 0:05:00 mgcp-pat 0:05:00
timeout sip 0:30:00 sip_media 0:02:00 sip-invite 0:03:00 sip-disconnect 0:02:00
timeout uauth 0:05:00 absolute
! Configure Local authentication for firewall management (For accessing the Firewall you need to
!use the username/password configured later).
aaa authentication serial console LOCAL
aaa authentication telnet console LOCAL
```

```
aaa authentication ssh console LOCAL
no snmp-server location
no snmp-server contact
snmp-server enable traps snmp authentication linkup linkdown coldstart
! Allow internal hosts to telnet to the device
telnet 192.168.1.0 255.255.255.0 inside
telnet timeout 5
! Allow an external management host to ssh from outside for firewall management
ssh 100.100.100.1 255.255.255.255 outside
ssh timeout 5
console timeout 0
dhcpd auto_config outside
! Assign a DNS server to internal hosts
dhcpd dns 200.200.200.1
!
! Assign IP addresses to internal hosts
dhcpd address 192.168.1.10-192.168.1.40 inside
dhcpd enable inside
!
!
! Configure here the username and password for accessing the device
username admin password secretpass privilege 15
```

16.1.3 ASA 5505 with Microsoft SBS Server on the Inside

A very common network scenario that I encounter all the time is to have a Cisco ASA 5505 working as Internet Border device and also a **Microsoft Small Business Server** (SBS) connected to the internal LAN network. This is suitable for small businesses and SOHO environments and offers an economical solution with great features. Although the best solution would be to have the SBS server isolated on a DMZ zone instead of directly connected to the internal LAN, here we assume that we have just a Basic License on ASA 5505 which does not allow DMZ configuration.

The requirement is to have all internal hosts (users' computers) to browse the Internet and also enable access from the Internet towards the SBS server. The example below will work for any SBS version (2003, 2008, 2011 etc). Depending on which services on the SBS you want to allow access from the Internet, you will need to allow the appropriate ports from the firewall. In our example below we assume that we have a single static Public IP address (100.1.1.1) configured on the outside interface of the ASA. This means that we will need to configure port redirection on the ASA in order to redirect the required traffic to the internal SBS Server (e.g traffic from internet to IP 100.1.1.1 / port 80 will be redirected to internal IP 192.168.1.100 / port 80 (SBS Server).

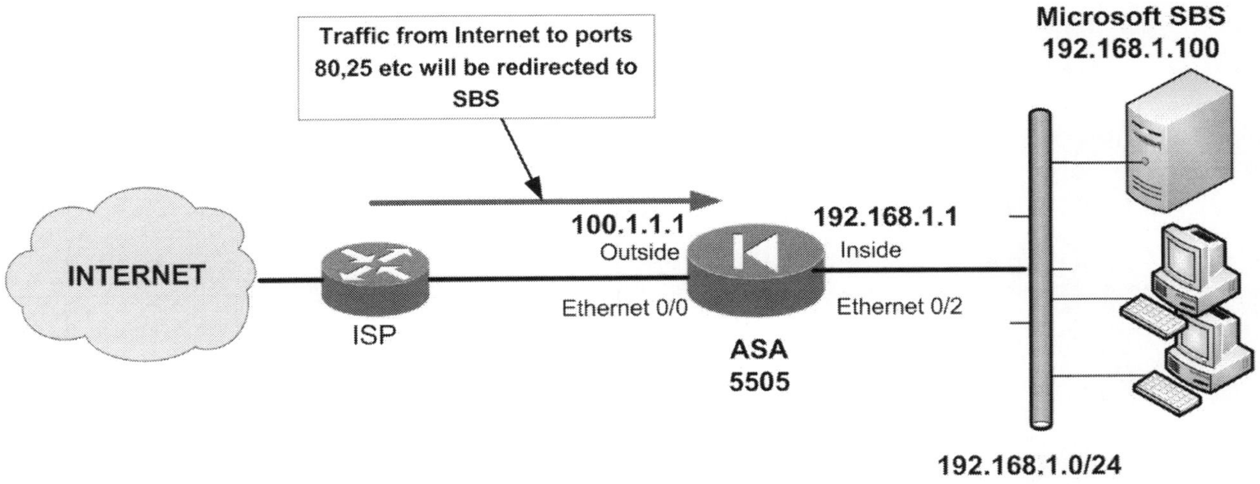

Let's see the complete configuration below. The commands with Bold are important.

```
ASA-5505# show run
: Saved
:
!
hostname ASA-5505
domain-name test.com
enable password xxxxxxxxxxxxxxxx encrypted
names
!
interface Vlan1
 nameif inside
 security-level 100
 ip address 192.168.1.1 255.255.255.0
!
interface Vlan2
 nameif outside
 security-level 0
 ip address 100.1.1.1 255.255.255.252
!
! Assign Eth0/0 to vlan 2.
interface Ethernet0/0
 switchport access vlan 2
!
! The rest are by default assigned to vlan 1. No need to change anything.
!
interface Ethernet0/1
!
interface Ethernet0/2
!
interface Ethernet0/3
!
interface Ethernet0/4
!
interface Ethernet0/5
!
interface Ethernet0/6
!
interface Ethernet0/7
!
ftp mode passive
dns server-group DefaultDNS
 domain-name test.com

! Create an ACL on the outside that will allow access to the SBS Server. Modify the ACL below
!according to which ports you actually need for accessing the SBS server.
access-list outside_in extended permit tcp any host 192.168.1.100 eq 80
```

```
access-list outside_in extended permit tcp any host 192.168.1.100 eq 25
access-list outside_in extended permit tcp any host 192.168.1.100 eq 443
access-list outside_in extended permit tcp any host 192.168.1.100 eq 3389
access-list outside_in extended deny ip any any log
pager lines 24
logging asdm informational
mtu inside 1500
mtu outside 1500
mtu DMZ 1500
icmp unreachable rate-limit 1 burst-size 1
arp timeout 14400

! Do PAT on the outside interface
object network internal_lan
  subnet 192.168.1.0 255.255.255.0
  nat (inside,outside) dynamic interface

! Create static port redirections towards the internal SBS Server. Modify the commands below
!according to which ports you actually need for accessing the SBS server.
! Note that we use the keyword "interface" because the mapped IP is the one assigned on the
!outside interface.
object network sbs_server_static_80
  host 192.168.1.100
  nat (inside,outside) static interface service tcp 80 80

object network sbs_server_static_25
  host 192.168.1.100
  nat (inside,outside) static interface service tcp 25 25

object network sbs_server_static_443
  host 192.168.1.100
  nat (inside,outside) static interface service tcp 443 443

object network sbs_server_static_3389
  host 192.168.1.100
  nat (inside,outside) static interface service tcp 3389 3389

! Apply the ACL we have created above to the outside interface
access-group outside_in in interface outside

route outside 0.0.0.0 0.0.0.0 100.1.1.2 1
timeout xlate 3:00:00
timeout conn 1:00:00 half-closed 0:10:00 udp 0:02:00 icmp 0:00:02
timeout sunrpc 0:10:00 h323 0:05:00 h225 1:00:00 mgcp 0:05:00 mgcp-pat 0:05:00
timeout sip 0:30:00 sip_media 0:02:00 sip-invite 0:03:00 sip-disconnect 0:02:00
timeout uauth 0:05:00 absolute
! Configure Local authentication for firewall management (For accessing the Firewall you need to
!use the username/password configured later).
```

```
aaa authentication serial console LOCAL
aaa authentication telnet console LOCAL
aaa authentication ssh console LOCAL
no snmp-server location
no snmp-server contact
snmp-server enable traps snmp authentication linkup linkdown coldstart
! Allow internal hosts to telnet to the device
telnet 192.168.1.0 255.255.255.0 inside
telnet timeout 5
! Allow an external management host to ssh from outside for firewall management
ssh 100.100.100.1 255.255.255.255 outside
ssh timeout 5
console timeout 0
! Assign a DNS server to internal hosts
dhcpd dns 200.200.200.1
!
! Assign IP addresses to internal hosts
dhcpd address 192.168.1.20-192.168.1.50 inside
dhcpd enable inside
!
![some commands omitted]

! Configure here the username and password for accessing the device
username admin password secretpass privilege 15
```

16.1.4 ASA 5505 with PPPoE Internet Access

For Broadband DSL or Cable access connectivity, many ISPs provide Point to Point over Ethernet (PPPoE) access, as will be described in this example scenario. If the ISP supplies you with a username/password for internet access, this means that you need to configure your ASA as PPPoE client. Most often, in this setup the ISP provides you also with a Modem which will bridge the DSL or Cable connectivity between the Customer Premises Equipment (ASA 5505 in our case) and the ISP equipment. In the following typical environment the ISP is providing Public IP address to the ASA via PPPoE.

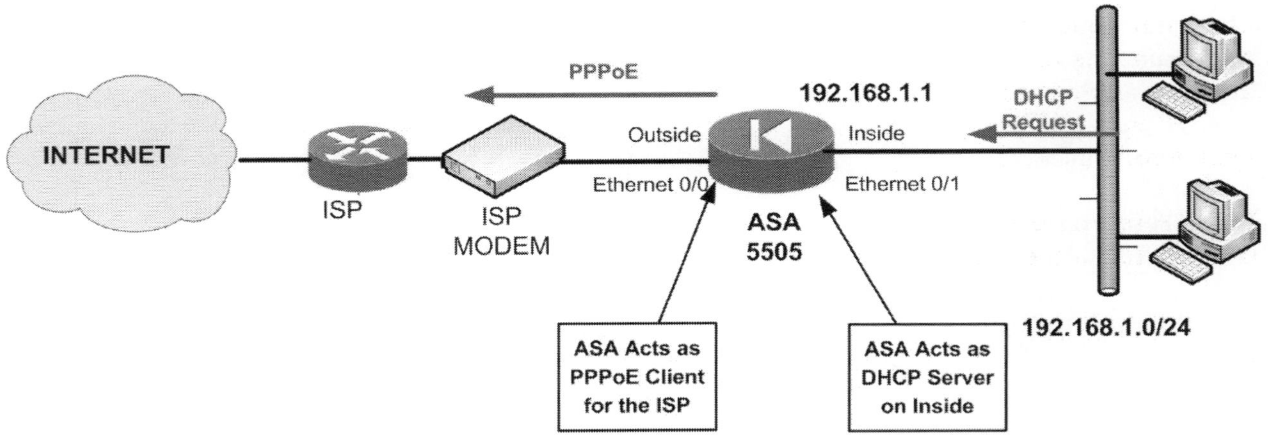

Let's see the complete configuration below. The commands with Bold are important.

ASA-5505# show run
: Saved
!
hostname ASA-5505
domain-name test.com
enable password xxxxxxxxxxxxxxxx encrypted
names
!
! Vlan 1 is assigned by default to all ports Ethernet0/1 to 0/7 which belong to the inside zone.
interface Vlan1
 nameif inside
 security-level 100
 ip address 192.168.1.1 255.255.255.0
!
! Vlan 2 is assigned to port Ethernet0/0 which belongs to the outside zone.
interface Vlan2
 nameif outside
 security-level 0
! Configure this VLAN as PPPoE Client and associate the pppoe group "ATT"
pppoe client vpdn group ATT
ip address pppoe setroute
!
! Assign Eth0/0 to vlan 2.
interface Ethernet0/0
 switchport access vlan 2
!
! By default, Eth0/1 to 0/7 are assigned to vlan 1. No need to change anything.
interface Ethernet0/1
!
interface Ethernet0/2
!
interface Ethernet0/3
!
interface Ethernet0/4
!
interface Ethernet0/5
!
interface Ethernet0/6
!
interface Ethernet0/7
!
ftp mode passive
dns server-group DefaultDNS
 domain-name test.com

! Create an ACL on the outside that will allow only echo-reply for troubleshooting purposes. Use a !deny all with log at the end to monitor any attacks coming from outside.
access-list outside_in extended permit icmp any any echo-reply
access-list outside_in extended deny ip any any log
pager lines 24
logging asdm informational
mtu inside 1500
! Configure the outside MTU as 1492 since there is an extra 8-byte overhead for PPPoE
mtu outside 1492
icmp unreachable rate-limit 1 burst-size 1
arp timeout 14400
! Do PAT using the outside interface address
object network internal_lan
  subnet 192.168.1.0 255.255.255.0
  nat (inside,outside) dynamic interface

access-group outside_in in interface outside
timeout xlate 3:00:00
timeout conn 1:00:00 half-closed 0:10:00 udp 0:02:00 icmp 0:00:02
timeout sunrpc 0:10:00 h323 0:05:00 h225 1:00:00 mgcp 0:05:00 mgcp-pat 0:05:00
timeout sip 0:30:00 sip_media 0:02:00 sip-invite 0:03:00 sip-disconnect 0:02:00
timeout uauth 0:05:00 absolute
! Configure Local authentication for firewall management (For accessing the Firewall you need to !use the username/password configured later).
aaa authentication serial console LOCAL
aaa authentication telnet console LOCAL
aaa authentication ssh console LOCAL
no snmp-server location
no snmp-server contact
snmp-server enable traps snmp authentication linkup linkdown coldstart
! Allow internal hosts to telnet to the device
telnet 192.168.1.0 255.255.255.0 inside
telnet timeout 5
! Allow an external management host to ssh from outside for firewall management
ssh 100.100.100.1 255.255.255.255 outside
ssh timeout 5
console timeout 0

! Next create the "ATT" pppoe group with the ISP connection details
vpdn group ATT request dialout pppoe
vpdn group ATT localname *[ENTER ISP USERNAME HERE]*
vpdn group ATT ppp authentication chap *[or PAP, depends on your ISP settings]*
vpdn username *[ENTER ISP USERNAME HERE]* password *[ENTER ISP PASSWORD HERE]*

! Assign a DNS server to internal hosts
dhcpd dns 200.200.200.1
!
! Assign IP addresses to internal hosts

```
dhcpd address 192.168.1.10-192.168.1.40 inside
dhcpd enable inside
!
! Configure here the username and password for accessing the device
username admin password secretpass privilege 15
```

16.2 ASA VPN Configuration Examples

16.2.1 Hub-and-Spoke IPSec VPN with Dynamic IP Spoke

This is a very common and useful scenario which you can scale it to a bigger number of Spokes depending on your network topology. Many Enterprises usually have a big Central site (HUB) which shares data resources with several remote Branches (SPOKES). You can build a WAN data network between your Central and Branch sites using dedicated communication lines (very expensive) or you can use cheap Internet connectivity to build a private IPSEC Hub-and-Spoke VPN, as illustrated in the example network below. The central Hub site and one Spoke site have static IP addresses, whereas the second Spoke site has Dynamic IP address. To setup our Hub-and-Spoke VPN, we need to create two Site-to-Site IPSEC VPN tunnels between Central – Branch1 and Central – Branch2. Note that this example uses the traditional IKEv1 IPSEC.

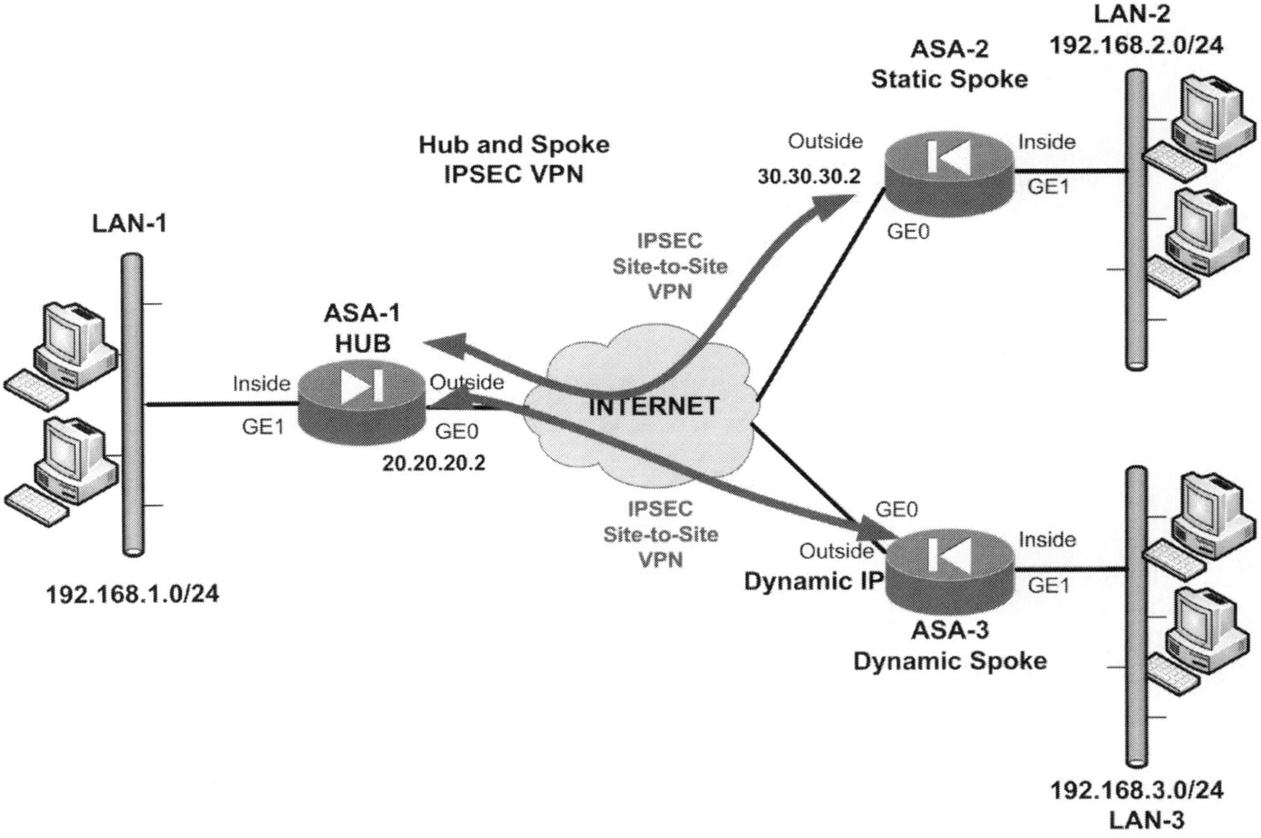

Let's see the complete configuration below. The commands with Bold are important.

ASA-1 (HUB)

hostname ASA1
enable password 8Ry2YjIyt7RRXU24 encrypted
passwd 2KFQnbNIdI.2KYOU encrypted
names
!
interface GigabitEthernet0
 nameif outside
 security-level 0
 ip address 20.20.20.2 255.255.255.0
!
interface GigabitEthernet1
 nameif inside
 security-level 100
 ip address 192.168.1.1 255.255.255.0
!
ftp mode passive

!Create objects with all local and remote LAN subnets
object network obj-local
 subnet 192.168.1.0 255.255.255.0
object network obj-remote1
 subnet 192.168.2.0 255.255.255.0
object network obj-remote2
 subnet 192.168.3.0 255.255.255.0
object network internal-lan
 subnet 192.168.1.0 255.255.255.0

access-list outside_in extended permit icmp any any echo-reply
access-list outside_in extended deny ip any any log

! Select the Interesting Traffic to be encrypted
access-list VPN-ACL1 extended permit ip 192.168.1.0 255.255.255.0 192.168.2.0 255.255.255.0
access-list VPN-ACL2 extended permit ip 192.168.1.0 255.255.255.0 192.168.3.0 255.255.255.0
pager lines 24
mtu outside 1500
mtu inside 1500
icmp unreachable rate-limit 1 burst-size 1
no asdm history enable
arp timeout 14400

```
! Do not translate VPN Traffic
nat (inside,outside) 1 source static obj-local obj-local destination static obj-remote1 obj-remote1
nat (inside,outside) 2 source static obj-local obj-local destination static obj-remote2 obj-remote2
!
!Do PAT for the internal LAN using ASA outside interface
object network internal-lan
 nat (inside,outside) dynamic interface

access-group outside_in in interface outside
route outside 0.0.0.0 0.0.0.0 20.20.20.1 1
timeout xlate 3:00:00
timeout conn 1:00:00 half-closed 0:10:00 udp 0:02:00 icmp 0:00:02
timeout sunrpc 0:10:00 h323 0:05:00 h225 1:00:00 mgcp 0:05:00 mgcp-pat 0:05:00
timeout sip 0:30:00 sip_media 0:02:00 sip-invite 0:03:00 sip-disconnect 0:02:00
timeout sip-provisional-media 0:02:00 uauth 0:05:00 absolute
timeout tcp-proxy-reassembly 0:01:00
timeout floating-conn 0:00:00
dynamic-access-policy-record DfltAccessPolicy
user-identity default-domain LOCAL
no snmp-server location
no snmp-server contact
snmp-server enable traps snmp authentication linkup linkdown coldstart warmstart

aaa authentication ssh console LOCAL
aaa authentication serial console LOCAL
aaa authentication telnet console LOCAL

! Create a Phase 2 transform set for encryption and authentication protocols.
crypto ipsec ikev1 transform-set TRSET esp-3des esp-md5-hmac

!Create a Dynamic crypto map for the Spoke ASA with Dynamic IP address.

crypto dynamic-map DYNMAP 10 match address VPN-ACL2
crypto dynamic-map DYNMAP 10 set ikev1 transform-set TRSET

!Create a main crypto map and attach the static and dynamic crypto maps
crypto map VPNMAP 5 match address VPN-ACL1
crypto map VPNMAP 5 set peer 30.30.30.2
crypto map VPNMAP 5 set ikev1 transform-set TRSET
crypto map VPNMAP 10 ipsec-isakmp dynamic DYNMAP

!Attach the main crypto map on outside interface
crypto map VPNMAP interface outside

!Configure and enable the Phase1 isakmp policy
crypto isakmp identity address
```

crypto ikev1 enable outside
crypto ikev1 policy 10
authentication pre-share
encryption 3des
hash sha
group 2
lifetime 86400

telnet timeout 5
ssh timeout 5
console timeout 0
threat-detection basic-threat
threat-detection statistics access-list
no threat-detection statistics tcp-intercept

!The following tunnel group (DefaultL2LGroup) is used for the Dynamic IP Spoke
tunnel-group DefaultL2LGroup ipsec-attributes
ikev1 pre-shared-key secretkey2

!The following tunnel group (30.30.30.2) is used for the static IP Spoke
tunnel-group 30.30.30.2 type ipsec-l2l
tunnel-group 30.30.30.2 ipsec-attributes
ikev1 pre-shared-key secretkey1
!
!
username admin password secretpass privilege 15

![other commands omitted]

ASA-2 (Static IP Spoke)

hostname ASA2
enable password 8Ry2YjIyt7RRXU24 encrypted
passwd 2KFQnbNIdI.2KYOU encrypted
names
!
interface GigabitEthernet0
nameif outside
security-level 0
ip address 30.30.30.2 255.255.255.0
!
interface GigabitEthernet1
nameif inside
security-level 100
ip address 192.168.2.1 255.255.255.0
!
ftp mode passive

```
!Create objects with all local and remote LAN subnets
object network obj-local
 subnet 192.168.2.0 255.255.255.0
object network obj-remote
 subnet 192.168.1.0 255.255.255.0
object network internal-lan
 subnet 192.168.2.0 255.255.255.0

access-list outside_in extended permit icmp any any echo-reply
access-list outside_in extended deny ip any any log
! Select the Interesting Traffic to be encrypted
access-list VPN-ACL extended permit ip 192.168.2.0 255.255.255.0 192.168.1.0
255.255.255.0
pager lines 24
mtu outside 1500
mtu inside 1500
icmp unreachable rate-limit 1 burst-size 1
no asdm history enable
arp timeout 14400

! Do not translate VPN Traffic
nat (inside,outside) source static obj-local obj-local destination static obj-remote obj-remote
!
!Do PAT for the internal LAN using ASA outside interface
object network internal-lan
 nat (inside,outside) dynamic interface

access-group outside_in in interface outside
route outside 0.0.0.0 0.0.0.0 30.30.30.1 1
timeout xlate 3:00:00
timeout conn 1:00:00 half-closed 0:10:00 udp 0:02:00 icmp 0:00:02
timeout sunrpc 0:10:00 h323 0:05:00 h225 1:00:00 mgcp 0:05:00 mgcp-pat 0:05:00
timeout sip 0:30:00 sip_media 0:02:00 sip-invite 0:03:00 sip-disconnect 0:02:00
timeout sip-provisional-media 0:02:00 uauth 0:05:00 absolute
timeout tcp-proxy-reassembly 0:01:00
timeout floating-conn 0:00:00
dynamic-access-policy-record DfltAccessPolicy
user-identity default-domain LOCAL
no snmp-server location
no snmp-server contact
snmp-server enable traps snmp authentication linkup linkdown coldstart warmstart
aaa authentication ssh console LOCAL
aaa authentication serial console LOCAL
aaa authentication telnet console LOCAL

! Create a Phase 2 transform set for encryption and authentication protocols.
crypto ipsec ikev1 transform-set TRSET esp-3des esp-md5-hmac
```

```
!Create a main crypto map for the tunnel with the Hub Site
crypto map VPNMAP 5 match address VPN-ACL
crypto map VPNMAP 5 set peer 20.20.20.2
crypto map VPNMAP 5 set ikev1 transform-set TRSET
crypto map VPNMAP interface outside

!Configure and enable the Phase1 isakmp policy
crypto isakmp identity address
crypto ikev1 enable outside
crypto ikev1 policy 10
 authentication pre-share
 encryption 3des
 hash sha
 group 2
 lifetime 86400
telnet timeout 5
ssh timeout 5
console timeout 0
threat-detection basic-threat
threat-detection statistics access-list
no threat-detection statistics tcp-intercept

!Tunnel group with the central Hub site
tunnel-group 20.20.20.2 type ipsec-l2l
tunnel-group 20.20.20.2 ipsec-attributes
 ikev1 pre-shared-key secretkey1
!
!
username admin password secretpass privilege 15

![other commands omitted]
```

ASA-3 (Dynamic IP Spoke)

```
hostname ASA3
enable password 8Ry2YjIyt7RRXU24 encrypted
passwd 2KFQnbNIdI.2KYOU encrypted
names
!
!Outside Interface receives a dynamic IP address using DHCP from the ISP
interface GigabitEthernet0
 nameif outside
 security-level 0
 ip address dhcp setroute
!
```

```
interface GigabitEthernet1
 nameif inside
 security-level 100
 ip address 192.168.3.1 255.255.255.0
!
ftp mode passive

!Create objects with all local and remote LAN subnets
object network obj-local
 subnet 192.168.3.0 255.255.255.0
object network obj-remote
 subnet 192.168.1.0 255.255.255.0
object network internal-lan
 subnet 192.168.3.0 255.255.255.0

access-list outside_in extended permit icmp any any echo-reply
access-list outside_in extended deny ip any any log

!Select VPN traffic
access-list VPN-ACL extended permit ip 192.168.3.0 255.255.255.0 192.168.1.0
255.255.255.0
pager lines 24
mtu outside 1500
mtu inside 1500
icmp unreachable rate-limit 1 burst-size 1
no asdm history enable
arp timeout 14400

! Do not translate VPN Traffic
nat (inside,outside) source static obj-local obj-local destination static obj-remote obj-remote
!
!Do PAT for the internal LAN using ASA outside interface
object network internal-lan
 nat (inside,outside) dynamic interface
access-group outside_in in interface outside
timeout xlate 3:00:00
timeout conn 1:00:00 half-closed 0:10:00 udp 0:02:00 icmp 0:00:02
timeout sunrpc 0:10:00 h323 0:05:00 h225 1:00:00 mgcp 0:05:00 mgcp-pat 0:05:00
timeout sip 0:30:00 sip_media 0:02:00 sip-invite 0:03:00 sip-disconnect 0:02:00
timeout sip-provisional-media 0:02:00 uauth 0:05:00 absolute
timeout tcp-proxy-reassembly 0:01:00
timeout floating-conn 0:00:00
dynamic-access-policy-record DfltAccessPolicy
user-identity default-domain LOCAL
no snmp-server location
no snmp-server contact
snmp-server enable traps snmp authentication linkup linkdown coldstart warmstart
```

```
aaa authentication ssh console LOCAL
aaa authentication serial console LOCAL
aaa authentication telnet console LOCAL

! Create a Phase 2 transform set for encryption and authentication protocols.
crypto ipsec ikev1 transform-set TRSET esp-3des esp-md5-hmac

!Configure a main crypto map with the central Hub Site
crypto map VPNMAP 5 match address VPN-ACL
crypto map VPNMAP 5 set peer 20.20.20.2
crypto map VPNMAP 5 set ikev1 transform-set TRSET
crypto map VPNMAP interface outside

!Configure and enable the Phase1 isakmp policy
crypto isakmp identity address
crypto ikev1 enable outside
crypto ikev1 policy 10
 authentication pre-share
 encryption 3des
 hash sha
 group 2
 lifetime 86400
telnet timeout 5
ssh timeout 5
console timeout 0
threat-detection basic-threat
threat-detection statistics access-list
no threat-detection statistics tcp-intercept

!Tunnel group with the central Hub site
tunnel-group 20.20.20.2 type ipsec-l2l
tunnel-group 20.20.20.2 ipsec-attributes
 ikev1 pre-shared-key secretkey2
!
!
username admin password secretpass privilege 15

![other commands omitted]
```

16.2.2 Site-to-Site IKEv2 IPSec VPN between two ASA

The legacy IKEv1 IPSEC VPN has seen widespread implementation over the years in millions of site-to-site VPNs. Its successor, IKEv2 IPSEC, has started to take its position into the VPN networking space. Right now we are in a transitional stage where many enterprises are implementing IKEv2 VPNs while they still have legacy tunnels using IKEv1 IPSEC. In this configuration example we have two ASA firewalls with site-to-site VPN using the new IKEv2 IPSEC standard.

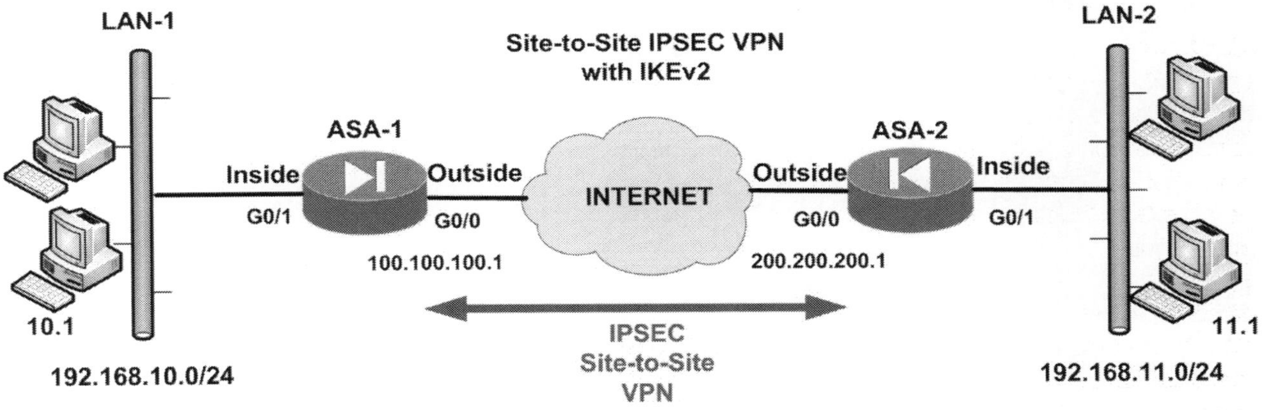

Let's see the complete configuration below. The commands with Bold are important.

ASA-1

ASA-1# sh run

```
!
hostname ASA-1
enable password 8Ry2YjIyt7RRXU24 encrypted
passwd 2KFQnbNIdI.2KYOU encrypted
names
!
interface GigabitEthernet0
 nameif outside
 security-level 0
 ip address 100.100.100.1 255.255.255.0
!
interface GigabitEthernet1
 nameif inside
 security-level 100
 ip address 192.168.10.254 255.255.255.0
!
interface GigabitEthernet2
 shutdown
 no nameif
 no security-level
 no ip address
!
interface GigabitEthernet3
 shutdown
 no nameif
 no security-level
 no ip address
!
interface GigabitEthernet4
 shutdown
 no nameif
 no security-level
 no ip address
!
interface GigabitEthernet5
 shutdown
 no nameif
 no security-level
 no ip address
!
ftp mode passive
!Create network objects for the local and remote subnets
object network obj-local
 subnet 192.168.10.0 255.255.255.0
```

object network obj-remote
subnet 192.168.11.0 255.255.255.0
object network internal-lan
subnet 192.168.10.0 255.255.255.0

access-list outside_in extended permit icmp any any echo-reply
access-list outside_in extended deny ip any any log

!Define VPN interesting traffic with an ACL
access-list VPN-ACL extended permit ip 192.168.10.0 255.255.255.0 192.168.11.0 255.255.255.0
pager lines 24
mtu outside 1500
mtu inside 1500
icmp unreachable rate-limit 1 burst-size 1
no asdm history enable
arp timeout 14400

!NAT Exemption for VPN traffic
nat (inside,outside) source static obj-local obj-local destination static obj-remote obj-remote
!
!PAT for the inside network
object network internal-lan
nat (inside,outside) dynamic interface

access-group outside_in in interface outside
route outside 0.0.0.0 0.0.0.0 100.100.100.2 1
timeout xlate 3:00:00
timeout conn 1:00:00 half-closed 0:10:00 udp 0:02:00 icmp 0:00:02
timeout sunrpc 0:10:00 h323 0:05:00 h225 1:00:00 mgcp 0:05:00 mgcp-pat 0:05:00
timeout sip 0:30:00 sip_media 0:02:00 sip-invite 0:03:00 sip-disconnect 0:02:00
timeout sip-provisional-media 0:02:00 uauth 0:05:00 absolute
timeout tcp-proxy-reassembly 0:01:00
timeout floating-conn 0:00:00
dynamic-access-policy-record DfltAccessPolicy
user-identity default-domain LOCAL
no snmp-server location
no snmp-server contact
snmp-server enable traps snmp authentication linkup linkdown coldstart warmstart

!Create IKEv2 IPSEC Proposal
crypto ipsec ikev2 ipsec-proposal IKEv2-AES-SHA
protocol esp encryption aes
protocol esp integrity sha-1

!main crypto map which binds several ipsec settings together
crypto map outside_map 1 match address VPN-ACL
crypto map outside_map 1 set peer 200.200.200.1

crypto map outside_map 1 set ikev2 ipsec-proposal IKEv2-AES-SHA
crypto map outside_map interface outside

!IKEv2 policy (similar to Phase 1 in ikev1)
crypto ikev2 policy 1
encryption aes 3des
integrity sha md5
group 2
prf sha
lifetime seconds 86400
crypto ikev2 enable outside
telnet timeout 5
ssh timeout 5
console timeout 0
threat-detection basic-threat
threat-detection statistics access-list
no threat-detection statistics tcp-intercept

!Allow ikev2 as tunnel protocol
group-policy GroupPolicy1 internal
group-policy GroupPolicy1 attributes
vpn-tunnel-protocol ikev2
tunnel-group 200.200.200.1 type ipsec-l2l
tunnel-group 200.200.200.1 general-attributes
default-group-policy GroupPolicy1

!Define both a local and remote pre-shared keys. They must be reverse on the other site
tunnel-group 200.200.200.1 ipsec-attributes
ikev2 remote-authentication pre-shared-key cisco1
ikev2 local-authentication pre-shared-key cisco1234
!
!
[other commands omitted]

ASA-2

hostname ASA-2
enable password 8Ry2YjIyt7RRXU24 encrypted
passwd 2KFQnbNIdI.2KYOU encrypted
names
!
interface GigabitEthernet0
nameif outside
security-level 0
ip address 200.200.200.1 255.255.255.0

```
!
interface GigabitEthernet1
 nameif inside
 security-level 100
 ip address 192.168.11.254 255.255.255.0
!
interface GigabitEthernet2
 shutdown
 no nameif
 no security-level
 no ip address
!
interface GigabitEthernet3
 shutdown
 no nameif
 no security-level
 no ip address
!
interface GigabitEthernet4
 shutdown
 no nameif
 no security-level
 no ip address
!
interface GigabitEthernet5
 shutdown
 no nameif
 no security-level
 no ip address
!
ftp mode passive
!Create network objects for the local and remote subnets
object network obj-local
 subnet 192.168.11.0 255.255.255.0
object network obj-remote
 subnet 192.168.10.0 255.255.255.0
object network internal-lan
 subnet 192.168.11.0 255.255.255.0
access-list outside_in extended permit icmp any any echo-reply
access-list outside_in extended deny ip any any log

!Define VPN interesting traffic with an ACL
access-list VPN-ACL extended permit ip 192.168.11.0 255.255.255.0 192.168.10.0
255.255.255.0
pager lines 24
mtu outside 1500
mtu inside 1500
icmp unreachable rate-limit 1 burst-size 1
```

no asdm history enable
arp timeout 14400

!NAT Exemption for VPN traffic
nat (inside,outside) source static obj-local obj-local destination static obj-remote obj-remote
!
!PAT for the inside network
object network internal-lan
nat (inside,outside) dynamic interface
access-group outside_in in interface outside
route outside 0.0.0.0 0.0.0.0 200.200.200.2 1
timeout xlate 3:00:00
timeout conn 1:00:00 half-closed 0:10:00 udp 0:02:00 icmp 0:00:02
timeout sunrpc 0:10:00 h323 0:05:00 h225 1:00:00 mgcp 0:05:00 mgcp-pat 0:05:00
timeout sip 0:30:00 sip_media 0:02:00 sip-invite 0:03:00 sip-disconnect 0:02:00
timeout sip-provisional-media 0:02:00 uauth 0:05:00 absolute
timeout tcp-proxy-reassembly 0:01:00
timeout floating-conn 0:00:00
dynamic-access-policy-record DfltAccessPolicy
user-identity default-domain LOCAL
no snmp-server location
no snmp-server contact
snmp-server enable traps snmp authentication linkup linkdown coldstart warmstart

!Create IKEv2 IPSEC Proposal
crypto ipsec ikev2 ipsec-proposal IKEv2-AES-SHA
protocol esp encryption aes
protocol esp integrity sha-1

!main crypto map which binds several ipsec settings together
crypto map outside_map 1 match address VPN-ACL
crypto map outside_map 1 set peer 100.100.100.1
crypto map outside_map 1 set ikev2 ipsec-proposal IKEv2-AES-SHA
crypto map outside_map interface outside

!IKEv2 policy (similar to Phase 1 in ikev1)
crypto ikev2 policy 1
encryption aes 3des
integrity sha md5
group 2
prf sha
lifetime seconds 86400
crypto ikev2 enable outside
telnet timeout 5
ssh timeout 5
console timeout 0
threat-detection basic-threat
threat-detection statistics access-list

no threat-detection statistics tcp-intercept

!Allow ikev2 as tunnel protocol
group-policy GroupPolicy1 internal
group-policy GroupPolicy1 attributes
vpn-tunnel-protocol ikev2
tunnel-group 100.100.100.1 type ipsec-l2l
tunnel-group 100.100.100.1 general-attributes
default-group-policy GroupPolicy1

!Define both a local and remote pre-shared keys. They must be reverse on the other site
tunnel-group 100.100.100.1 ipsec-attributes
ikev2 remote-authentication pre-shared-key cisco1234
ikev2 local-authentication pre-shared-key cisco1
!
!
[other commands omitted]

16.2.3 Remote Access VPN with IKEv1, IKEv2 and SSL on the same ASA Device

After configuring the ASA in this scenario you will have a device that can support almost all types of remote access VPN technologies supported by Cisco ASA. Specifically, we will configure the ASA to accommodate remote access VPNs using the legacy IKEv1 IPSEC VPN, the new IKEv2 IPSEC VPN and also SSL VPNs. The first VPN type (IKEv1 IPSEC) requires the Cisco VPN client software installed on the user's computer. The other two VPN types (IKEv2 and SSL VPN) will work with the new Anyconnect Secure Mobility Client (version 3.x and above) as we have described in the main ASA book.

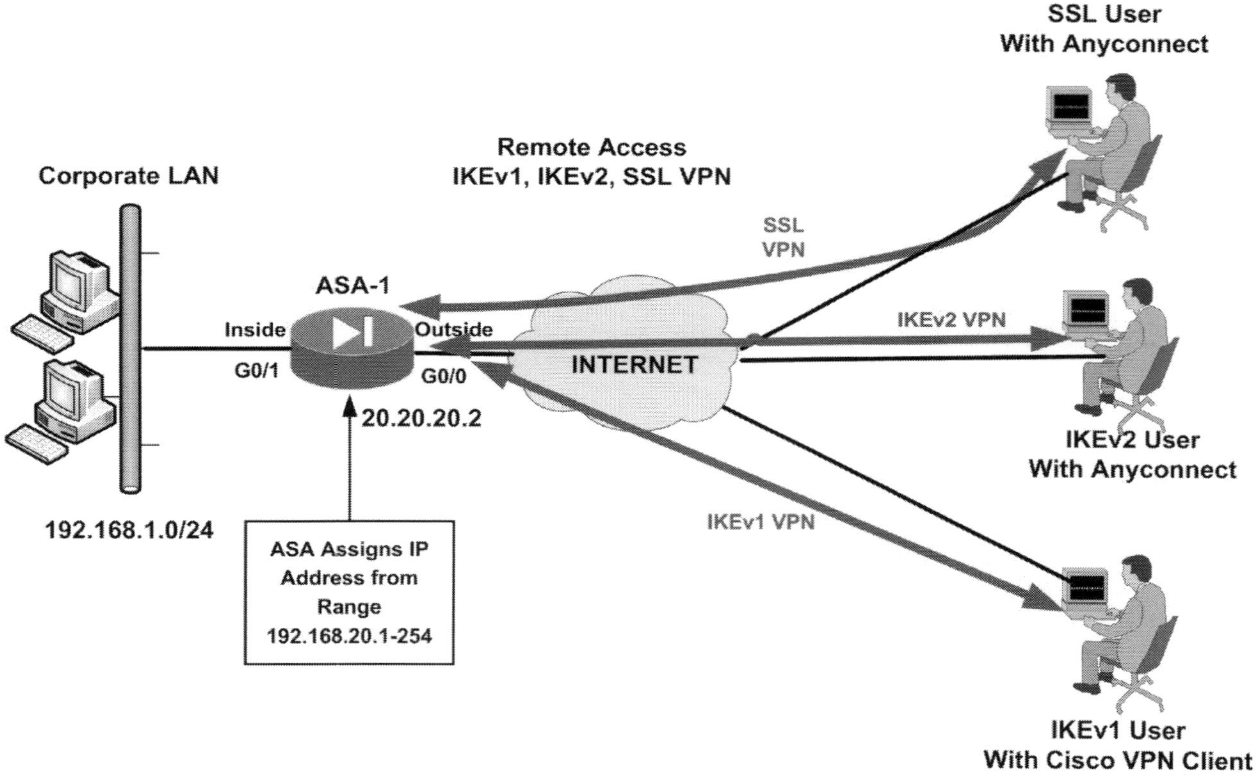

The following configuration has several pre-requisite settings that need to be in place in order to work. Specifically you need to create an Anyconnect XML Profile for the IKEv2 VPN as we have described in the main book. Optionally you can have also an XML Profile for the SSL VPN tunnel. These XML profiles must be created and copied to the flash of the ASA. Also, you must create RSA keys in order to generate a self-signed ASA certificate for the IKEv2 VPN (as we have described before). You can have also certificates signed from a third party CA instead of self-signed. Let's see the complete configuration below:

!Its important to configure a hostname and domain name since we will use certificates
hostname vpnasa
domain-name mycompany.com
enable password 8Ry2YjIyt7RRXU24 encrypted
passwd 2KFQnbNIdI.2KYOU encrypted
names
!
interface GigabitEthernet0
 nameif outside
 security-level 0
 ip address 20.20.20.2 255.255.255.0
!
interface GigabitEthernet1
 nameif inside
 security-level 100
 ip address 192.168.1.1 255.255.255.0
!
![some commands omitted]
!
!Its important to have correct clock settings and time-zone
clock timezone EEST 2
clock summer-time EEDT recurring last Sun Mar 3:00 last Sun Oct 4:00
dns server-group DefaultDNS
 domain-name mycompany.com

!Create network objects for the local LAN and for the VPN pool
object network obj-local
 subnet 192.168.1.0 255.255.255.0
object network obj-vpnpool
 subnet 192.168.20.0 255.255.255.0
object network FOR_PAT
 subnet 192.168.1.0 255.255.255.0

!split-tunnel ACL to enable split tunneling feature
access-list split-tunnel standard permit 192.168.1.0 255.255.255.0
pager lines 24
mtu outside 1500
mtu inside 1500

!IP Pool to assign addresses to remote users
ip local pool VPNpool 192.168.20.1-192.168.20.254 mask 255.255.255.0
icmp unreachable rate-limit 1 burst-size 1
no asdm history enable
arp timeout 14400

!PAT Configuration for the internal LAN
nat (inside,outside) source dynamic FOR_PAT interface

!NAT Exemption for the VPN traffic
nat (inside,outside) source static obj-local obj-local destination static obj-vpnpool obj-vpnpool no-proxy-arp route-lookup

route outside 0.0.0.0 0.0.0.0 20.20.20.1 1
timeout xlate 3:00:00
timeout conn 1:00:00 half-closed 0:10:00 udp 0:02:00 icmp 0:00:02
timeout sunrpc 0:10:00 h323 0:05:00 h225 1:00:00 mgcp 0:05:00 mgcp-pat 0:05:00
timeout sip 0:30:00 sip_media 0:02:00 sip-invite 0:03:00 sip-disconnect 0:02:00
timeout sip-provisional-media 0:02:00 uauth 0:05:00 absolute
timeout tcp-proxy-reassembly 0:01:00
timeout floating-conn 0:00:00
dynamic-access-policy-record DfltAccessPolicy
user-identity default-domain LOCAL
http redirect outside 80
no snmp-server location
no snmp-server contact
snmp-server enable traps snmp authentication linkup linkdown coldstart warmstart

!Phase2 IPSEC Configuration for IKEv1
crypto ipsec ikev1 transform-set IKEv1-TS esp-3des esp-sha-hmac

!IPSEC Proposal (Phase2) Configuration for IKEv2
crypto ipsec ikev2 ipsec-proposal AES-3DES
 protocol esp encryption aes 3des
 protocol esp integrity sha-1 md5

!Create Dynamic Crypto maps for IKEv1 and IKEv2
crypto dynamic-map DYN_MAP 5 set ikev1 transform-set IKEv1-TS
crypto dynamic-map DYN_MAP 10 set ikev2 ipsec-proposal AES-3DES

!Attach the dynamic crypto map above to a static crypto map
crypto map OUTSIDE_MAP 10 ipsec-isakmp dynamic DYN_MAP
crypto map OUTSIDE_MAP interface outside

!This is the Trustpoint for the self-signed certificate
crypto ca trustpoint SELF-TP
 enrollment self
 subject-name CN=vpnasa.mycompany.com
 keypair rsakeys
 crl configure

!The following is created automatically when you generate the self-signed certificate
crypto ca certificate chain SELF-TP
 certificate 26239652

    308201ff 30820168 a0030201 02020426 23965230 0d06092a 864886f7 0d010105
    05003044 311d301b 06035504 03131476 706e6173 612e6d79 636f6d70 616e792e
    636f6d31 23302106 092a8648 86f70d01 09021614 76706e61 73612e6d 79636f6d

70616e79 2e636f6d 301e170d 31333131 32373137 32353231 5a170d32 33313132
35313732 3532315a 3044311d 301b0603 55040313 1476706e 6173612e 6d79636f
6d70616e 792e636f 6d312330 2106092a 864886f7 0d010902 16147670 6e617361
2e6d7963 6f6d7061 6e792e63 6f6d3081 9f300d06 092a8648 86f70d01 01010500
03818d00 30818902 8181008e acca3766 bb7b5d50 1d53e073 e40f1907 313ce6d1
6adea8a5 bd6371ff cdc68277 ca5d00a3 5c8b8ec3 385387e1 bb4ce3fe b0090129
c79cba4d 5a72de30 df5ef8df 3e298ffd 68082aaa 6a368bc1 45251713 7bc3c756
b73f3d1c eeef26ce 981f2a7d 25bc2dce ebff0c08 7c90c17c f537017a d7eee408
b35528a9 1ec9598c a62c5102 03010001 300d0609 2a864886 f70d0101 05050003
81810077 fe2dd664 da39f3b8 37bfac62 8b42c678 17fdaee3 84c61662 c665a1ff
29557768 796336b4 f4715bbb c162bdc5 b1f5e9fb d321d445 d8cb3559 0d43b3f6
10d7228f 245383e1 6c7132c9 6f742c4f 1fe4db48 a7020e6c 427e9000 bc334ca1
91e04a11 c9776eb2 348f9e96 c1505349 4dab886a e4302059 be1414eb 5c76fdec 8857a9
quit

crypto isakmp identity address

!Create ikev2 isakmp policy
crypto ikev2 policy 1
encryption aes
integrity sha
group 5 2
prf sha
lifetime seconds 86400

!Enable client-services and TrustPoint SSL authentication for IKEv2
crypto ikev2 enable outside client-services port 443
crypto ikev2 remote-access trustpoint SELF-TP

crypto ikev1 enable outside

!Create ikev1 isakmp policy
crypto ikev1 policy 10
authentication pre-share
encryption 3des
hash sha
group 2
lifetime 86400

telnet timeout 5
ssh timeout 5
console timeout 0
threat-detection basic-threat
threat-detection statistics access-list
no threat-detection statistics tcp-intercept

```
ssl trust-point SELF-TP outside

!Setting for the Anyconnect VPNs (SSL and IKEv2)
webvpn
 enable outside
 anyconnect image disk0:/anyconnect-win-3.1.04072-k9.pkg 1
!the following XML profiles must be copied to ASA flash (disk0)
 anyconnect profiles ikev2profile disk0:/ikev2profile.xml
 anyconnect profiles sslprofile disk0:/sslprofile.xml
 anyconnect enable
 tunnel-group-list enable

!Configure separate VPN group policies for each type of VPN users
!This is the VPN policy for SSL VPN remote access users
group-policy SSL-USERS-POLICY internal
group-policy SSL-USERS-POLICY attributes
 dns-server value 192.168.1.15
 vpn-tunnel-protocol ssl-client ssl-clientless
 split-tunnel-policy tunnelspecified
 split-tunnel-network-list value split-tunnel
 webvpn
  anyconnect keep-installer installed
  anyconnect dpd-interval client 20
  anyconnect profiles value sslprofile type user
  anyconnect ask none default anyconnect

!This is the VPN policy for IKEv2 VPN remote access users
group-policy IKEv2-USERS-POLICY internal
group-policy IKEv2-USERS-POLICY attributes
 dns-server value 192.168.1.15
 vpn-tunnel-protocol ikev2 ssl-client
 split-tunnel-policy tunnelspecified
 split-tunnel-network-list value split-tunnel
 webvpn
  anyconnect keep-installer installed
  anyconnect dpd-interval client 20
  anyconnect profiles value ikev2profile type user
  anyconnect ask none default anyconnect

!This is the VPN policy for legacy IKEv1 VPN remote access users
group-policy IKEv1-USERS-POLICY internal
group-policy IKEv1-USERS-POLICY attributes
 dns-server value 192.168.1.15
 vpn-tunnel-protocol ikev1
 split-tunnel-policy tunnelspecified
 split-tunnel-network-list value split-tunnel

!Create local users for each type of remote access users
```

```
username ssluser password kmUcA9cVGIaUJEA6 encrypted
username ikev2user password z59Qxp4jZFQvrhoQ encrypted
username ikev1user password z59Qxp4jZFQvrhoQ encrypted

username admin password f3UhLvUj1QsXsuK7 encrypted privilege 15


!Configure separate tunnel groups for each type of VPN
!For IKEv2
tunnel-group ikev2remoteaccess type remote-access
tunnel-group ikev2remoteaccess general-attributes
 address-pool VPNpool
 default-group-policy IKEv2-USERS-POLICY

tunnel-group ikev2remoteaccess webvpn-attributes
 group-alias ikev2_users enable

!For SSL VPN
tunnel-group sslremoteaccess type remote-access
tunnel-group sslremoteaccess general-attributes
 address-pool VPNpool
 default-group-policy SSL-USERS-POLICY

tunnel-group sslremoteaccess webvpn-attributes
 group-alias sslvpn_users enable

!For IKEv1 VPN
tunnel-group ikev1remoteaccess type remote-access
tunnel-group ikev1remoteaccess general-attributes
 address-pool VPNpool
 default-group-policy IKEv1-USERS-POLICY

tunnel-group ikev1remoteaccess ipsec-attributes
 ikev1 pre-shared-key secretgroupkey
!
![other command omitted]
```

16.2.4 Anyconnect SSL VPN with Microsoft Active Directory Authentication

This is a scenario used frequently by many enterprises which have an internal Microsoft Active Directory (AD) server containing all users' credentials. Instead of configuring local usernames/passwords on the ASA device for authenticating the remote access users, you can use the existing AD to authenticate the users with their domain accounts. One important thing to keep in mind is that you must create an AD user account which has the privileges to login, search and retrieve account information from the AD. Here we used the username "**admin**" as an example. You must use a proper username which has enough privileges to be able to search/read/lookup users in the LDAP server. The ASA will use this "admin" user account to connect to the AD (whenever a remote user tries to authenticate) in order to lookup the remote user credentials and confirm the user authentication.

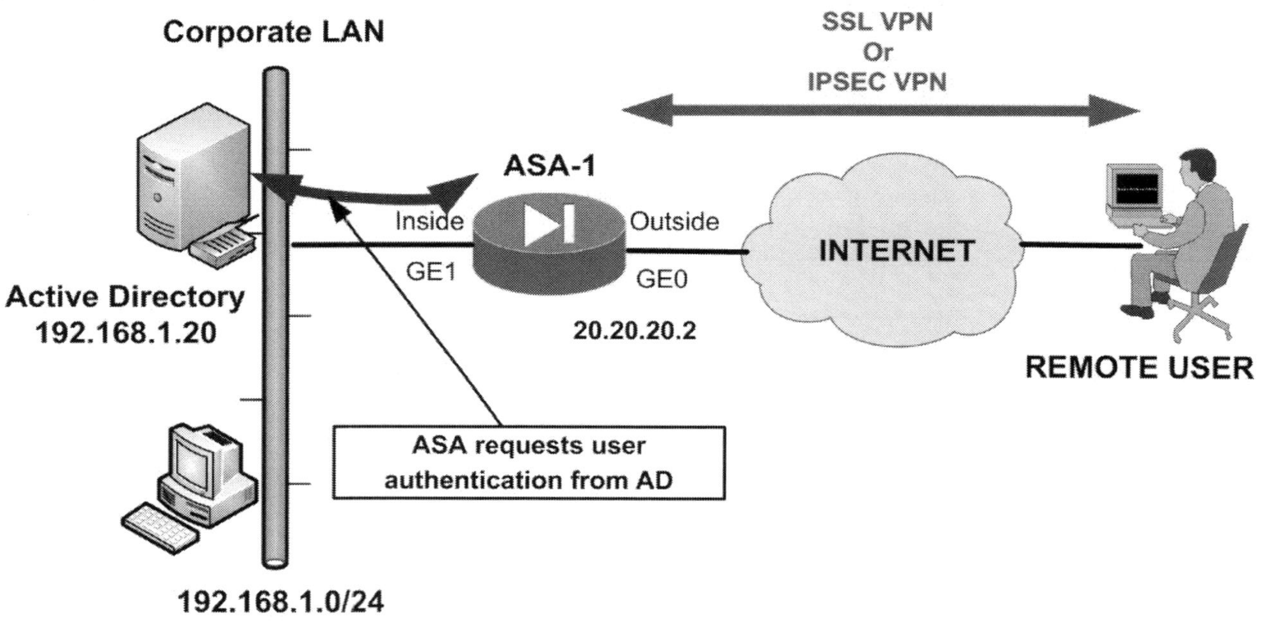

Let's see the configuration below based on the diagram above.

hostname ASA1
enable password 8Ry2YjIyt7RRXU24 encrypted
passwd 2KFQnbNIdI.2KYOU encrypted
names
!
interface GigabitEthernet0
 nameif outside
 security-level 0
 ip address 20.20.20.2 255.255.255.0
!
interface GigabitEthernet1
 nameif inside
 security-level 100
 ip address 192.168.1.1 255.255.255.0
!
![other interface commands omitted]
ftp mode passive

!network objects for the local LAN and VPN pool
object network obj-local
 subnet 192.168.1.0 255.255.255.0
object network obj-vpnpool
 subnet 192.168.5.0 255.255.255.0
object network FOR_PAT
 subnet 192.168.1.0 255.255.255.0

access-list split-tunnel standard permit 192.168.1.0 255.255.255.0
pager lines 24
mtu outside 1500
mtu inside 1500

ip local pool VPNpool 192.168.5.1-192.168.5.20 mask 255.255.255.0
icmp unreachable rate-limit 1 burst-size 1
no asdm history enable
arp timeout 14400

!NAT exemption for VPN traffic
nat (inside,outside) source static obj-local obj-local destination static obj-vpnpool obj-vpnpool no-proxy-arp route-lookup

nat (inside,outside) source dynamic FOR_PAT interface

route outside 0.0.0.0 0.0.0.0 20.20.20.1 1
timeout xlate 3:00:00
timeout conn 1:00:00 half-closed 0:10:00 udp 0:02:00 icmp 0:00:02
timeout sunrpc 0:10:00 h323 0:05:00 h225 1:00:00 mgcp 0:05:00 mgcp-pat 0:05:00
timeout sip 0:30:00 sip_media 0:02:00 sip-invite 0:03:00 sip-disconnect 0:02:00
timeout sip-provisional-media 0:02:00 uauth 0:05:00 absolute

timeout tcp-proxy-reassembly 0:01:00
timeout floating-conn 0:00:00
dynamic-access-policy-record DfltAccessPolicy

!Configure the ASA to communicate with an internal AAA server using LDAP protocol
!(Microsoft AD uses LDAP) and the server-type will be Microsoft. The user "admin" with
!password "cisco123" must be created on the AD as we've discussed above. Also, the base DN
!tree must be obtained from the AD. Also "sAMAccountName" must be used by default

aaa-server AD-SERVER protocol ldap
aaa-server AD-SERVER (inside) host 192.168.1.20
 ldap-base-dn dc=mycompany, dc=com
 ldap-scope subtree
 ldap-naming-attribute sAMAccountName
 ldap-login-password cisco123
 ldap-login-dn cn=admin, cn=users, dc=mycompany, dc=com
 server-type microsoft

user-identity default-domain LOCAL

http redirect outside 80
no snmp-server location
no snmp-server contact
snmp-server enable traps snmp authentication linkup linkdown coldstart warmstart
telnet timeout 5
ssh timeout 5
console timeout 0
threat-detection basic-threat
threat-detection statistics access-list
no threat-detection statistics tcp-intercept

!Configure the SSL WebVPN
webvpn
 enable outside
 anyconnect image disk0:/anyconnect-win-3.1.03103-k9.pkg 1
 anyconnect enable
 tunnel-group-list enable

group-policy Anyconnect-Policy internal
group-policy Anyconnect-Policy attributes
 dns-server value 192.168.1.15
 vpn-tunnel-protocol ssl-client
 split-tunnel-policy tunnelspecified
 split-tunnel-network-list value split-tunnel
 webvpn
  anyconnect keep-installer installed
  anyconnect dpd-interval client 20
  anyconnect ask none default anyconnect

```
tunnel-group telecommuters type remote-access


!Here, specify the AD-SERVER configured above as the authentication server for this tunnel
tunnel-group telecommuters general-attributes
 address-pool VPNpool
 authentication-server-group AD-SERVER
 default-group-policy Anyconnect-Policy

tunnel-group telecommuters webvpn-attributes
 group-alias sslgroup_users enable
!
![other commands omitted]
```

16.2.5 Special site-to-site IPSEC VPN between two ASA with Controlled VPN access

In this configuration scenario we will discuss a site-to-site IPSEC VPN implementation between two ASA devices. However, this will not be the classical simple site-to-site VPN scenario that you find everywhere but a more enhanced version of it. One of the sites will be a central headquarters (HQ) site with 2 internal network subnets (LAN1 and LAN2) and a DMZ subnet. The other site will be a remote Branch site again using Cisco ASA firewall as border Internet device (ASA2).

In a regular site-to-site VPN scenario, the two sites will have full LAN access between them over the VPN tunnel by default. In our special scenario here the remote branch site will have full network access only to the HQ DMZ subnet BUT restricted access to the two internal LAN networks of the HQ site. Specifically, the branch site will be allowed to access only a Web Server in Internal LAN1 of HQ and an Email Server in Internal LAN2 of HQ.

The above scenario will demonstrate several concepts in addition to the classical site-to-site ASA IPSEC VPN configuration. It will show how to pass multiple networks inside a VPN tunnel, how to access a DMZ via a VPN, how to restrict VPN traffic to specific hosts and ports etc.

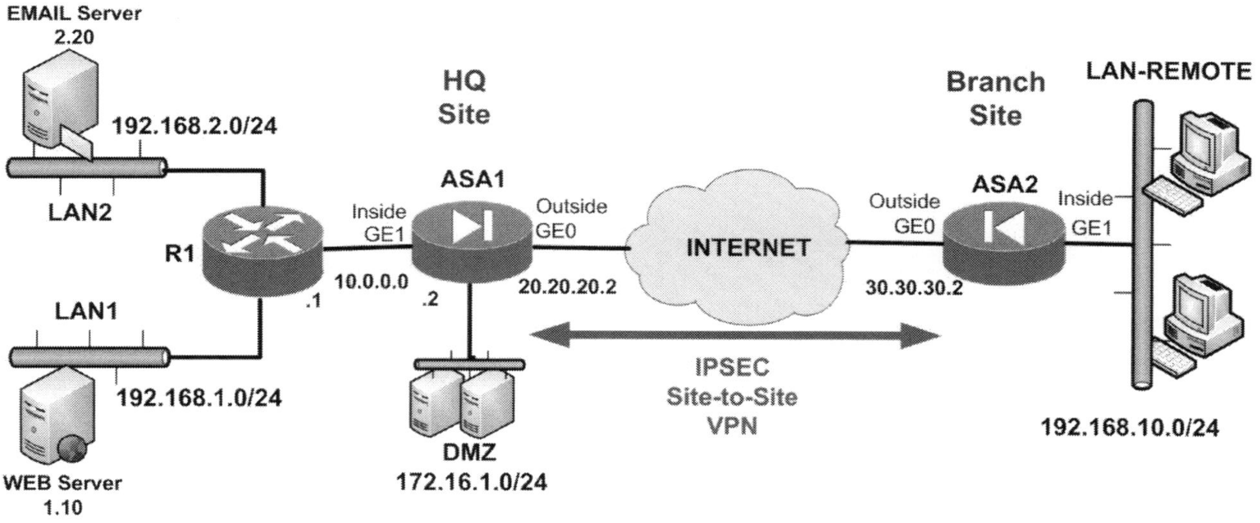

Let's see the configuration for both ASA devices below:

ASA1 (HQ Site)

```
hostname ASA1
enable password 8Ry2YjIyt7RRXU24 encrypted
passwd 2KFQnbNIdI.2KYOU encrypted
names
!
interface GigabitEthernet0
 nameif outside
 security-level 0
 ip address 20.20.20.2 255.255.255.0
!
interface GigabitEthernet1
 nameif inside
 security-level 100
 ip address 10.0.0.2 255.255.255.0
!
interface GigabitEthernet2
 nameif dmz
 security-level 50
 ip address 172.16.1.1 255.255.255.0
!
![other interface commands omitted]
!
ftp mode passive
!Create network objects for the local and remote LANs
object network LAN1
 subnet 192.168.1.0 255.255.255.0
object network LAN2
 subnet 192.168.2.0 255.255.255.0
object network DMZ-LAN
 subnet 172.16.1.0 255.255.255.0
object network obj-remote
 subnet 192.168.10.0 255.255.255.0

!Create ACL to match the VPN traffic you want to encrypt
access-list VPN-ACL extended permit ip 192.168.1.0 255.255.255.0 192.168.10.0
255.255.255.0
access-list VPN-ACL extended permit ip 192.168.2.0 255.255.255.0 192.168.10.0
255.255.255.0
access-list VPN-ACL extended permit ip 172.16.1.0 255.255.255.0 192.168.10.0
255.255.255.0

!The outside ACL must explicitly allow IPSEC VPN protocols (ESP, AH, isakmp) and also allow
!access from remote LAN to DMZ and to Web Server and Email Server
access-list outside_in extended permit esp host 30.30.30.2 host 20.20.20.2
access-list outside_in extended permit ah host 30.30.30.2 host 20.20.20.2
access-list outside_in extended permit udp host 30.30.30.2 host 20.20.20.2 eq isakmp
```

access-list outside_in extended permit ip 192.168.10.0 255.255.255.0 172.16.1.0 255.255.255.0
access-list outside_in extended permit tcp 192.168.10.0 255.255.255.0 host 192.168.1.10 eq 80
access-list outside_in extended permit tcp 192.168.10.0 255.255.255.0 host 192.168.2.20 eq 25

pager lines 24
mtu outside 1500
mtu inside 1500
mtu dmz 1500
icmp unreachable rate-limit 1 burst-size 1
no asdm history enable
arp timeout 14400

!Create the required NAT Exemptions for VPN traffic
nat (inside,outside) source static LAN1 LAN1 destination static obj-remote obj-remote
nat (inside,outside) source static LAN2 LAN2 destination static obj-remote obj-remote
nat (dmz,outside) source static DMZ-LAN DMZ-LAN destination static obj-remote obj-remote

access-group outside_in in interface outside
route outside 0.0.0.0 0.0.0.0 20.20.20.1 1
route inside 192.168.1.0 255.255.255.0 10.0.0.1 1
route inside 192.168.2.0 255.255.255.0 10.0.0.1 1
timeout xlate 3:00:00
timeout conn 1:00:00 half-closed 0:10:00 udp 0:02:00 icmp 0:00:02
timeout sunrpc 0:10:00 h323 0:05:00 h225 1:00:00 mgcp 0:05:00 mgcp-pat 0:05:00
timeout sip 0:30:00 sip_media 0:02:00 sip-invite 0:03:00 sip-disconnect 0:02:00
timeout sip-provisional-media 0:02:00 uauth 0:05:00 absolute
timeout tcp-proxy-reassembly 0:01:00
timeout floating-conn 0:00:00
dynamic-access-policy-record DfltAccessPolicy
user-identity default-domain LOCAL
no snmp-server location
no snmp-server contact
snmp-server enable traps snmp authentication linkup linkdown coldstart warmstart

!This command is important. It disables the mechanism to automatically allow all VPN traffic,
!so that you can control which VPN traffic you want to allow with the outside ACL
no sysopt connection permit-vpn

!The following commands configure IKEv1 IPSEC VPN parameters
crypto ipsec ikev1 transform-set TRSET esp-aes esp-sha-hmac

crypto map VPNMAP 10 match address VPN-ACL
crypto map VPNMAP 10 set peer 30.30.30.2
crypto map VPNMAP 10 set ikev1 transform-set TRSET

crypto map VPNMAP interface outside

crypto isakmp identity address
crypto ikev1 enable outside
crypto ikev1 policy 10
 authentication pre-share
 encryption aes
 hash sha
 group 2
 lifetime 86400
telnet timeout 5
ssh timeout 5
console timeout 0
threat-detection basic-threat
threat-detection statistics access-list
no threat-detection statistics tcp-intercept
tunnel-group 30.30.30.2 type ipsec-l2l
tunnel-group 30.30.30.2 ipsec-attributes
 ikev1 pre-shared-key secretkey1
!
!
![other commands omitted]

ASA2 (Branch Site)

hostname ASA2
enable password 8Ry2YjIyt7RRXU24 encrypted
passwd 2KFQnbNIdI.2KYOU encrypted
names
!
interface GigabitEthernet0
 nameif outside
 security-level 0
 ip address 30.30.30.2 255.255.255.0
!
interface GigabitEthernet1
 nameif inside
 security-level 100
 ip address 192.168.10.1 255.255.255.0
!
![other interface commands omitted]
!
ftp mode passive
!Create network objects for the local and remote LANs
object network LAN1
 subnet 192.168.1.0 255.255.255.0

object network LAN2
subnet 192.168.2.0 255.255.255.0
object network DMZ-LAN
subnet 172.16.1.0 255.255.255.0
object network obj-local
subnet 192.168.10.0 255.255.255.0
!Create ACL to match the VPN traffic you want to encrypt
access-list VPN-ACL extended permit ip 192.168.10.0 255.255.255.0 192.168.1.0 255.255.255.0
access-list VPN-ACL extended permit ip 192.168.10.0 255.255.255.0 192.168.2.0 255.255.255.0
access-list VPN-ACL extended permit ip 192.168.10.0 255.255.255.0 172.16.1.0 255.255.255.0

pager lines 24
mtu outside 1500
mtu inside 1500
mtu dmz 1500
icmp unreachable rate-limit 1 burst-size 1
no asdm history enable
arp timeout 14400

!Create the required NAT Exemptions for VPN traffic
nat (inside,outside) source static obj-local obj-local destination static LAN1 LAN1
nat (inside,outside) source static obj-local obj-local destination static LAN2 LAN2
nat (inside,outside) source static obj-local obj-local destination static DMZ-LAN DMZ-LAN

route outside 0.0.0.0 0.0.0.0 30.30.30.1 1

timeout xlate 3:00:00
timeout conn 1:00:00 half-closed 0:10:00 udp 0:02:00 icmp 0:00:02
timeout sunrpc 0:10:00 h323 0:05:00 h225 1:00:00 mgcp 0:05:00 mgcp-pat 0:05:00
timeout sip 0:30:00 sip_media 0:02:00 sip-invite 0:03:00 sip-disconnect 0:02:00
timeout sip-provisional-media 0:02:00 uauth 0:05:00 absolute
timeout tcp-proxy-reassembly 0:01:00
timeout floating-conn 0:00:00
dynamic-access-policy-record DfltAccessPolicy
user-identity default-domain LOCAL
no snmp-server location
no snmp-server contact
snmp-server enable traps snmp authentication linkup linkdown coldstart warmstart

!The following commands configure IKEv1 IPSEC VPN parameters
crypto ipsec ikev1 transform-set TRSET esp-aes esp-sha-hmac
crypto map VPNMAP 10 match address VPN-ACL
crypto map VPNMAP 10 set peer 20.20.20.2
crypto map VPNMAP 10 set ikev1 transform-set TRSET

```
crypto map VPNMAP interface outside

crypto isakmp identity address
crypto ikev1 enable outside

crypto ikev1 policy 10
 authentication pre-share
 encryption aes
 hash sha
 group 2
 lifetime 86400
telnet timeout 5
ssh timeout 5
console timeout 0
threat-detection basic-threat
threat-detection statistics access-list
no threat-detection statistics tcp-intercept

tunnel-group 20.20.20.2 type ipsec-l2l
tunnel-group 20.20.20.2 ipsec-attributes
 ikev1 pre-shared-key secretkey1
!
!
![other commands omitted]
```

16.3 General Configuration Examples

16.3.1 ASA Firewall with DMZ and two Internal Zones

In this scenario we will illustrate an ASA 5500 series Firewall (any model except 5505) with four security zones. One Outside, one DMZ, and two Internal Zones. The two Internal zones will be implemented on the same physical interface (Ge0/1) using two subinterfaces (Ge0/1.10 and Ge0/1.20). The DMZ zone will host a Web Server and an Email Server. We will use static NAT for the DMZ servers to translate their private IP addresses to public (Static NAT for private IP 10.0.0.2 to public IP 100.1.1.2 and Static NAT for private IP 10.0.0.3 to public IP 100.1.1.3). Also we will impose traffic restrictions to the two Internal Zones. **Inside1** users will be allowed to access only Web and Email, and **Inside2** users will have unrestricted Internet access.

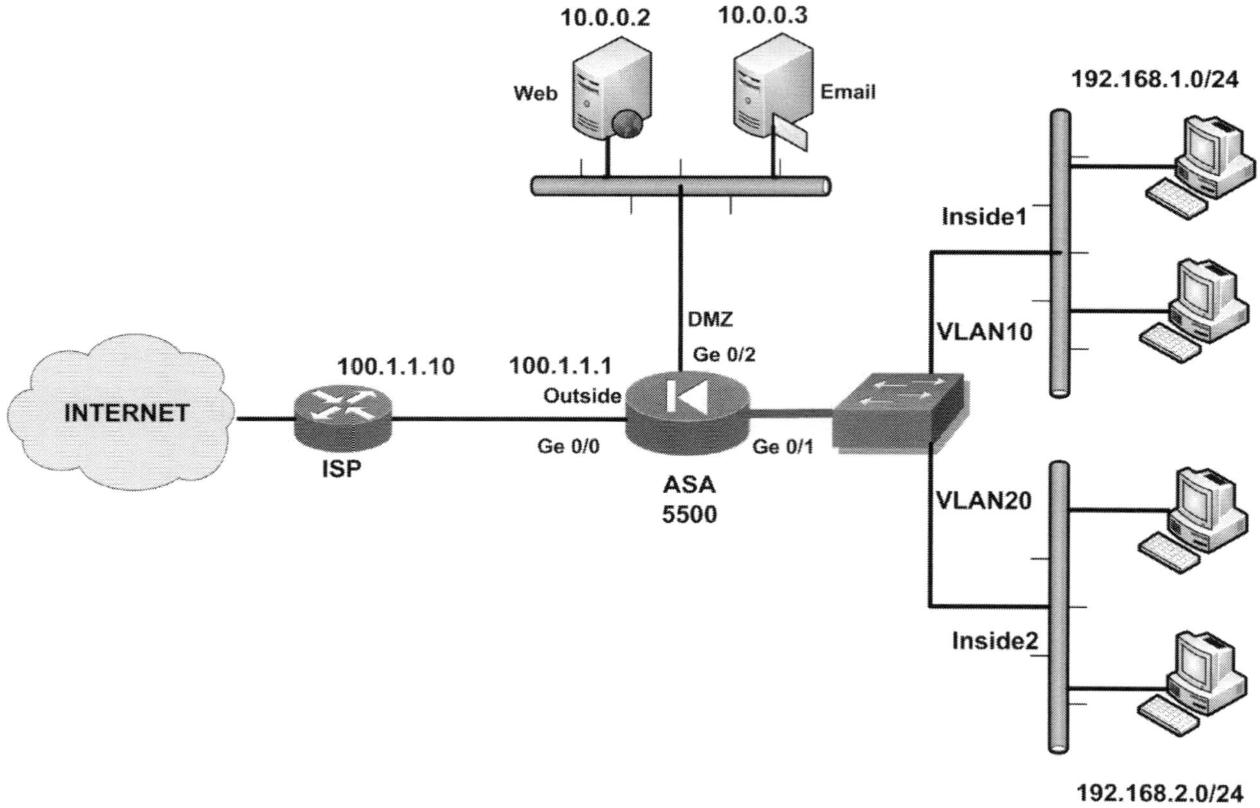

Let's see the complete configuration below. The commands with Bold are important.

```
ASA-5500# show run
: Saved
:
!
hostname ASA-5500
domain-name test.com
enable password xxxxxxxxxxxxxxxxx encrypted
!
interface GigabitEthernet0/0
 description CONNECTION TO OUTSIDE INTERNET
 speed 100
 duplex full
 nameif outside
 security-level 0
 ip address 100.1.1.1 255.255.255.0
!
! Use the same Physical Interface Ge0/1 to create two internal zones using Vlans
interface GigabitEthernet0/1
 no nameif
 no security-level
 no ip address
!
interface GigabitEthernet0/1.10
 description CONNECTION TO INSIDE 1
 vlan 10
 nameif inside1
 security-level 80
 ip address 192.168.1.1 255.255.255.0
!
interface GigabitEthernet0/1.20
 description CONNECTION TO INSIDE 2
 vlan 20
 nameif inside2
 security-level 90
 ip address 192.168.2.1 255.255.255.0
!
interface GigabitEthernet0/2
 description CONNECTION TO DMZ
 nameif DMZ
 security-level 50
 ip address 10.0.0.1 255.255.255.0
!
interface GigabitEthernet0/3
 shutdown
 no nameif
 no security-level
 no ip address
!
```

```
interface Management0/0
 shutdown
 no nameif
 no security-level
 no ip address
!
banner motd          ** W A R N I N G **
banner motd Unauthorized access prohibited. All access is
banner motd monitored, and trespassers shall be prosecuted
banner motd to the fullest extent of the law.
no ftp mode passive
dns server-group DefaultDNS
 domain-name test.com

!Create a service object with the Web Ports
object-group service WEB-PORTS tcp
 port-object eq 80
 port-object eq 443

! Allow access from Internet to our Web Server and Email Server. Notice that we use the private IP
access-list OUTSIDE_IN extended permit tcp any host 10.0.0.2 object-group WEB-PORTS
access-list OUTSIDE_IN extended permit tcp any host 10.0.0.3 eq 25

! Inside1 zone is only allowed to access web and email
access-list INSIDE1_IN extended permit tcp 192.168.1.0 255.255.255.0 any eq http
access-list INSIDE1_IN extended permit tcp 192.168.1.0 255.255.255.0 any eq https
access-list INSIDE1_IN extended permit tcp 192.168.1.0 255.255.255.0 any eq smtp
access-list INSIDE1_IN extended permit tcp 192.168.1.0 255.255.255.0 any eq pop3
access-list INSIDE1_IN extended permit udp 192.168.1.0 255.255.255.0 any eq dns

! Inside2 zone is allowed to access all protocols
access-list INSIDE2_IN extended permit ip 192.168.2.0 255.255.255.0 any

! Do PAT on the Outside and DMZ interfaces for internal hosts
object network internal_lan1_outside
   subnet 192.168.1.0 255.255.255.0
   nat (inside1,outside) dynamic interface

object network internal_lan1_dmz
   subnet 192.168.1.0 255.255.255.0
   nat (inside1,DMZ) dynamic interface

object network internal_lan2_outside
   subnet 192.168.2.0 255.255.255.0
   nat (inside2,outside) dynamic interface
```

```
object network internal_lan2_dmz
  subnet 192.168.2.0 255.255.255.0
  nat (inside2,DMZ) dynamic interface

! Create permanent static NAT mappings for our DMZ servers.
object network web_static
  host 10.0.0.2
  nat (DMZ,outside) static 100.1.1.2

object network email_static
  host 10.0.0.3
  nat (DMZ,outside) static 100.1.1.3

!Apply ACLs on the proper interfaces
access-group OUTSIDE_IN in interface outside
access-group INSIDE1_IN in interface inside1
access-group INSIDE2_IN in interface inside2

route outside 0.0.0.0 0.0.0.0 100.1.1.10 1

!create local user for firewall administration
username admin password secretpass privilege 15

aaa authentication serial console LOCAL
aaa authentication ssh console LOCAL
aaa authentication telnet console LOCAL

!Allow ssh from zone inside1
ssh 192.168.1.0 255.255.255.0 inside1
ssh timeout 20
ssh version 2
console timeout 0
!

![other commands omitted]...
```

16.3.2 How to Block Access to specific Websites with Cisco ASA

The ASA can provide a simple solution for restricting web access to specific websites. However, it is NOT a replacement for a full-featured URL filtering solution. There are a few methods to block access to websites. These methods include regular expressions (regex) together with Modular Policy Framework (MPF), finding the IP address of the website and blocking with ACL, and using FQDN in an ACL. The first method (regex with MPF) works well with HTTP websites but it will not work at all if the website uses HTTPs. The second method (blocking the IP with ACL) will work only for simple websites which have a static IP but it will be difficult to work for dynamic websites (such as Facebook, Twitter etc) which have many different IP addresses which change all the time. The third method (using FQDN in an ACL) is the one which we will describe here.

From ASA version 8.4(2) and later, Access Control Lists (ACL) can contain an object which represents a Fully Qualified Domain Name (FQDN). So, inside an ACL you can allow or deny access to hosts using their FQDN name instead of their IP address. You can therefore deny access to website **www.facebook.com** by denying access to FQDN object "**www.facebook.com"** inside the ACL. The ASA will need to resolve all possible IP addresses of the FQDN and will dynamically insert several "deny IP" entries for these IP addresses in the ACL. Therefore you must specify what DNS server the ASA can use in order to resolve IP addresses for the FQDNs.

In our example network below, we want to restrict access to **www.website.com** which resolves to IP address 2.2.2.2. The ASA will use the internal DNS server (or any other DNS) to resolve the IP and put a "deny IP" entry in the inbound ACL applied on the "inside" interface.

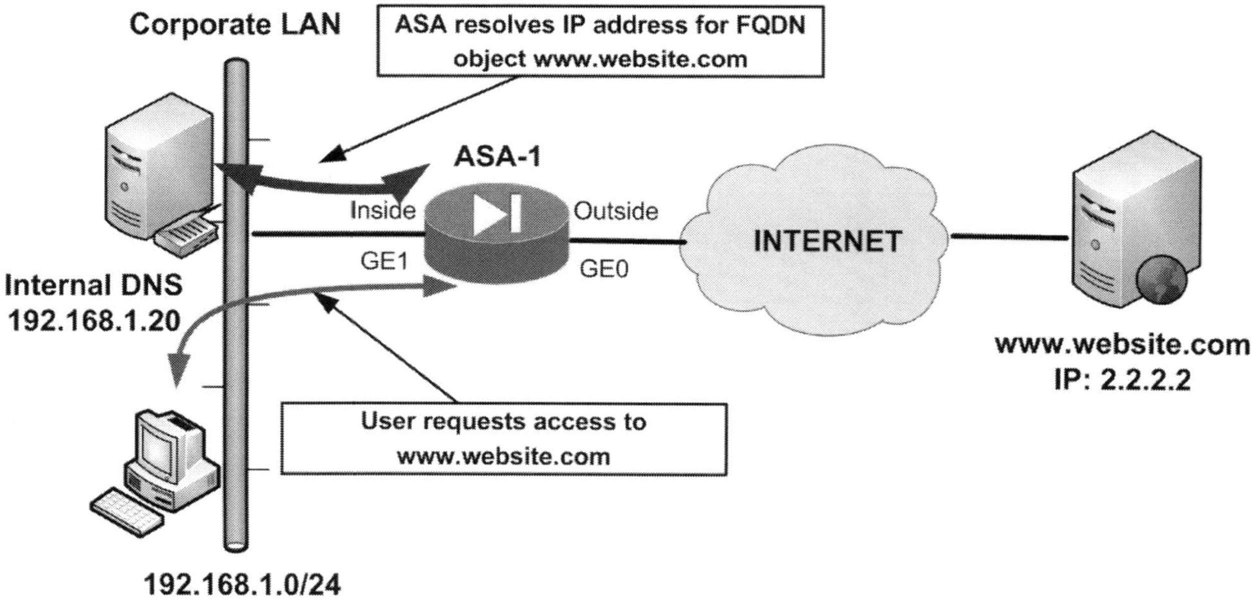

ASA-1

```
hostname ASA-1
domain-name mycompany.com
enable password 8Ry2YjIyt7RRXU24 encrypted
passwd 2KFQnbNIdI.2KYOU encrypted
names
!
interface GigabitEthernet0
 nameif outside
 security-level 0
 ip address 20.20.20.2 255.255.255.0
!
interface GigabitEthernet1
 nameif inside
 security-level 100
 ip address 192.168.1.1
!
![other interface commands omitted]
!
ftp mode passive

!Specify which DNS server to use for resolving FQDN domains.
dns domain-lookup inside
dns server-group DefaultDNS
 name-server 192.168.1.20
 domain-name mycompany.com

!Create FQDN objects for website we want to block. Block both the www and non-www domains
object network obj-www.website.com
 fqdn www.website.com

object network obj-website.com
 fqdn website.com

!Add the FQDN objects above to an ACL applied inbound on the inside interface
access-list INSIDE-IN extended deny ip any object obj-www.website.com
access-list INSIDE-IN extended deny ip any object obj-website.com
access-list INSIDE-IN extended permit ip any any

!Apply the ACL above to the inside interface
access-group INSIDE-IN in interface inside

![other commands omitted]
```

Conclusion:

If you have studied carefully the information presented in this Book, I'm confident that you will be able to tackle the most common ASA configuration scenarios that you will encounter in your professional career. The purpose of this Book was to provide you the Foundation concepts for designing and implementing one of the most popular hardware firewalls in the market, the Cisco Adaptive Security Appliance. I know that the features, concepts and configuration capabilities that the Cisco ASA Firewall supports are much more than what is presented here. However, with the foundation base that this Book provided you, it's fairly easy from now on to build up your knowledge with extra information provided from other Cisco documents for the ASA firewall.

Again, thank you for purchasing and reading this Book. It has been a pleasure writing this handbook, and I really hope that you have enjoyed it as well.

You can check out my Networking related Blog http://www.networkstraining.com for more technical tips and tutorials about Cisco products and solutions. You can also register your email address at my Blog above in order to receive news and updates about my books and other Cisco technical tips.

I will be glad to answer any questions you may have at admin@networkstraining.com

GOOD LUCK TO YOUR PROFESSIONAL CAREER

Index:

7262114R00164

Printed in Great Britain
by Amazon.co.uk, Ltd.,
Marston Gate.